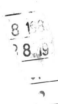

NEW PERSPECTIVES ON

# Coleridge and Wordsworth

# New Perspectives on Coleridge and Wordsworth  SELECTED

## PAPERS FROM THE ENGLISH INSTITUTE

*Edited with a Foreword*

*by* GEOFFREY H. HARTMAN

NEW YORK AND LONDON

COLUMBIA UNIVERSITY PRESS 1972

Acknowledgment is made to Alfred A. Knopf, Inc.,
for permission to quote several lines from the
poetry of Wallace Stevens.

**Library of Congress Cataloging in Publication Data**

English Institute.
    New perspectives on Coleridge and Wordsworth.

    Essays presented at the 1970 and 1971 English
Institutes.
    Includes bibliographical references.
    1. Coleridge, Samuel Taylor, 1772–1834.
2. Wordsworth, William, 1770–1850.  I. Hartman,
Geoffrey H., ed.  II. Title.
PR4484.E5   1972      821'.7'09      72-3738
ISBN 0-231-03679-5

To the two members of the original
Supervising Committee present at the
Thirtieth Session of the English Institute

## Rudolf Kirk

*"onlie begetter" and first secretary*

## &

## Robert Spiller

*inaugurator of the English Institute Essays*

# FOREWORD

*In* 1970 and 1971 the English Institute offered as part of its program bicentenary conferences, on Wordsworth and Coleridge respectively. The four papers on Coleridge gathered here are from the conference directed by Professor Harold Bloom; the two on Wordsworth from that directed by me. I have added an essay of my own which focuses on the idea and movement of literary history from Akenside to Coleridge. Of the essays not printed, that of Walter J. Ong, S.J., on "Romantic Difference and the Poetics of Technology," can be found in his recent book, *Rhetoric, Romance and Technology* (Ithaca and London, 1971).

What strikes one in the present collection is a blend of the conventional and the new. The two essays on Wordsworth interpret freshly what used to be called the Romantic "shift of sensibility." Mr. Johnston's "The Idiom of Vision" shows again how important the eye was to the poet, and how he mediated between visual and visionary. Perception became a language for Wordsworth, and the poem a developed perception. The two lyrics analyzed by him in detail, "St. Paul's" and "A Night-Piece," had remained marginal, but now throw a new light on such "tops of speculation" as the ascent of Snowdon. Mr. Johnston grapples not only with Wordsworth but also with a conflict in contemporary ideas about him. Is Wordsworth a nature poet or a reluctant visionary? This conflict may actually reflect an antinomy in the idea of the Modern. Attempting to break through to nature (to more direct possibilities of feeling and speaking), Wordsworth discovered the apocalyptic tenor of this attempt, and so draws back from (re-veils) revelation. Modernism as we have come to know it —and Post-Modernism too—is perhaps less conscious than Wordsworth of a contradiction that besets its desire for the unmediated. The new, quasi-erotic simplicity it claims is strangely apocalyptic in vigor of demand.

Wordsworth's definition of genius, as "a widening of the sphere of human sensibility," is well known. For Mr. Hollander, poetry leads also to a widened *representation* of sensibility. The poet gives us new concepts of sound as well as new sounds. Technology could say (like Freud in another context), "The poets were there before me." Words like "image" and "reflection" refer primarily to ideas of sight, but Wordsworth is haunted by "images of voice," by natural sounds that move beyond echo or physical richochet into resonance and myth. His soundscapes redeem a silence of concepts as well as the spiritual vacancy of his solitaries. Yet increase of sensibility, said Wordsworth, was to be "for the delight, honor and benefit of human nature." The poet's acoustics remain orphic. He integrates or humanizes techniques whose troubled exploitation is now upon us: for him "sound" is "music" still. Mr. Hollander's work-in-progress allows us to glimpse an integrated history of the arts, verifiably concrete in its approach, and which projects itself as a history of sensory representation.

The first two essays on Coleridge also show an interest in "representation" as distinguished from, simply, "mimesis." Mr. Cooke's "Manipulation of Space" is thematic in approach, but its important link to an older type of image study is complemented by a subtle sense of how space becomes a Bachelardian "revery of the will." It can also be, of course, a "revery of repose," and we are made to see the intimate connection between Coleridge's fearful sense of space and his desire for method and self-definition. The word "manipulation" points, in fact, to the strongly rhetorical aspects of Coleridge's verse, and so to the problematics of willing or fabricating a self.

Mr. Fletcher ends, rather than begins, with a traditional literary term. His "personification" is a resting-point after strange seas of thought. Yet "personification" rhymes with "positive negation" and contains a theory of symbols that was fully developed in Mr. Fletcher's book *Allegory*. Coleridge's use of personification (as in "Limbo," for example) is shown to be part evasion and part fixation—an appropriate type of figure for what is aptly called the "threshold poem." For Coleridge (and here the findings of several essays converge) anything can become a threshold, that is, precarious, a gateway guarded by demons. Time is as vulnerable as space to "stills" or "negations" which have a ghostly presence and must be represented as such, becoming "positive negations." By introducing, however, the formal concept of "sequence," Mr. Fletcher implies, like Mr. Cooke, that what is

experienced is also the will to form itself, which has a demonic element in it, like the "glittering eye" of Mariner or
rhetorician. Mr. Fletcher's closing distinctions between metaphor, synecdoche, and metonymy are, therefore, a bit deceptive, because they sound so cool and formalistic. They continue a type of analysis which, spurred by Jakobsonian
linguistics, and taking new courage from a rediscovery of
Nietzsche (that meditator of the will), is being developed in
France by such "grands rhétoriqueurs" as Michel Foucault,
Gérard Genette, Tzvetan Todorov, and—in this country—
Paul De Man. It is strange to think that what started with
I. A. Richards in the 1920s and passed into American criticism
through the academic study of traditional rhetoric (Empson,
Wallerstein, Tuve, Ong) is now returning to the Anglo-Amer-
ican domain via France. Yet, on reflection, the figure of Ken-
neth Burke also emerges as extravagant pater.

The last two essays are concerned with the problem of influence, but in very different ways. Mr. McFarland shows the
exact nature of the debt Coleridge owed to Tetens, a psychol-
ogist-philosopher of the German Enlightenment. The threefold
division of imagination in the *Biographia Literaria* derives
from Tetens and helped Coleridge in his quest for a "self-active" mental principle that would deliver him from the passive implications of associationist psychology. Moreover, by a
deeply Coleridgean connectivity this quest is related not only
to the poet's interest in systematic philosophy but also to his
ongoing, passionate endeavor to reconcile head and heart, the
impersonal or pantheistic and the personalist or Johannine
God. In extending the context of influence Mr. McFarland
also extends the chain of influence and leads us beyond Te-

tens to Leibniz, Plato, and the importance of theology. He strengthens the one consensus Coleridge scholarship seems to have reached: that Coleridge's greatness, whatever else it may be, or not be, is as a religious thinker.

Mr. Bloom's essay proposes an important transformation of influence studies. Some years ago Lionel Trilling asked us to reconsider the astrological origin of the word "influence," "a word intended to express a mystery. It means a flowing-in, but not as a tributary river. . . . Before the idea of influence we ought to be far more puzzled than we are" ("The Sense of the Past"). For Mr. Bloom the relation of past and present is that of person to person, a dialogue in which someone is bound to live another's life, as poet competes with poet for his own, significant difference. His literary history is a "war in heaven" rather than a progressive idealization of major figures. The question of influence is, of course, particularly appropriate to a writer whose reputation has been haunted, from De Quincey to Norman Fruman, by the plagiarism issue. But Mr. Bloom has generalized the issue to cover the "revisionary" relation of every new poet to his precursor. It is narrowed too, because there is no significant relation except between poets of the first order. Plagiarism thus becomes a matter for Grub Street. The real "anxiety" lies elsewhere, closer to the fear of possession or vampirism. "The eyes of the great dead yet look through ours" (J. L. Lowes).

"The death of the father is my shepherd," writes Marvin Bell, "he maketh me . . . versions of wanting." Mr. Bloom's six versions define nothing less than the life (or death) cycle of poets genuinely in touch with a sublime tradition. My own paper on the theme of the Evening Star also describes this

conflict of artist with art, or with a "westering" of great poetry. I describe it, however, from a perspective that stays in
the realm of poetical superstition—of veiled yet irreducible
terms.

GEOFFREY H. HARTMAN

*Yale University*
*January, 1972*

# CONTENTS

NEW PERSPECTIVES ON

*Coleridge and Wordsworth*

KENNETH R. JOHNSTON

THE IDIOM OF VISION

_During_ his imaginary correspondence with history, Saul Bellow's Herzog dashes off this urgent note to Martin Heidegger: "Dear Doktor Professor Heidegger, I should like to know what you mean by the expression 'the fall into the quotidian.' When did this fall occur? Where were we standing when it happened?" Well may Herzog ask. With eight hundred unpublished pages on Romanticism lurking in his closet, and his faith invested in the possibility that human life may yet have transcendental dimensions, he wants to know exactly when and where these possibilities fell to the ground.

One of the persistent, if minor, conditions of "the fall into the quotidian" engineered by post-Hegelian philosophy was the reluctance of sympathetic idealists to put the Herzogian question to the great Romantic writers who are, ostensibly, Heidegger's opposites on the question of transcendence. For example, what do Romantic poets mean by "vision"? In many

interpretations of Romantic poetry, unfavorable as well as fa-
vorable, there is a tendency to hypostasize The Vision out of
all contexts, without regard for differences between and
within poets' *œuvres*. Naturally this leads to reductionism:
"If you've seen one . . ." Then, enter Doktor Professor
Heidegger—stage left or stage right, depending on the critic's
attitude toward transcendence. New directions meet old on
this issue. The words "visionary" and "apocalyptic" are sometimes used as loosely in contemporary interpretations of Romanticism as the words "transcendental" and "mystical" were
a generation ago, and George Poulet's claim—that the "secular ecstasies" of the Romantic poets parallel Christian mys-
tics' vision of the divine *totum simul*—requires a firm sense
of the limits of analogy if claims about the Romantic imagination are to avoid the old charge of spilt religion.[1]

What then do the Romantic poets mean by "vision"? When
do these visions occur? That is, at what point in a poem has
something visionary taken place? Where are we, as readers,
standing when it happens, and how do we know that it has
happened?

The questions are crucial in the case of Wordsworth, because Wordsworth tells us that the fall into the quotidian is
not a Fall but the occasion for ascent into vision:

> I must tread on shadowy ground, must sink
> Deep—and, aloft ascending, breathe in worlds
> To which the heaven of heavens is but a veil.
>
> (*The Recluse*, I.i.781–83)

These new worlds are in "the Mind of Man," which, "when
wedded to this goodly universe," shall find true Paradise "a
simple produce of the common day." Something like this,

stripped of its rhetorical excitement, may also be behind Heidegger's phrase, in which case we see that Herzog lacks the
courage of his own Romantic convictions. Yet when we come
fresh upon Wordsworth's descriptions of vision, or of his
lesser "spots of time," we can be as perplexed as Herzog.
How can these moments possibly be sublime? We are often
at a loss to say what, if anything, has happened, let alone determine "to what point, and how,/The mind is lord and
master—outward sense/The obedient servant of her will"
(*The Prelude,* XII.221–23). Especially, it is hard to tell when
ordinary sight transmutes into vision in Wordsworth's poetry
—but this difficulty is, as much as anything else, the very essence of his genius.

Wordsworth's ecstasies are often so obscure that the sympathetic critic is only too willing to take Wordsworth's interpretation as a whole truth. When, for example, he concludes
his description of stealing eggs from ravens' nests with this
cry—

> With what strange utterance did the loud dry wind
> Blow through my ear! the sky seemed not a sky
> Of earth—and with what motion moved the clouds!—

we often need the straightforward puzzlement of students to
remind us that these exclamatory assertions sound like questions on first reading: What strange utterance indeed? And
with what motion *did* the clouds move? It is hard not to take
refuge in the deep sonority of Wordsworth's own interpretation of the event ("Dust as we are, the immortal spirit
grows/Like harmony in music . . ."), or to explain somewhat
lamely that the mysterious inexplicability of Wordsworth's
perceptions transmutes his questions into a form of praise.

Nevertheless, if the experience described is significant as poetry it must mean something in itself, prior to the poet's interpretive commentary upon it. And indeed it does, if we look
closely enough:

> Oh! when I have hung
> Above the raven's nest, by knots of grass
> And half-inch fissures in the slippery rock
> But ill-sustained, and almost (so it seemed)
> Suspended by the blast that blew amain,
> Shouldering the naked crag, oh, at that time
> While on the perilous ridge I hung alone,
> With what strange utterance did the loud dry wind
> Blow through my ear . . .        (*The Prelude*, I.330–37)

The long build-up of anticipation ("Oh! when . . . ," "oh, at
that time . . .") leads us to expect dramatic closure, but
Wordsworth's exclamations are questions disguised as assertions, and they extend the narrative line—or leave it hanging
—while only seeming to close it.[2] Yet a meaning has already
been predicated in the imagery. The boy hangs suspended
between the *shoulder* of the wind and the *naked* crag. The
personification could not be less obvious, and Wordsworth
carefully hedges it ("almost," "so it seemed"), yet the hint has
evidently been given, that nature's giant forms supported him
as a boy, even in theft, and thus nurtured him with fear as
well as beauty. The nakedness of the crag takes (or recovers)
a little of human feeling from the cliché—naked rocks—by
virtue of its proximity to the metaphor of the wind's shoulder.
The process is an instance of the "conferring, the abstracting,
and the modifying powers of Imagination" which Wordsworth explained in the Preface of 1815 with reference to the

composite image of the old man/rock/sea beast in "Resolution and Independence." It is also an example of one of the
most important recent insights into Wordsworth's poetry, the
recognition that the meaning of his visions is implicit in the
process by which they are described.[3]

Nevertheless, it is as easy to gloss over the difficulty of
Wordsworth's visionary sublimities as it is to reject them out
of hand for their obscurity. It is easy because Wordsworth
makes it easy. Most of his visionary descriptions appear in
contexts which carefully prepare the reader before the fact
and interpret it back to him afterwards, like a verse translation from the Egotistical Sublime into discursive High Quotidian. The pattern established in Book I of *The Prelude,* of
intensely emotional concrete descriptions alternated with
highly rhetorical abstract interpretations, pervades all fourteen books in some degree, and is especially apparent—
annoying, many would say—in the climactic vision from
Snowdon. These interpretive passages were often composed
separately from and later than the visionary descriptions to
which they are attached. The descriptions themselves usually
began their literary life as imagistic notebook jottings, but
Wordsworth rarely let them venture into public without a
chaperoning interpretation that guides the reader's response
away from the awkwardness and oddity of the poet's descriptive language: its apparently inconsequential exclamations, its
repetitiveness, bothersome double negatives, redundant cau-
tions and qualifiers, etc. Thus it takes a certain effort to con-
front this language squarely. Yet these peculiarities of
language, long thought to be signs of crudity and ineptness,
are probably the key to, and the highest expression of,
Wordsworth's verbal artistry. Taken together, they are a body

of idiomatic expressions with their own grammatical consistency, and they constitute Wordsworth's successful realization of his theoretical claim to have written in the language of common men as it is modified by passion and high emotion.

Recently the question of Wordsworth's obscure emotionalism has been interpreted from two different but complementary viewpoints, both of which aim to define the final cause or intention of Wordsworth's poetry. Writing from the perspective of a phenomenology of mind, Geoffrey Hartman examines the interstices of Wordsworth's heightened language and finds in them evidence of the poet's "consciousness of self raised to an apocalyptic pitch." [4] The magnificence of Wordsworth's achievement is for Hartman his determined and successful effort to bind his self-conscious Imagination to Nature, principally by means of a variously repeated mythic action in which Nature is portrayed as leading Imagination away from apocalyptic self-isolation and, simultaneously, beyond itself to love of man.[5] Richard Onorato, analyzing the psychological oddities of Wordsworth's visionary language from a Freudian perspective, sees them as manifestations of the poet's preconscious effort to hide from himself the fact that he is projecting onto Nature desires which were traumatically sundered from normal development by the death of his mother when he was eight. Onorato is far from simplistic; he is not saying that Nature was Wordsworth's mother-substitute. Rather, he interprets Wordsworth's recurrent effort to see *through* Nature into "the life of things" as a poetic idealization of the infant's sense of full identity between himself and everything around him—a sense which is focused in the figure of the mother. By age eight, Wordsworth like most children had long outgrown this primitive stage of consciousness, but according to Onorato his mother's death undid his normal development and led him to seek, "almost in spite of himself, a deeper reality in solitude and Nature"—deeper, that is, than the everyday reality of Mother Nature.[6]

These summations are inadequate to the theses advanced by Hartman and Onorato, and it must be stressed that neither account is reductive of Wordsworth's genius. Still, even their appreciation of Wordsworth's achievement will sound condescending to readers who imagine that Wordsworth has been "found out" in false pretensions about Nature—readers, that is, who believe Wordsworth to be a poet of Nature, of transcendence through or relationship to Nature, in ways which assume that "Nature" or "transcendence" or "relationship" is a metaphysical given that everyone knows and understands in common. It seems to me, however, that Hartman and Onorato have taken us closer to understanding Wordsworth's real achievement and real pretensions—which are, if anything, more pretentious than anything ever said about his nature worship. Specifically, they can lead us to reconsider how the sense Wordsworth conveys of transcendence and relationship in Nature is earned, not given, and how his poems are the enactment or creation of a faith, not simply the expression of it. It has been all too easy to speak of Wordsworth's Nature as though we knew from childhood what he meant. A certain insouciance comes into our manner once we set up—or silently assume—an easy dichotomy between a literalistic conception of Nature and a quasi-religious impression of transcendence. A recent book says, "Wordsworth is good at describing trees." Such observations do little to advance the crucial task of reinterpreting the nature of imaginative literature to a culture saturated with ersatz mimesis; they

strengthen rather than weaken the assumption that the literary artist is primarily dependent on an extrinsic subject
matter for his language. The needful effort of revisionary criticism represented here by Hartman and Onorato is already
well under way, but it raises certain alarms in its implicit po-
lemic against subject matter, especially in the case of Wordsworth, who has, to speak oddly, *more* subject matter than any
other poet in the language. Wordsworth's great faith is in Nature, the extrinsic, what is "out there," and in the *excursive*
power of Imagination to go out to meet it. Hence it can be
unsettling or aggravating to hear that his true subject matter
is self-consciousness, or to gain the impression, as one can
from reading Onorato, that "Nature" is Wordsworth's own
largest instance of poetic diction. For assuredly Wordsworth
does describe trees. Neither Hartman nor Onorato denies the
real importance of external Nature and other people to
Wordsworth's poetry, but the polemical demands of displac-
ing the Arnoldian Wordsworth with the Bradleyan Wordsworth have put a strain on our patient understandings, and
perhaps we need a touch of the Paterian Wordsworth to help
keep the new balance in trim. At least it seems so to me, that
"the function of the critic of Wordsworth" described by Pater
a century ago is very salutary just now, especially in the
method of procedure he recommends. It is to

> trace the action of his unique, incommunicable faculty,
> that strange, mystical sense of a life in natural things,
> and of man's life as a part of nature, drawing strength
> and color and character from local influences, from hills
> and streams, and from natural sights and sounds. Well!
> that is the *virtue*, the active principle in Wordsworth's
> poetry; and then the function of the critic of Wordsworth

is to follow up that active principle, to disengage it, to
mark the degree in which it penetrates his verse.
(Preface to *Studies in the History of the Renaissance*,
1873)

In the bulk of the remainder of this essay, I will be looking
closely at one poem, "A Night-Piece," to suggest that it is a
paradigm of Wordsworth's representation of visionary potential in Nature because of the intricate, odd ways in which it
shows phenomenal processes imbedded in apocalyptic structures. Conversely, I will suggest briefly that another poem,
the little-known manuscript poem called "St. Paul's," is paradigmatic of the ways in which apocalyptic pressures are inherent in his poems which seem to avoid vision. They are
useful paradigms because their dominant visuality under-
scores the crucial relationship between sight and vision in his
work, and, further, because they turn upon Wordsworth's use
of an image—the veil—which is structurally and archetypally
central to any discussion of poems pretending to "re-*vela-
tion*." In the realms of consciousness, Wordsworth is our first
and greatest border poet. Hence we do well to focus attention
on the details of those moments when he passes from one
state of being to another (or at least intimates that there *is*
another—"something evermore about to be"), from sight to
vision, or from veiled to unveiled vision. We will be struck by
the subtleties of his control over language; oddities that appear at first merely awkward turn out to be related in mean-
ingfully linguistic patterns. Moreover, the fact of control is
not neutral, it implies a meaning in and of itself: namely, that
different modes of being, though manifestly different, are
manifestly contiguous. They border; they touch. Wordsworth's high valuation of "moods by form or image unpro-

faned" does not imply that he felt a necessary separation between these moods and others where a natural image is
paramount. If transcendence lies across a border or behind a
veil, the value of Nature on the near side of the crossing is as
clear as ever: it is the path or temple through which one approaches the veiled shrine of the "mystery of man" (*The Prelude*, XII.272). Wordsworth's vigilance against the tyranny of
the bodily eye does not mean that the visual aspects of his visions can be separated from something in them conceived to
be "truly" visionary; such a separation was for him the ultimate tyranny, or trauma.

II

## A Night-Piece [7]

(Composed Jan. 25, 1798; published 1815)

          —The sky is overcast
With a continuous cloud of texture close,
Heavy and wan, all whitened by the Moon,
Which through that veil is indistinctly seen,
A dull, contracted circle, yielding light          5
So feebly spread that not a shadow falls,
Chequering the ground—from rock, plant, tree, or tower.
At length a pleasant instantaneous gleam
Startles the pensive traveller while he treads
His lonesome path, with unobserving eye          10
Bent earthwards; he looks up—the clouds are split
Asunder,—and above his head he sees
The clear Moon, and the glory of the heavens.
There, in a black-blue vault she sails along,
Followed by multitudes of stars, that, small          15
And sharp, and bright, along the dark abyss

Drive as she drives: how fast they wheel away,
Yet vanish not!—the wind is in the tree,
But they are silent;—still they roll along
Immeasurably distant; and the vault,                              20
Built round by those white clouds, enormous clouds,
Still deepens its unfathomable depth.
At length the Vision closes; and the mind,
Not undisturbed by the delight it feels,
Which slowly settles into peaceful calm,                          25
Is left to muse upon the solemn scene.

The poem draws together most of the issues raised in my introduction. Herzog's questions apply: Does something happen in "A Night-Piece" or not? That is, is it a complete event with its own coherence, or does it plead for explanation? Is the event quotidian or visionary—or both at once? Finally, is it a poem or a fragment? (All of these questions apply equally to "St. Paul's.")

That "A Night-Piece" is an antecedent of the kind of experience Wordsworth imagines in the Snowdon description has often been noted, with the suggestion that it is also a prototype of that "emblem of a mind/ That feeds upon infinity." [8] Its fitness as a visionary paradigm is established by scholarly precedent, since it is a favorite point of reference for introductory observations about Romantic or Wordsworthian visions.[9] Usually, however, it is presented as an incomplete or inferior form of visionary poetry.[10] Certainly it is less magnificent than many moments of vision in *The Prelude*, but I will argue that it is in all essentials parallel to them, and well deserving of Wordsworth's recommending it in particular among his Poems of the Imagination (along with "Yew Trees") for "the imaginative power displayed in them." Crabb

Robinson's puzzled response to Wordsworth's choice of models neatly captures the mixed quality of strength and difficulty which Wordsworth's visions present to their readers: "They are fine, but I believe I do not understand in what their excellence consists. Wordsworth, as Hazlitt has well observed, has a pride in deriving no aid from his subject. It is the mere power which he is conscious of exerting in which he delights, not the production of a work in which men rejoice on account of the sympathies and sensibilities it excites in them." [11] To my mind, the tension in "A Night-Piece" runs in exactly the opposite direction—that is, it strikes one's sensibilities more immediately as an exciting description of night than as evidence of the poet's self-conscious exertion of his imaginative powers. But the poetic issue is certainly one of tension, and Robinson accurately states the problem which understanding "A Night-Piece" helps to solve in all of Wordsworth's visionary poems.

As in the Snowdon vision, which is indebted to the earlier poem,[12] the tension in "A Night-Piece" is between a scene of dull blankness and one of deep brilliance. It is tempting to phrase this as a tension between earth and heaven, but the poem will not support such an organizing view. True, the difference between feelings of finite limitation and infinite expanse is basic to it, but its tension is temporal rather than spatial like Snowdon's. The poem moves temporally from an initially obstructed relationship between earth and sky—but with the cloud-veil in the sky representing the obstruction—through a two-part sequence of relationship, first sudden and brilliant, then gradual and subdued. But the second stage of relationship is as earth-bound as the initial situation of blankness. This in a sense is the whole point, the completed statement, of the poem.

"A Night-Piece" is therefore an imagist narrative; meaning arises from the development of its imagery. It expresses a tension like the tension of thought, but it is impossible to know what makes the traveler "pensive" before the vision or what is the objective content of his peaceful musing afterwards. Wordsworth does not interpret for us as he does in *The Prelude*, and the only way the reader can "muse upon the solemn scene" in anything like the traveler's frame of mind is by subduing himself to the poem's imagery. As is so often his wont, Wordsworth here describes his soul "Remembering how she felt, but what she felt/ Remembering not . . ." (*The Prelude*, II.316–17).

It took a long time for Wordsworth to recognize that "A Night-Piece" was largely complete in its original form. Based originally upon an entry in Dorothy's journal, it was simply labeled "Fragment" in the *Christabel Notebook*. Wordsworth added the title, polished a few phrases, and added three clarifying lines while preparing the poem for the edition of 1815.[13] Even in its original form, however, "A Night-Piece" is no more fragmentary than "Kubla Khan," that most famous of all Romantic pseudo-fragments. Like Coleridge's poem, Wordsworth's reveals a principle of coherence based on an implicit tension between a mysterious natural scene and an apocalyptic dimension which opens up inside it. A simple but plausible explanation of the difference between the "Fragment" of 1798 and the "Night-Piece" of 1815 is that poems that seemed fragmentary to Wordsworth and Coleridge in the earliest days of their mutual experimentation were gradually recognized to be unified works of art—what we today regard as characteristic Romantic poems.[14] Certainly both men had composed scores of similar pieces in the interim.

The title signals Wordsworth's recognition of the full po-

tential of his early fragment, drawing our attention to the
highly visual, almost painterly aspects of the poem—
theatrical set design is perhaps its most appropriate visual
analogue. Of course we must allow Wordsworth any poet's
right to stick a title on a fragment and call it a poem. In this
respect the colloquial sense of the title is perfectly just, suggesting a short descriptive piece. But a "night-piece" is,
strictly speaking, the name of a sub-genre of landscape painting which the Renaissance made the domain of romance. It
may have come to Wordsworth as a result of his friendship
with Sir George Beaumont, which stimulated his interest in
painterly visual effects. The antiphony of Shakespeare's Lorenzo and Jessica, "On such a night . . . , On such a night
. . . ," expresses the generic *donnée* of all such paintings, and
Herrick's poems are their first straightforward literary embod-
iment in English. However, as with most of the topoi of romance, there is a dark underside, a dialectical antithesis. It is
touched on lightly in the allusions to tragedy which filter
through Lorenzo and Jessica's sweet sighing, but it is expressed most strongly in the darkly flaming night-pieces of
Grunewald (c.1460–1528) and Altdorfer (c. 1480–1538). Especially in Elsheimer's "Flight into Egypt" (c. 1600), the genre
startlingly intimates apocalypse in the midst of pastoral romance.[15] This is the same tension which gives life to "Kubla
Khan"; it is implicit in the title Wordsworth affixed to his
onetime fragment and runs throughout the poem.

The poem actually proceeds in such a way as to minimize
or, rather, equalize the tensions it establishes between limitation and boundlessness. But though Wordsworth skillfully
"perceptualizes" an event which hints at transcending ordinary perception, the poem's visual excitement deserves notice,

the better to see how he checks himself. Visual drama is certainly the primary thrust of the poem, but a cursory reading
of it, especially under the influence of our recent enthusiasm
for things visionary, might see nothing but epiphany and ecstasy. On the other hand, Jonathan Wordsworth has called
the emotion of "A Night-Piece" "quite ordinary," relative to
the Snowdon description, meaning that it describes a qualita-
tively lesser experience.[16] But the ordinariness or extraordi-
nariness of emotions is moot, especially in poems, and we
must look for firmer criteria to determine such qualitative distinctions as whether "A Night-Piece" is or is not typical of
Wordsworth's description of vision.

The striking effect of the moonlight depends on the dim
darkness preceding it; hence the function of the entire first
sentence (ll. 1–7) is an extended operation in dimming the
lights. The description of the light moves downward, from its
source in the sky, to the cloud, to the feeble light shining
through the cloud, to the absence not only of light but of
shadow, to a heavy Alexandrine conclusion accented by spon-
dees: "not a shadow falls,/ . . . from rock, plant, tree, or
tower." [17] Disjunction between states of consciousness begins
with "startles" in an initial, accented position in line 9, and
the vision opens in earnest in line 11. There, syntax is dis-
rupted by caesuras strongly marked with dashes ("excitement
is an unusual and irregular state of mind; ideas and feelings
do not, in that state, succeed each other in accustomed
order"; Preface of 1798). On a first reading, line 11 may seem
end-stopped, so that the actual moment of revelation is doubly emphasized when we realize that "split" is enjambed to
"Asunder," and this realization, passing in an instant, is immediately brought up short by another caesura. With its

eccentric caesura, line 12 seems short, and indeed has only four accents in ten syllables. The sense of excitement moves swiftly through the next seven lines, with more broken syntax and simple, single-accent words (five lines have nine words each). The adjectives are commonplace and, notably in the description of the stars, are as far separated from their noun as coherence will allow. The placement and simplicity of these adjectives is significantly different from the opening lines, where the adjectives almost submerge their noun. (For example, in line 3 it is easier to read "heavy" and "wan" as modifying cloud, or even sky, than to read them grammatically for what they are, extensions of the adjectival modification of "texture"—a noun which in turn is an elaboration of still another adjective, "continuous.") Thus the sharp discreteness of the language in lines 11–19 parallels and supports the distinct and rapid motion of the planets which is the subject matter or content of the vision.

Nevertheless, a full view of the poem will recognize that it is structured in such a way that its excitement does not transcend natural processes. It only puts them, for a moment, in eternal perspective: the stars, "how fast they wheel away,/Yet vanish not!"

Wordsworth's control is evident particularly in his manipulation of visual imagery to achieve spectacular lighting effects without becoming stagey. The laconic phrase "At length," which opens and closes the vision, is conscious artistry, and not only in its parallel placement. In her journal account of the experience, Dorothy wrote "at once," certainly a more idiomatic or cliché phrase for visual excitement: all of a sudden. In his first version, Wordsworth wrote "at last," a phrase which is at the opposite extreme from "at once" as an expression of juncture. Then he chose "at length," the least definite, most mediate of the three possibilities. It is the nature of visions to be extraordinary and beyond the idiomatic descriptive powers of ordinary language, so it is perhaps a contradiction in terms to speak of Wordsworth's idiom-of-vision, or to say that "at once" is more cliché than idiomatic. But in a sense it is the intention of Wordsworth's greatest poetry to render vision idiomatic, avoiding on the one hand clichés which overcontrol it (cf. Coleridge's "Religious Musings"), and on the other hand avoiding expressions and images which are too unique to be intelligible (as Blake and Shelley often did not).

Insofar as there is a Wordsworthian idiom of vision, line 8 exemplifies an important element in it: "At length a pleasant instantaneous gleam." It is an almost diagrammatically regular bridge between stages of consciousness, a construction of mutually canceling connotations which makes the movement from blankness to brilliance a progression by stages rather than leaps. "At length" and "pleasant" are on one side of a fulcrum of emotional connotations, "instantaneous" and "gleam" on the other. There is, moreover, a faintly oxymoronic quality in the "pleasant instantaneous" combination. Bennett Weaver long ago adduced the visionary thrust of nouns like "gleam" and "flash" in Wordsworth's poetry.[18] Now that the pendulum of cultural value and critical practice is swinging away from Wordsworth the nature poet to Wordsworth the visionary, we need to remind ourselves of the adjectives that so often accompany these nouns. Here I feel the sense of the phrase as, instantaneous-but-pleasant-nonetheless, or pleasant-even-though-instantaneous. As in Wordsworth's famous description of Nature's twin ministry of Fear and Beauty, there is never a complete break between one stage of emotion and the next. (Cf. Nature's *"fearless* visitings, or those / That come with *soft* alarm, like *hurtless* light / Opening the *peaceful* clouds." These adjectives of cautious revelation, Nature's ministry of Beauty, are then linked to, not separated from, the ministry of Fear, which is characterized by "sever*er* interventions, ministry / *More* palpable." The comparatives make us see the ministry of Fear in the light of Beauty's "fearless" visits. *The Prelude,* I.352–56.)

Taking line 8, then, as an "exchange" between emotions, we no sooner come upon the verb activating the subjective effect of the vision ("startles") than we find movement once more impeded by the belated introduction of the perceiving subject. He traipses into the poem, passive to his verb. As is often the case in Wordsworth's visionary descriptions, emotional effect is paramount, and prior to conscious response. This poem is titled "A Night-Piece," not, say, "Man Traveling," and emotion is represented in its vision almost to the exclusion of the traveler, "who, and what he was— / The transitory Being that beheld / This Vision" (*The Recluse,* I.i.849–51). Every descriptive word modifying the bare narrative essentials (traveler, path, eye) links the human subject to the earth-bound blankness of the first sentence: "Pensive," "lonesome," "unobserving," "earthwards." Half of these adjectives were added to the poem when Wordsworth was readying it for publication; [19] he almost exactly doubles the effect he wishes to achieve. The human figure is linked to the dullness of the opening scene in order that he may be linked, at least in implication, to the visionary change which comes over the landscape. Even the traveler's motive verb, "treads," connects aurally with the word "spread," which describes the feeble power of the light, and thus contrasts his initial motion more sharply with the verbs of visionary action to follow: split, sails, drives, wheel, roll.

What principally stamps the vision as Wordsworthian, however, in the dialectical terms I am using, are the repetitions and redundancies of his visual description proper: "drive . . . drives," "silent . . . still . . . still," "clouds . . . clouds," and the subtle construction, brought to perfection in "Tintern Abbey" six months later, of a verb returned upon itself as its own object: [20] "deepens its unfathomable depth." Like his faint oxymorons and double negatives, Wordsworth's repetitions are functional, not sloppy craftsmanship, and cannot easily be faulted except by critical standards which say, as though poetry were a class in elementary composition, that words should not be repeated in proximity to each other. Here, as in the opening lines of "Tintern Abbey," such repetitions are signs of proximities more essential to Wordsworth than literary decorum: the close interrelation between the constituent elements of the vision, and between them and his *visionnaire malgre lui.*

The stars "drive" as the moon "drives." The verb implies friction, connoting a sense of weighty motion much like that Keats achieves with the word "swims" describing the motion of the planet in "On First Looking into Chapman's Homer." The verb impinges upon the glitter and speed of the stars with the steadier light and port of the moon, thus anticipating and reinforcing the paradox toward which all these repetitions tend: "how fast they wheel away,/Yet vanish not!"

The word "still," coming immediately after "silent," is a mild punning of sight into sound, of the kind Roger Murray has shown to be characteristic of Wordsworth's reduction of

rhetorical figures to their lowest common denominator.[21] Like
the wind-tossed tree, the stars are in motion, but unlike the
tree, silently. And continuously: the dialectic between the
senses of sound and sight reasserts itself at the word "Immeasurably," where the idea of never-broken silence merges
into the idea of everlasting motion. These countervailing patterns are so common in Wordsworth they could almost be reduced to a formula: aural absence : visual presence : : visual
presence : aural absence. Here, as David Ferry says more
simply and succinctly, silence and light are joined to contrast
with sound and darkness.[22] Jonathan Wordsworth says the
wind in the tree is "just a noise" and has "quite false associations" because it does not develop into a version of Wordsworth's "correspondent breeze." [23] Again, the observation is
true but its interpretation is moot; the issue is whether images that are not explicitly stretched to their full metaphysical implications by the poet may still be said to carry a significance of their own, greater than the barren naturalism of
"just a noise" or the invidious comparison of "false associations." Be that as it may, "still" is primarily a word of visual
description in "A Night-Piece," and its repetition in line 22
connects one visible motion with another, the driving-wheel-
ing-rolling motion of the stars to the slower movement of the
clouds. This connection, which could hardly be more tenuous,
is important, because it links the interconnected movement of
the visionary foci, moon and stars, to the similarly connected
movement of the clouds (which, we must remember, are part
of the nonvisionary topography of "A Night-Piece").

The evidence of Wordsworth's revisions helps us to understand his intention here. In the *Christabel Notebook* he tried
the following alternative for what is now line 21: [the vault],

"Built round by those huge clouds retains its form." [24] This is half the idea Wordsworth wants to convey: the cloud-vault remains coherent as the cloud-veil breaks apart over the moon, thus setting off "the glory of the heavens." But the *Notebook* line is too static, because not only does Wordsworth see the vault retain its form, he sees it as dynamically *intensifying* its form. It is deep but it becomes deeper; it becomes more like what it is; it stays the same but changes. Thus we see clearly in the MSS what is more subtly present in the printed poem, that the continual deepening of the clouds parallels the motion at the heart of the vision: the stars' wheeling away without ever vanishing.

The repetitions and redundancies in the description of the vision are for Wordsworth a means for simultaneously suggesting and controlling the movement of mind from imperception, to perception, to vision. They are nature's checks and balances upon vision, enabling the mind to move back from vision to perception, or nature. For about five lines, beginning with the key word "Asunder," the drama of the vision has moved quickly and smoothly. But beginning with the repetitions connecting the moon and stars the language begins to get more complicated, slowing down visual and verbal movement for a gradual "reentry" into the world of nature. This is not to say that line 22 is undramatic; quite the contrary, it is mysteriously magnificent. Yet its grandeur is closer to the earth than anything else in the vision because it returns our attention to the clouds, once a veil of "texture close," now a vault of "unfathomable depth." The sides of the vault are, so to speak, the rended edges of the veil of line 4. Line 22 represents nature's analogue to the paradox of the stars' movement, the last stage of a three-part vision: first, "the clear Moon,

and the glory of the heavens"; secondly, the stars, "how fast
they wheel away/Yet vanish not"; thirdly, the cloud-vault
"Still deepens its unfathomable depth."

Before looking at the last four lines of "A Night-Piece," it is
instructive at this point to pursue David Ferry's observation
that the clouds change, metaphorically, from a veil obscuring
vision to a vault defining it. Ferry's "sacramentalist" reading
sees this shift in metaphor as an emphasis of drama, profund-
ity, and clarity: "ordinary nature both aids and obstructs the
'vision.'" [25] But from a different perspective—one in which
nature is not sacramental but is represented as a real presence in itself—the fact that the cloud-veil changes from visual obstruction to visual aid implies that natural limitations
upon vision are helpful not only to emphasize visionary experience but also to keep it in perspective—almost literally so.
By its contrasting of ground and background of vision, "A
Night-Piece" intimates that the dimensions of natural experience run very deep, almost to eternity, but the same contrast
also suggests that the eternal dimension would not be recognized without the natural scene. Literally, it would lack
focus. Ferry says the depth of the vault is shown by its "contrast" with the clouds, but what is the vault without the
clouds? The separation Ferry wants to make between the "sacramental" Wordsworth and the "mystical" Wordsworth is
implicit in this admittedly minuscule point. According to
Ferry, the wind in the trees and the clouds (as "contrasted"
to the vault) are "something of a distraction to the traveler.
The moon itself, by this view, is but a symbol for the metaphysical world." [26] But the clouds and the sound of the wind,
though assuredly *different* from "the glory of the heavens" in

metaphysical status, are distractions only if one assumes (as Ferry does) that Wordsworth desires an immediate, total union with infinity. But this it seems to me is not the case. The image of the cloud-vault and the sound of the wind in the trees, like other images and verbal constructions throughout the poem, function in the poem precisely to suggest and yet avoid such a union. In saying this I am following half the thesis of Geoffrey Hartman, though I am not sure I would want to assign Wordsworth's motive to fear of apocalypse.[27] That "A Night-Piece" seeks to avoid apocalypse I think is evident; why it should do so is another, larger question. It shows that Wordsworth, far from being indifferent or antagonistic to Nature, re-creates its simulacra with painstaking care in moments which seem determined to transcend Nature. This I take it is the other side of the coin of Hartman's dialectical argument.

When "at length" the vision closes, a double negative ("not undisturbed") is Wordsworth's careful way—somewhat awkward—of acknowledging emotional effect. His double negatives are of a piece with his habit of defining his experience by saying what it is not, as in the Ode and "Tintern Abbey." [28] Like the phrase "pleasant instantaneous" they function as crude oxymorons. Here, "not undisturbed" allows the poet to acknowledge emotion while simultaneously asserting that the emotion was not overwhelming—not, in a word, unnatural. Having acknowledged, somewhat grudgingly, a delightful disturbance, Wordsworth goes on to reduce emotional intensity in every substantive term of the following line: "*slowly settles* into *peaceful calm.*" "Peaceful calm," far from being an oxymoron, is almost a tautology, but it works in the same direction as the oxymorons and double negatives —to exert its particular species of control over the description of vision.

Finally, the brilliant interruption of the moonlight changes the observer as well as the scene. It has made the traveler observant; obviously this is the point of the poem. The final adjective "solemn" is a transferred epithet, an aspect of the wayfarer's state of mind gained from, but quietly shifted back onto, his surroundings. The clouds have transmuted back again from vault to veil, but the veil is now a mediator, not an obstruction. The landscape is no longer "feebly" lit to the traveler's eye, even though its measurable light must be nearly identical to the opening scene's; its "solemn" light is the afterglow of vision.

The cumulative effect of all these details is to intimate, almost invisibly, the *conjunctive* character of the vision. A man suddenly discovers himself to be standing between heaven and earth, standing, moreover, as a link between them. The traveler does not simply apprehend or suffer this dualism, he *is* the dualism—without him it does not exist. The two spheres are brought together not so much by, as in, man; recognizing his mediate position, he defines his being. It has been said that landscape in Romantic poetry functions like the Muse of classical poetic fiction; it also functions like the text in modern critical theory. Like the Muse, it is invoked as a source of power, and like the text, it is given meaning by participation. Any statement about the meaning of "A Night-Piece" will have to acknowledge that, above all, the poem represents the process by which the traveler's consciousness is transformed from dullness to ecstasy to meditative calm. No meditation arises from the traveler, as at the end of the Snow-

don vision, but the pattern of visionary imagery is very close
to that of Snowdon. It may be objected that the significance I
am attributing to "A Night-Piece," as a model, depends upon
prior knowledge of Wordsworth's more famous descriptions of
vision. While this is true—and in a sense is precisely my
point—it is not necessary to have Snowdon in mind to see
what special, organized arrangements of language are at
work here. The meaning of "A Night-Piece," like most of
Wordsworth's descriptions of vision, resides in the process it
describes: simultaneously disjunctive and conjunctive, the
very type of a great consummation in which Mind and Nature are imagined as exquisitely fitted to each other, yet remain distinct.


III

There is neither space nor need for a detailed examination
of "St. Paul's," the poem which I propose as a paradigm dia-
lectically the contrary of "A Night-Piece." Indeed, I quote it
here as much to draw attention to a neglected minor master-
piece as to support a thesis. Also, the fact that Coleridge was
the cause of the "conflicting thoughts" which give the poem
its tension makes it especially appropriate for the present volume.

St. Paul's [29]

(Composed March-April, 1808; published 1947)

Press'd with conflicting thoughts of love and fear
I parted from thee, Friend, and took my way
Through the great City, pacing with an eye
Downcast, ear sleeping, and feet masterless

That were sufficient guide unto themselves                    5
And step by step went pensively. Now, mark!
Not how my trouble was entirely hush'd,
(That might not be) but how, by sudden gift,
Gift of Imagination's holy power,
My Soul in her uneasiness received                           10
An anchor of stability. —It chanced
That while I thus was pacing, I raised up
My heavy eyes and instantly beheld,
Saw at a glance in that familiar spot
A visionary scene—a length of street                         15
Laid open in its morning quietness,
Deep, hollow, unobstructed, vacant, smooth,
And white with winter's purest white, as fair,
As fresh and spotless as he ever sheds
On field or mountain. Moving Form was none                   20
Save here and there a shadowy Passenger
Slow, shadowy, silent, dusky, and beyond
And high above this winding length of street,
This moveless and unpeopled avenue,
Pure, silent, solemn, beautiful, was seen                    25
The huge majestic Temple of St. Paul
In awful sequestration, through a veil,
Through its own sacred veil of falling snow.

The obvious differences between "St. Paul's" and "A
Night-Piece" involve both process and content. The vision is
veiled, not unveiled. True, something is seen through the veil,
but the veil is the end of the visionary process rather than the
beginning. (The veil in "A Night-Piece" is also part of the
end of the vision, but by being transformed from a veil into a
vault.) Secondly, the content of the vision is emphatically
static ("an anchor of stability") in contrast to the dynamic

movement of the spheres in "A Night-Piece." And surely the specifically religious character of the visionary focus can be ascribed to differences that run far deeper in Wordsworth's development than the literal difference between the setting of the two poems. Nevertheless, his presentation of the effect of the vision is in all essentials comparable to the apocalyptic (i.e., uncovering) structure modeled in "A Night-Piece." There is the passive, head-down dullness of the observer at the beginning, the sudden start of the vision and the equally sudden braking of its impact (ll. 7–11), and the careful establishing of the appropriate perspective in which to view the vision (the unobstructed street parallels the cloud-vault). Furthermore, the various stages of the visionary process are here marked even more clearly than in "A Night-Piece," by lines of adjectives (ll. 17, 22, 25) which simultaneously describe and demarcate the street, the pedestrians, and the temple. Stylistically, they are flaws which Wordsworth might have removed had he polished the poem for publication, but they are interesting manuscript evidence of the structural form of his visions (cf. the three stages of the Simplon and Snowdon visions).

Still, we may ask what has happened, beyond a rather obvious linking of "Imagination's holy power" to an external religious object. What disparate elements have been yoked together here to make us assent to Wordsworth's characteristic claim that a "familiar spot" has become "a visionary scene"? Wordsworth was puzzled enough by this question to refrain from ever putting the poem forward in public. In a letter to Beaumont he expressed amazement that this image of London should ever have fixed itself so deeply in his mind. "I cannot say how much I was affected at this unthought-of sight in such a place, and what a blessing I felt there is in habits of exalted imagination." [30] He hews doggedly to his belief that cities are death to imagination. Yet in both the poem and the letter, city and country are the polar opposites linked together as loci of inspiration. The statement of "St. Paul's" could be reduced in paraphrase to this: Even here, in London of all places, imagination comes in aid of feeling. The street carries an appearance of imaginative power to Wordsworth which he accommodates by attributing to the street the dimensions of a Westmoreland valley. This use of metaphor is the same as in the Westminster Bridge sonnet. In strictly imagistic terms, the snow-veil itself is the mediating link between the unveiled and veiled stages of the vision, like the cloud-veil/vault in "A Night-Piece." It is nature's mantle in the country and St. Paul's veil in the city.

It might be said that "St. Paul's," written in the spring of 1808, stands as a symbolic exit from the Great Decade, just as "A Night-Piece" stands like a beacon at the beginning. But the suggestion must be withdrawn as soon as it is offered, because both poems represent kinds of visionary poetry that appear throughout Wordsworth's career and cannot be contained inside the troublesomely convenient category of a Great Decade. The pattern symbolized by "A Night-Piece" is now well known and respected, but as a mode of poem writing it exists in a dialectical relationship with the kind of visionary poetry represented by "St. Paul's." This kind of poem is neither well known nor widely honored, but it is apparent throughout Wordsworth's cannon, in such diverse poems as Book IV of *The Excursion, Peter Bell,* and the late *Evening Voluntaries,* the lengthy manuscript poems "Home at Grasmere" and "The Tuft of Primroses," and such lyrics as the address "To the Clouds" and "To a Highland Girl." A mixed lot, textually and critically. It would take another essay to distinguish them, as Poems of the Imagination, from the different imaginative mode represented by "A Night-Piece." Here it is sufficient to note that many of them, including "St. Paul's," have associations with the incomplete *Recluse* project which to later generations of scholars has remained one of the central enigmas of Wordsworth's genius.[31] "A Night-Piece" is a paradigm of the visionary Wordsworth of *The Prelude;* "St. Paul's" is a paradigm of the differently visionary poet of *The Recluse.* The latter is a failed poet, but certainly not an unknown one. Many of his works are extant. He is more elusive —reclusive—than the epically modern egoist of *The Prelude,* but his works constitute a kind of shadow epic in the magnificence both of their conception and of their failure. They represent an elusive poetic ideal which has informed many creative efforts of the last two hundred years, one that we do well to keep in mind in weighing the importance of Nature in Wordsworth's poetry, and of subject matter generally in artistic creation of all kinds.

IV

Twenty years ago, on the centenary of Wordsworth's death, Lionel Trilling observed that Wordsworth is "not an attractive and not an intellectual possibility" in contemporary culture, owing to his incapacity for tragedy, violence, and "all that is fierce and feral and consciously heroic and charismatic in our literature." Trilling lamented the situation. He saw that modern literature's fascination with elemental instincts and memories owed a great debt to Wordsworth, a debt ob-

scured by the unattractiveness of his moral and religious seriousness. Only the universities, said Trilling, keep Wordsworth alive.[32]

Twenty years later, the universities have more than repaid
Trilling's confidence. The Wordsworth set before us by contemporary academic criticism has rather more affinity with
modern culture than he had in 1950. Some might complain
we have got the Wordsworth we deserve, tailored to the
apocalyptic taste of our times. Reinterpretations of Romanticism, especially of Blake, are always susceptible to the temptations of enthusiasm and short-range relevance.[33] But in the
most sophisticated and meticulous works on Wordsworth, one
can discern the beginnings of an effort to heal the breach
Trilling deplored in our appreciation of Wordsworth, the
breach between the unattractive poet of moral responsibility
and the attractive poet of instinctual egoism. In these studies
Wordsworth appears not as a poet of apocalypse but as one
who offers an attractive and intellectually possible critique of
the apocalyptic and pseudo-apocalyptic impulses of our time.

The possibility of this fundamental readjustment in Wordsworth's reputation was brought home to me again as I read
one of Professor Trilling's most recent diagnoses of our cultural ills, "Authenticity and the Modern Unconscious." [34]
Here he takes to task the putative metaphysicians of the new
"counter-culture," Herbert Marcuse, Norman O. Brown, and
R. D. Laing. What most disturbs him in the writings of the
latter two is their celebration of the "divine madness" of the
fully liberated unconscious, what we may call its potential for
apocalyptic assertion of Self against the institutionalized "in-
sanity" of technological society. Trilling now writes more as a
Freudian than as a Wordsworthian or Arnoldian, but it is just

at this point—that is, the nature and value of selfhood in modern society—that the possibility seems greatest of reuniting the Arnoldian Wordsworth ("Wordsworth's poetry is great because of the extraordinary power with which Wordsworth feels the joy offered to us in nature") and the Bradleyan Wordsworth ("the 'mystic,' 'visionary,' 'sublime' aspect of Wordsworth's poetry must not be slighted . . . in Wordsworth's poetry, everything is natural, but everything is apocalyptic").

One of the most vexing phrases in recent Wordsworth scholarship is Geoffrey Hartman's claim that Imagination in Wordsworth's poetry is "consciousness of self raised to an apocalyptic pitch." The similarity of this level of consciousness to that extolled by Brown and Laing is obvious, but it is so often quoted out of context that Hartman has seemed to play Blake to Wordsworth's Milton, claiming he is of the devil's party without knowing it. But, as Hartman's recent retrospective essay makes perfectly clear, his view of Wordsworth has always been more on the side of Trilling's critique, though he is more confident than Trilling about Wordsworth's ability to meet the "devils" on their own ground. Hartman describes a Wordsworth who has tasted deeply the attractions of apocalyptic selfhood, yet who submits himself, of his own volition, to the struggle of turning away from solipsism to nature, man, and society. The mechanism of this turning is of profound interest today. Why and how should it occur? Freudian psychology has developed an extensive vocabulary to describe it, but the drama of its operation is everywhere in Wordsworth's poetry, though oftentimes in language that veils what is actually happening.

What the more important critics have shown us during the

last twenty years is the real difficulty of Wordsworth's poetry, and how its difficulty is intimately related to his personal difficulties in making himself into the poet he was. An "ennobling interchange" between inner and outer worlds was Wordsworth's solution to a problem, but it is not a solution to the problem of reading his poetry. Another troublesome phrase of Hartman's, in this connection, is his characterization of the Snowdon episode as "Wordsworth's most astonishing avoidance of apocalypse." When I first read it, I resented what I took to be its implication, that Wordsworth had failed to measure up to the exigencies of Hartman's thesis. Now I believe Hartman has shown us how Wordsworth faced an ultimate transcendental temptation and faced it down. It is easy to be swayed by the gloriously obfuscating rhetoric of Wordsworth's interpretation of the Snowdon vision, swayed, that is, from confronting his repeated circling round the idea that the man of genius is like a god ("that glorious faculty/That higher minds bear with them as their own"), or more than "like" ("In soul of more than mortal privilege"). What is astonishing is not Wordsworth's cowardly failure to embrace apocalypse but his determination not to. We greatly underestimate him if, recognizing the temptations of universal egotism, we do not appreciate the heroism—feral and fierce indeed—of turning it to something else.

Wordsworth's turning back from the veil of apocalyptic vision, documented in this essay in his intricate efforts at verbal control, his constant impeding of the visionary thrust of his verse by repetition and redundancy, by faint oxymorons, double negatives, and banal tautologies, must be understood with one additional proviso. Wordsworth did not become a conser-

vative only at middle age; the entire arc of his development
was an effort to learn how to conserve imagination:

> the hiding places of man's power
> Open; I would approach them, but they close.
> I see by glimpses now; when age comes on,
> May scarcely see at all . . . (*The Prelude*, XII.279–82)

His turning toward Nature away from Self is always done in
the name of the proper culture of individual feelings. This is
what he said in the Preface of 1800, and this was the testimony of his greatest interpreters in the nineteenth century,
Arnold, Pater, and Mill. When Mill said that Wordsworth is
"the poet of unpoetical natures," he identified him as the first
poet of modern culture. We are all unpoetical natures now,
and the other poets that Mill paid lip service to, poets of "poetical natures," of "deeper and loftier" feelings, have, it appears, gone forever.[35]

If the long reaction against Wordsworth the poet of nature
and of feeling is nearing an end, and if it comes about paradoxically by means of those who stress his apocalyptic egotism, it comes at an apt time. Trilling characterized our society at mid-century as "the iron time," paraphrasing Arnold;
the times are less rigid now, but it takes courage to say that
our new fluidity is absolutely to be preferred, and we are all
the more in need of guides. Wordsworth cannot save us, but
he can at least help us to recognize ourselves. For example,
Trilling begins his essay on the new cults of personal authenticity with an exordium on the decline of narrative, in literature, in history-writing, and in individuals' sense of themselves. Others have referred to "the death of the past." What

is to be mourned in this death, says Trilling, is the loss of the
essential *weightiness* of human nature. And without weight,
without character in the old-fashioned sense, the temptation
to individualized apocalypse is all too great, as anyone connected with university life in the past decade can testify.
What Trilling says about narrative and the sense of the past
is obviously germane to Wordsworth's faith in memory, but it
also applies by analogy to his sense of Nature. Our sense of
place suffers in travail as much as our sense of time; too
many people don't know where they're from in either sense.
We must largely grant the diagnostic insights of Marcuse,
Brown, and Laing, physicians of the plastic age. But we will
make little headway with either Wordsworth the nature poet
or Wordsworth the poet of consciousness unless we allow that
he creates our sense of Nature in his poems as much as he
creates our sense of transcendence. His argument founders
when it rests literally on Nature, for what is literal Nature?
"Where man is not, nature is barren"—it is not impossible to
imagine Blake's proverb in Wordsworth's mouth. Nature is
"out there," always, but its essential thereness must be affirmed by consciousness, and to that extent, created. Despite
all we know about its debt to eighteenth-century epistemol-
ogy and Edward Young, there is still something to ponder in
Wordsworth's testimonial to

> the mighty world
> Of eye, and ear—both what they half create,
> And what perceive          ("Tintern Abbey," ll. 105–7)

Wallace Stevens remarks somewhere that the motive of poetry arises from the poet's sense of being in a place that is not
his place and not his self. The poet recognizes, articulates,

and thus defeats displacement. Wordsworth knew well the "feeling that I was not for that hour,/Nor for that place" (*The Prelude*, III.81–82). He made determined efforts of obscure language to veil his isolation, but no one can deny he always responded to it affirmatively, with a still greater determination to create a faith that this earth can be our place and self. On this ground "old" and "new" Wordsworthians can surely meet.

## NOTES

1. J. Hillis Miller, "Geneva or Paris? The Recent Work of Georges Poulet," *University of Toronto Quarterly*, XXIX (1970), 214, 217. Cf. M. H. Abrams's claim that Romantic writers "undertook . . . to save traditional concepts, schemes, and values which had been based on the relation of the Creator to his creature and creation." *Natural Supernaturalism* (New York, 1971), p. 13. As a description of writers' conscious motive or intention, this otherwise exemplary statement implies that the Romantics were second-stage Reformers, purifying metaphysics as the first Reformers had purified ethics and belief.

2. This is an example of what I would call the "veiled" or "invisible" predicate in Wordsworth's grammar of vision. Compare his assertion that the "sands of Westmoreland, the creeks and bays/ Of Cumbria's rocky limits" can testify to his "unconscious intercourse with beauty":

> they can tell
> *How*, when the Sea threw off his evening shade,
> And to the shepherd's hut on distant hills
> Sent welcome notice of the rising moon,
> *How I have stood*, to fancies such as these
> A stranger, linking with the spectacle
> No conscious memory of a kindred sight,
> And bringing with me no peculiar sense

Of quietness or peace; *yet I have stood,*
*Even* while mine eye hath moved o'er many a league
Of shining water, gathering as it seemed,
Through every hair-breadth in that field of light,
New pleasure like a bee among the flowers.

(*The Prelude*, I.567-80; italics added)

They never do tell *how* he stood; the passage gradually elides its anticipated predicate until the assertion becomes simply the fact *that* he has stood and looked at nature. Cf. the sentence in "Tintern Abbey" beginning, "And so I dare to hope . . ." (ll. 65–72). Even after long acquaintance with it, one sometimes expects it to move forward to closure: i.e., "And so I dare to hope . . . [*that* something good will result]." But the predicative force of the demonstrative adjective is actually carried by the word "so," and the sentence looks backward for its predicate rather than forward: "And so [*thus*: "with pleasing thoughts / That in this moment there is life and food / For future years," ll. 63–65] I dare to hope . . ." His hope thus appears to be a general mental condition, like his "unconscious intercourse with beauty," not a wish whose object can be specified.

3. Herbert Lindenberger, *On Wordsworth's "Prelude"* (Princeton, 1963), pp. 73–74, 90–91; Alex King, *Wordsworth and the Artist's Vision* (London, 1966), pp. 62–79; Karl Kroeber, "The Relevance and Irrelevance of Romanticism," *Studies in Romanticism*, IX (Fall, 1970), 303–4.

4. Geoffrey H. Hartman, *Wordsworth's Poetry, 1787–1814* (New Haven, 1964), p. 17.

5. See Hartman's prefatory essay, "Retrospect 1971," in a new printing of *Wordsworth's Poetry* (New Haven, 1971), pp. xi–xx.

6. Richard J. Onorato, *The Character of the Poet: Wordsworth in "The Prelude"* (Princeton, 1971), pp. 25, 68–69.

7. *The Poetical Works of William Wordsworth*, Vol. II, ed. Ernest de Selincourt and Helen Darbishire, 2d ed. (Oxford, 1952), pp. 208–9. (Third in the "Poems of the Imagination" sequence.)

8. James Kissane, " 'A Night-Piece': Wordsworth's Emblem of the Mind," *Modern Language Notes*, LXXXI (1956), 183–86.

9. Karl Kroeber, *Romantic Narrative Art* (Madison, 1960), pp. 51–53; David Ferry, *The Limits of Mortality* (Middletown, Conn., 1959), pp. 30–31; Frederick Garber, *Wordsworth and the Poetry of Encounter* (Urbana, Ill., 1971), pp. 80–85.

10. Jonathan Wordsworth, "The Climbing of Snowdon," *Bicentenary Wordsworth Studies*, ed. Jonathan Wordsworth (Ithaca, N.Y., 1970), pp. 454–56; Thomas Vogler, *Preludes to Vision* (Berkeley, 1970), pp. 83–85.

11. *Henry Crabb Robinson on Books and Their Writers*, ed. Edith J. Morley (London, 1938), I, 166–67.

12. Jonathan Wordsworth, "The Climbing of Snowdon," p. 456.

13. Beth Darlington, "Two Early Texts: *A Night-Piece* and *The Discharged Soldier*," *Bicentenary Wordsworth Studies*, pp. 426, 431–32.

14. Karl Kroeber nicely observes that a modern poet would probably concentrate on the epiphanic emotion at the center of the poem while down-playing its narrative elements, whereas a neoclassical poet would have fleshed out the narrative with appropriate moral and philosophical applications. *Romantic Narrative Art*, p. 53.

15. Kenneth Clark, *Landscape into Art* (London, 1949), pp. 37–42, 51–52.

16. Jonathan Wordsworth, "The Climbing of Snowdon," p. 455.

17. Darlington, "Two Early Texts," p. 431. Wordsworth improved the dramatic finality of this line from his original draft, which read: [the moon] "chequers not the ground / With any shadow—plant, or tower, or tree." The influence of one of his own most memorable lines is apparent: "Rolled round in earth's diurnal course, / With rocks, and stones, and trees."

18. Bennett Weaver, "Forms and Images," *Studies in Philology*, XXXV (1938), 433–45.

19. Darlington, "Two Early Texts," pp. 431–32.

20. Geoffrey H. Hartman, *The Unmediated Vision* (New Haven, 1954), p. 24.

21. Roger Murray, *Wordsworth's Style: Figures and Themes in the "Lyrical Ballads" of 1800* (Lincoln, Nebr., 1967), pp. 131–42.

22. Ferry, *Limits of Mortality*, p. 30.

23. Jonathan Wordsworth, "The Climbing of Snowdon," p. 455.

24. Darlington, "Two Early Texts," p. 432. Judging by MS variants, this is the only line in the description of the vision proper that gave Wordsworth much trouble in revision; as noted above, he had considerably more difficulty with the lines describing the scene before the vision opens.

25. Ferry, *Limits of Mortality*, p. 31.          26. *Ibid.*

27. Hartman, *Wordsworth's Poetry*, pp. 60–65.

28. E. de Selincourt, ed., *Poetical Works*, II, 503.

29. *Ibid.*, IV (Oxford, 1947), 374–75. (Appendix B: Poems Either Never Printed by Wordsworth or Not Included in the Edition 1849–50.) The title is supplied by De Selincourt.

30. *The Letters of William and Dorothy Wordsworth*, Vol. II, *The Middle Years*, Part I (1806–11), ed. E. de Selincourt, 2d ed. rev. by Mary Moorman (Oxford, 1969), p. 209.

31. Mary Moorman, *William Wordsworth*, II (Oxford, 1965), 130–31. Some of the poems cited have suggestive connections in Wordsworth's MSS. MS I of "To the Clouds" is on the verso of MS I of *Peter Bell*, and MS 2 contains also "The Tuft of Primroses" and "St. Paul's." (*Poetical Works*, II, 524.)

32. Lionel Trilling, "Wordsworth and the Iron Time," *Wordsworth: Centenary Studies*, ed. Gilbert Dunklin (Princeton, 1951), pp. 131, 150.

33. Recent articles aimed at rescuing Blake from contemporary irrationalisms are: Harold Bloom, "First and Last Romantics," and

Karl Kroeber, "The Relevance and Irrelevance of Romanticism," *Studies in Romanticism*, IX (Fall, 1970), 225–32, 297–306, respectively.

34. *Commentary*, LII (September, 1971), 39–50. The essay is a revised version of the last of six lectures on sincerity and authenticity delivered by Professor Trilling during his recent tenure as Charles Eliot Norton Professor of Poetry at Harvard. Publication of the entire series is forthcoming from Harvard University Press.

35. John Stuart Mill, *Autobiography* (1873), Chap. V: "A Crisis in My Mental History. One Stage Onward."

JOHN HOLLANDER

# WORDSWORTH AND THE MUSIC OF SOUND

$In$ a strange little meditation written in 1919,[1] Rainer Maria Rilke recalls his earliest schoolboy experiments with a then recently invented cylinder phonograph, and how what stayed with him longest were his belief that, as he put it, "independent sound, taken from us and preserved outside us, would be unforgettable," and the image later to work on his fancy—not the sound from the horn but the markings traced on the cylinder. This unassimilated impression lay dormant, Rilke suggests, until awakened in another context: while a student later on at the Beaux-Arts, he had become fascinated with skeletal anatomy and had procured a skull upon which to meditate at night (if as in a baroque emblem, he does not say). A passing glance seems to have precipitated an involuntary memory:

> By candlelight—which is often so particularly alive and challenging—the coronal suture had become strikingly visible, and I knew at once what it reminded me of: one

of those unforgotten grooves, which had been scratched
in a little wax cylinder . . .

and he goes on to outline a fancy:

The coronal suture of the skull (this would first have to
be investigated) has—let us assume—a certain similarity
to the closely wavy line which the needle of a phonograph engraves on the receiving, rotating cylinder of the
apparatus. What if one changed the needle and directed
it on its return journey along a tracing which was not derived from the graphic translation of a sound, but existed
of itself naturally—well: to put it plainly, along the coronal suture, for example. What would happen? A sound
would necessarily result, a series of sounds, music . . . .
    Feelings—which? Incredulity, timidity, fear, awe—
which of all the feelings here possible prevents me from
suggesting a name for the primal sound which would
then make its appearance in the world . . . ?[2]

A subsequent expansion of technology and the evolution of
musical institutions over fifty years allows us to identify
Rilke's terrifying *Ur-geraüsch*, his "primal sound," as nothing
more awesome than the kind of *musique concrete* that is
probably more to be described than heard. But this matter of
technology is by no means trivial, I think, in the matter of the
history of the Imagination; Rilke's childhood toy, which for
the first time in history could can music, could thus provide a
far more remarkable mechanical model of memory than previously envisioned, and initiated a deeper imaginative discontinuity with acoustical antiquity than any broached since,
whether by tapes, happenings, or the solemnization of the
aleatory, the playful, and the boring. Electronic technology
might provide us with alternative emblems to Rilke's inter-

nalized *musica mundana,* his inaudible sounds of the heavenly vault inscribed in the arch of the human dome: we might think of an amplitude or frequency-modulated carrier wave, where the modulation by the imprinting of a sound transcription might stand easily for the imposition of consciousness of itself upon a mere act of hearing (or, by extension, for a humanization of an inert myth like the music of the spheres). We have grown up being able to flick a switch and thus plunge, *in medias res,* into the unprepared audibility of soundless music which has been going on unheard or suffering an Aeolian imprisonment; we can, with the twist of a knob, change the volume of musical sounds, or their enveloping timbre. We have, moreover, become accustomed to *underscoring,* to musical accompaniment of the visual beyond, and below, the projections of romantic desires for the *Gesammtkunstwerk;* and in a world increasingly flooded with piped-in sound, we have unwittingly had to accept the transformation of quiet music, magically coming from no visible source, into annoying noise.

There is an obvious parallel here with the imaginative status of the visual technologies—photographic, cinematic, projectional, and soon more available, perhaps, holographic —which have developed in the last century. Recent studies of Romantic imagery have underlined the ways in which visionary modes, at one moment in history, will anticipate the picturings of the as-yet-uninvented technologies of the visual. In a larger context, this is only part of the historical dialectic of science and poetry: discarded scientific models metamorphose into constellations of myth, and, in a recycling movement, industrial technolgies produce phenomena which unimaginatively duplicate some of the achieved visionary imagery in poetry of the past.

In this connection it might be remarked that the poetic treatment of the sounds of wind and water had achieved, by 1711, the full status of cliché; the great lullaby of eighteenth-century poetry is one of decorative words so emptied of their meaning that they have become musical sounds:

> Where-e'er you find "the cooling western breeze,"
> In the next line, it "whispers thro' the trees":
> If crystal streams "with pleasing murmurs creep,"
> The reader's threaten'd (not in vain) with "sleep":
> (Pope, *An Essay on Criticism*, 350–53)

Or consider for a moment this instance, with which we also might have begun: Thomas Warton in his MS notes on Spenser comments on some lines about the harp of Philisides, or Sir Philip Sidney, in "The Ruines of Time." The harp is rising into the sky to become, like its Orphean predecessor, the constellation Lyra,

> Whilst all the while most heavenly noyse was heard
> Of the strings, stirred with the warbling wind
> That wrought both ioy and sorrow in my mind . . .

And Warton comments, "What Spenser's imagination here beautifully feigns, is actually brought into execution in the Aeolian harp, the effect of whose music is exactly what our poet describes: 'That wroght both ioy and sorrow in my mind.' " [3] Leaving aside the appalling standards of acoustical and musical description, we are faced with the relation between the eighteenth-century toy and the image it parodies.

There are moments—for Whitman, say, or Hart Crane—when these domestications of revelation appear to be fulfillments of a kind of modal, as opposed to a moral, prophecy.

But in many ways the convenient reductions which invention affords—the overlaying of transparencies, for example, as a model of what must be accomplished, at the opening of "Tintern Abbey," by an intense mingling of terms drawn from landscape description and associationist psychology via the magical verb "connect"—such reductions will be read by poetic history as satanic paraodies of the poetic process. Only Romanticism itself, actually, could react with answering energy to the notion of automata simulating will, perception, or utterance. Such contemporary phenomena are frequently functional in glossing eighteenth- and nineteenth-century poetic imagery (students need only be reminded of the Antonioni films to grasp the para-emblematic qualities of the image of the poplar tree's shadow falling across the face of Marianna in her moated grange); but perhaps to remark on this is only to confirm their reductive status.

We need hardly be reminded, however, that the auditory realm is ever secondary to the kingdom of sight; and in these observations on the treatment of sound in Wordsworth's poetry, we shall be continually referred back to that secondariness by our want of a complementary term, in the aural dimension, to the word "visionary" in contrast with "visual." The records of Wordsworth's visionary hearing range from the formal "soundscapes" which Geoffrey Hartman has analyzed and named in the two long early topographical poems,[4] through the imaginatively dangerous remythologizing of natural music in the interesting and problematic ode "On the Power of Sound." In a section of it, the poet addresses echoes as "Ye Voices, and ye Shadows/ And Images of voice—"[5] and these very shadows and images of the exhortation are as much a succedaneum and prop as that of invoking reflections as "echoes of vision" would be a fancy. A British linguistic scholar has put rather well one aspect of this phenomenological commonplace: "sound stands more in need of external support than light, form or color; hence the greater frequency of the intrusion of outside elements into the description of acoustic phenomena." [6] The "external supports" here are those of metaphor. Shadow, and mirror-image in bronze or water, coexist in antiquity with echoes, and their personifications are parallel myths. But there is no analogue of painting of sculpture for the preservation of aural shades; until the invention of the phonograph, in fact, there is no way of recording sounds of discourse or music save by echoes or parrots. Nor can any dreams and imaginations of the ear save those of human discourse survive the feeble resources of the dreamer's reportage.

Thus, for example, while the afterimage of the daffodils can "flash upon" the inward eye, the immediate presence of the mountain echoes of a reciprocal poem composed two years later are "rebounds our inward ear / Catches sometimes from afar," [7] a kinetic characterization threatened, rather than elucidated, by the subsequent development of rubber balls. But the cultivation of this "inward ear" is nonetheless an important element in preparing for the representation of consciousness, and it is interesting to observe the parallels with, as well as the intersection of, the course of evolving an answerable diction which that element reveals. In 1802 Wordsworth had addressed his brother John as a "*silent* Poet" who "from the solitude / Of the vast sea didst bring a watchful heart / Still couchant, an inevitable ear, / And an eye practised like a blind man's touch." [8] But the openness of the sense of hearing is never the problem: crucial to the economy of the senses is the fact that we cannot close our ears as we do our eyes, and that vision is far more directional than hearing, which is not "To such a tender ball as th'eye confin'd" but, more like feeling, through all parts, at least of the head, "diffus'd." "A man, inasmuch as he has ears," said Emerson, "is accosted by the thunder and the birds." [9] It is more a matter of the availability of appropriate conceptualization for representing the experience of hearing.

The poetic treatment of sound as such has a rather foreshortened history. Acoustic science distinguishes between the natures of noises and musical tones by demonstrating that the fogmer result from vibrations at all frequencies within a band (and are thus, in a sense, more "general"), while the tones of music are produced by vibrations at a very few frequencies, carefully related mathematically. (It is this phenomenon, actually, which should inspire Pythagorean superstition, rather than the numerical ratios governing scales: the human ear performs what Leibniz called its "unconscious arithmetic" by distinguishing tone from noise as such. Ironically enough, an absolutely "pure" frequency, a concert-pitch $a$ of 440 cycles per second, has only during the last fifteen years become, through the legitimization of electronic instruments, which alone can produce such sounds, a tone rather than a modern, industrial, electric *noise*, part of the humming and buzzing and beeping of machinery.) From classical times through the Renaissance, the imaginative distinction between tone and noise had a moral content. Music, as represented by Orphean myths and those of *musica mundana*, was the sound of Creation, of what had been organized; noise, whether the thundering which might be read as cracks in nature's structure, ambiguous sea-sounds, or whatever, was the sound of chaos in its eternal effort to creep further back into nature. Human speech (which, for the modern acoustician, is structured *noise*) was conceptually closer to music than to inanimate nonmusical sounds. This left only the noises which were to be read as belonging to music's realm—the sounds of *nature* in the fullest sense, rather than merely a biological one, and these were assimilated through mythologizing. Echoes, the spirits inhabiting large natural concavities, were thus assimilated to musical spirits dwelling within the caves or shells of musical instruments (this becomes virtually a cliché of musical allusion in poetry from the seventeenth century on); the noise of moving water becomes an emblem of eloquence, and that sound, birdsong, and the rustling of foliage in the milder winds all enter, in pastoral tradition, into the conventional musical underscoring for the picture of the *locus amoenus*.[10]

Good sound must be music or speech, then; and insofar as any sound at all is to be considered beneficial or pleasurable, it must be metaphorically invoked as such. From this point of view, the catalogues of outdoor sounds which are so ubiquitous in eighteenth-century poetry and which are certainly derived from Renaissance descriptions of the *locus amoenus* expand beyond the conventional lists as more and more kinds of sound become part of the imaginative landscape. "Music to my ears," that is, means not only "what I'm glad to hear," but at another level "what I notice and what nourishes my aural attention." The sublime incorporates what had been previously considered the noises of chaos into the rural orchestra; torrents, the sounds of landslides, cataracts, thunder, and the sounds of storm all come to signal the authenticity of the *locus terribilis* even as the choir of birds and water and wind accompanies the lovely one, and the mingling of piping or song and waterfall in pastoral eclogue identifies a world in which poetry is creative and evocative force. There are other aspects of this incorporation, of course. We must not neglect the phenomenological consequences of the history of formal music itself; there is certainly some connection between the developing taste for the pianoforte, with its responsiveness to touch and its dynamic range, and the poetic interest in the gradations of volume as a quality, and even a mode, of sound.[11] By the end of the eighteenth century, this is being reflected in more general ways, and the so-called terraced dynamics of baroque music give way to rolling ground. This is the musical context for the emergence of the Romantic theme of auditory distancing as an aspect of the over-all cliché: "Alles wird in der Entfernung Poesie: ferne Berge, ferne Menschen, ferne Begebenheiten. Alles wird romantisch"[12]—distancing makes everything poetry, says Novalis, faraway hills, faraway humans, faraway happenings, and although he does not add "ferne Laute"—faraway sounds—Romantic tradition does so for him. Collins's Melancholy, in his ode "The Passions," to which I shall return, "from her wild sequester'd Seat, / In notes by Distance made more sweet, / Pour'd through the mellow *Horn* her pensive Soul."[13] By 1806, Wordsworth can adduce, almost as if quoting a received proverb, "sweetest melodies / Are those that are by distance made more sweet";[14] both he and Collins imply a post-Renaissance meaning for "sweet" in a musical context—in the seventeenth century it still means only "in tune" (cf. modern residual "sour notes")—moving toward "dear." It is as important to distinguish poetic conventions for the handling of sound from the records of actual attentive listening, as it is to interpret changing terminology correctly, though. Consider the following passage from Coleridge's notebooks: [15]

> . . . the moon is gone. The cock-crowing, too, has ceased. The Greta sounds on forever. But I hear only the ticking of my watch in the pen-place of my writing-desk and the far lower note of the noise of the fire, perpetual, yet seeming uncertain. It is the low voice of quiet change, of destruction doing its work little by little.

A splendid sketch, perhaps, for an unrendered soundscape, and before we can read its notations we must be assured that "low" refers to dynamic and not to pitch. Coleridge is forever jotting down such sketches, as he is continually raising questions about the possibilities of musical metaphor and the limits of received language; this attentive interest is not unconnected with his inability to write the ode on music which he occasionally projected.

But here is Thomas Warton's figure of Melancholy:

> Raptur'd thou sitt'st, while murmurs indistinct
> Of distant billows sooth thy pensive ear
> With hoarse and hollow sounds . . .[16]

and again, with religious music in mind:

> . . . or let me sit
> Far in sequester'd isles of the deep dome,
> There lonesome listen to the sacred sounds
> Which, as they lengthen through the Gothic vaults,
> In hollow murmurs reach my ravish'd ear.[17]

In both cases, the "hollow" quality of the sound has as little to do with an act of listening, *en plein air*, as the "ravish'd ear";

it derives from the first of Dryden's St. Cecilia's Day odes, and is about as accurate, in this context, as a black shadow in a landscape by Claude. Instead, it authenticates the sound by referring back to its source (the "hollow shell" of a lute or a nymph's cave—these coalesce in neoclassical poetry) and by generating evocations like those of the desert music in Goldsmith's deserted village:

> Along thy glades, a solitary guest,
> The hollow-sounding bittern guards its nest;
> Amidst thy desert walks the lapwing flies,
> And tires their ecchoes with unvaried cries.[18]

The bittern's booming sounds hollow, and thus empty of meaning, in an emptied world.

The hollow places give birth to music mythologized—the shell as synecdoche for "lyre"; the literal, technically termed "shell" of the Renaissance lute; the caves; the labyrinths of the ear which gradually become inevitable, as in Gray's lines from "The Progress of Poesy": "Or where Maeander's amber waves/ In Lingering Lab'rinths creep,/ How do your tuneful Echo's languish,/ Mute, but to the voice of Anguish?," [19] where the "airy shell" has contracted into what suggests both the semicircular canals and the as-yet-unpoetized seashell of Wordsworth and Landor. The confusion between the shell-as-instrument of neoclassic cliché and the truly new Romantic image of the seashell is too elaborate to be discussed here. But the generative hollows tend to appear in the background of reference even when no formal invocation of them is made. Thus, toward the end of "Tintern Abbey":

> . . . when thy mind
> Shall be a mansion for all lovely forms,

> Thy memory be as a dwelling-place
> For all sweet sounds and harmonies . . .[20]

no skulllike cave of memory is openly described, but the recorded sounds will surely exist there forever as rebounding,
undying echoes.

But these are hollows of potentiality. Goldsmith's hollow-
sounding bittern announces the mockery of sublime ruin. Its
solitariness distorts, rather than sensitizes, like that of Cowper's Selkirk for whom the tameness of the beasts around him
must be shocking, who never hears "the sweet music of
speech" and so can confess: "I start at the sound of my own."
Conversely, the village music of what Goldsmith calls "the
sounds of population" fall into the layered patterning of rural
music that, throughout the seventeenth and eighteenth centuries, provided the model for the representation of sound listened-to out of doors:

> Sweet was the sound when oft at evening's close,
> Up yonder hill the village murmur rose;
> There as I past with careless steps and slow,
> The mingling notes came softened from below;
> The swain responsive as the milk-maid sung,
>
> The sober herd that lowed to meet their young,
> The noisy geese that gabbled o'er the pool,
> The playful children just let loose from school,
> The watch-dog's voice that bayed the whispering wind,
> And the loud laugh that spoke the vacant mind,
> These all in sweet confusion sought the shade,
> And filled each pause the nightingale had made.[21]

"Responsive" usually occurs in pastoral to characterize the
echoing phenomenon in nature which confirms the poetic

character of the music of voice or instrument,[22] and the ironies here emerge when we see how close this is to the antipastoral urban catalogues of Swift in a poem like "A Description of the Morning." The point is that all the noises and voices enter into a polyphonic consort whose ancestry can be traced back to Spenser.

This is not the place to work out that genealogy; we shall simply recall the long tradition of soundscape accompanying the *locus amoenus* which was mentioned earlier. Classical and Renaissance traditions come together in the mingled vocal, instrumental, and natural music characterizing the Bower of Bliss. For Spenser, this mingling is sinister, mixing modes and systems and literary genres and betraying the pastoral conventions it sophisticatedly parodies, as the artificial vegetation betrays nature. But in his immediate seventeenth-century followers, the mixing of human and natural music becomes a positive presence in pastoral adaptation. Drayton, Browne, and Fletcher all convert traditional catalogues of birdsong into descriptions of contemporary broken-consort music, and provide a format for the quasi-visual representation of sounds, and eventually noises, in descriptive poetry.[23]

The layering of the voices, whether in Spenserian stanza or in couplets, suggests the vertical format of polyphonic parts in score, and even when this has become minimal it still informs the way in which the sequence of reported sounds must be read. They are antiphonal, choral, or both: thus Gray again,

> The Attic Warbler pours her throat
> Responsive to the cuckow's note,
> The untaught harmony of spring . . .[24]

is rehearsing an old baroque theme of the bird-concert (reinforced in seventeenth-century Northern painting, by the way,
by a minor genre that shows the brightly colored birds
perched among green, unruined choirs of foliage, all singing
from a book of musical notation held open by one of them).[25]
Aside from the literary convention, which helps to establish
the manifest musical image, there is the almost unwitting involvement of one of the oldest prosthetic metaphors which
aid our vestigial vocabulary of sound-description: *liquidity* is
used as early as Lucretius to describe birdsong.[26] In Renaissance pastoral, melody *pours* and sounds *fill* regions in such a
way that the very imagery of the solo melodic line is "attuned" to that which literally describes the moving of water
in brooks and streams which by convention *speak*, but in the
lovely places, *sing*.[27] Again, the problem of listening to nature
seems to be one not of the inevitability of ear, or even the unmediated act of listening, but rather in the storage and re-
trieval of what has been heard.

Variations and extensions of this model abound in eighteenth-century poetry. They range from orchestrations of
village noises and gothic echoes in Goldsmith and Blair, for
example, to the almost paradigmatic preservation of the
model that we should indeed expect to find in Dyer's "Grongar Hill":

> While the wanton Zephyr sings,
> And in the vale perfumes his wings;
> While the waters murmur deep;
> While the shepherd charms his sheep;
> While the birds unbounded fly,
> And with musick fill the sky,
> Now, ev'n now, my joys run high.[28]

Here are the harmonized delights of bucolic tradition, even to the juxtaposition of the sound and the smell of the moving air, a topos lurking everywhere in the Renaissance *locus amoenus*. Wordsworth's more formal musical orchestrations, in "An Evening Walk" and the "Descriptive Sketches," are chiefly remarkable for the fine tuning of their auditory attention, as well as for the way in which, in the former poem, they signal and accompany the fading out of a scene. In the 1790s he can give musical privilege, in that beautiful water-poem in remembrance of Collins, to the sound of "The dripping of the oar suspended," [29] as he can in another moment of silence (the silence that is audible when speech, rather than sound, has ceased), a decade later, to "the flapping of the flame, / Or kettle whispering its faint under-song." [30] But if in the earlier poems the music has become perfectly naturalized, the presentation of it has not. There is the almost emblematic treatment of an instrumental consort in the "Descriptive Sketches," mixing maids' voices, "twilight lute" (wisely removed, in the 1849 revision—Wordsworth had never heard a lute in his life), "village hum," fife, drum, and, finally, a wailing insect; this has a distinct neoclassical flavor, in its implicit assumptions of a modality proper to each instrument, rather in the manner, as shall be discussed shortly, of the Augustan ode for music. But even the more characteristically natural catalogues partake of this:

> An idle voice the sabbath region fills
> Of Deep that calls to Deep across the hills,
> Broke only by the melancholy sound
> Of drowsy bells for ever tinkling round;
> Faint wail of eagle melting into blue
> Beneath the cliffs, and pine-woods steady sugh;

The solitary heifer's deepen'd low;
Or rumbling heard remote of falling snow.[31]

This catalogue, we are told at its beginning, is free of all "irreligious sound" save at the end now, where the avalanche
demands that the sabbath be broken, and "the stranger seen
below, the boy/ Shouts from the echoing hills with savage
joy." The "wail of eagle melting into blue" is masterful for the
Miltonic syntax—the wail melts into the blue as the shrinking
sight of the bird does—and the layers of sound, lowering in
pitch while varying wildly in dynamic, timbre, and ordinary
signification, are beautifully adapted to the part-song model.
In the revision for the 1849 edition, Wordsworth adds a couplet, in this instance unwisely, for it destroys the effect of the
original closure. But it is a significant, almost querulous reductive glossing, as if to remind the reader of the lost model:
"All motions, sounds, and voices, far and nigh,/ Blend in a
music of tranquillity." [32]

The "blending" here is that of vertical musical harmony,
but another, older tradition lies behind it. The first musical
sounds to request and receive "authentic comment" from the
noises of nature are in Theocritus and Vergil, antiphonal at
first and then, with the Renaissance, polyphonic. The alternative to the carefully orchestrated "layered" page of music is
the blended duo of singing voice or instrument and the wind.
For English poetry of the later eighteenth century and after,
the only genuine music will be heard out of doors. For the
poetry of the Renaissance, the richly mythologized world of
music all took place, whether indoors or out, under the order-
ing, unifying, covering shell of the cosmos, a shell from which
noise, like chaos, was excluded. Augustan thought and rheto-

ric tended to trivialize that musical mythology, and during
the eighteenth century we can listen to chorded shells, lutes,
harps, lyres, ravishing voices, and so forth creeping out into
the generalized *locus amoenus* which all landscape becomes
and reauthenticating themselves with what the traditions of
speculative music from Aristotle on would have considered
breaths of inanimate air. The voices of fair singers start
blending with the wind, becoming sweetened by distance,
and so forth; the aeolian harp, an eighteenth-century house-
hold toy, becomes the basis of a profound and widespread
trope for imaginative utterance, and a kind of mythological
center for images of combining tone and noise, music and
sound.

There are moments in the history of this developing imagery when ambiguities and misunderstandings are possible.
Dr. Johnson, for example, who is seldom generous toward the
mythopoeic, seems to ignore the figurativeness of Gray's "rich
stream of music" at the opening of "The Progress of Poesy," a
stream that clearly starts "From Helicon's harmonious
springs." Perhaps it is because the stream of imagery itself repeats its poetic phylogeny, moving from the classical allusion
through the pastoral "laughing flowers" animated by the flow
of eloquence, to the regions of the unpremeditated in the
near-sublime lwndscape at the end of the strophe: "Now rowl-
ing down the steep amain,/ Headlong, impetuous, see it
pour:/ The rocks, and nodding groves rebellow to the roar."
"Gray," says Dr. Johnson,

> seems in his rapture to confound the images of spreading
> sound and running water. A "stream of music" may be al-
> lowed; but where does "music," however "smooth and
> strong," after having visited the "verdant vales" "rowl

down the steep amain," so that "rocks and nodding groves, rebellow to the roar"? If this be said of music, it is nonsense; if it be said of water, it is nothing to the purpose.[33]

But it is said of the water-sound-music figure, still linked to poetry by the Heliconian origin. Just as there had to be, one feels, at least one poem in which the neoclassical term "shell" for "stringed instrument" would be confused even by the poet himself with the recently invented Romantic singing seashell, there appear to have to be these transitional passages from the stock emblem or epithet into the more modulated images. A fanciful figure for this might be the sounds of a harpsichord sonata by Arne, say, heard outside the house and across a brook amid a gentle fanning of leaves. A historical fact is the addition, in the 1770s and thereafter, of the so-called Venetian-swell mechanism to English harpsichords, in a vain attempt to compete with the piano's ability to control dynamics and thus analogically to invoke shades of feeling.[34] Such a fact is figure enough.

Wordsworth never totally loses touch with conventions of musical imagery about natural noise, and such images keep reappearing long after more fully naturalized figures should have taken possession of the domain of sound. In the context of the musical epithets, the aural experience of the bower, in "Nutting," "Where fairy water-breaks do murmur on/ For ever" is astonishing, and more imaginatively than epistemologically revolutionary:

> I saw the sparkling foam,
> And—with my cheek on one of those green stones
> That fleeced with moss, under the shady trees,

Lay round me, scattered like a flock of sheep—
I heard the murmur and the murmuring sound . . .[35]

"The murmur *and* the murmuring sound"—as if the separation into two phenomena might begin to comprehend the interruption of actual stereophony occasioned by the one ear to
the ground and the other upward. One hears the natural and
one, the faery, one the literal water noises and the other the
figurative bleatings of the rocks becoming sheep in the poem
itself. This is one of the great anatomized acts of listening in
Wordsworth, occurring at a moment of shaded, perhaps sated
vision. It is the listening itself we are on the brink of hearing.

But consider for a moment a purportedly more casual report, a description of warblers in the *Guide to the Lakes:*

> . . . and their notes, when listened to by the side of
> broad still waters, or when heard in unison with the mur-
> muring of moutain-brooks, have the compass of their
> power enlarged accordingly. There is also an imaginative
> influence in the voice of the cuckoo, when that voice has
> taken possession of a deep mountain valley . . .[36]

There is an almost stepwise movement here from the acoustical fact that sound heard across still water is indeed ampli-
fied, to the *musical* phenomenon of the bird-brook duo
(where the enlargement of the "power" is in the attention, the
*listened-to* rather than the audible) and finally to the pure
figure of the conclusion (the voice of the cuckoo only "takes
possession" of the valley for the hearer who, in a special way,
has lost possession of his senses). Even in glossing his own
sound imagery, in the 1815 Preface, Wordsworth can move
from mythological acoustics into the wider realm of acoustic
mythology. He is commenting on the lines from the poem

which reject the nightingale's fabulous, night-denying music
for the internalized, self-hearing song of the stock dove,
whose "voice was buried among trees,/ Yet to be come at by
the breeze."

> . . . a metaphor expressing the love of *seclusion* by
> which this bird is marked; and characterizing its note as
> not partaking of the shrill and the piercing, and therefore
> more easily deadened by the intervening shade; yet a
> note so peculiar, and withal so pleasing, that the breeze,
> gifted with that love of sound which the poet feels, pene-
> trates the shade in which it is entombed, and conveys it
> to the ear of the listener.[37]

The meta-language employs an image more complex than
that of its object, for it is the listening, rather than the sound,
which is being embraced. Not only is the pictorially operative
word "shade" repeated twice (and in a context that calls only
for the acoustically insulating "foliage"), but in the whole last
part of the image it is caught up again and almost gothicized
("the shade in which it is entombed") by the near-pun on
"shade = ghost." And finally, the breeze, which conventionally
merely broadcasts, here becomes a fully realized form of the
genius of listening, of the activity of the ear.

Here particularly, vision has come so much to the aid of
hearing that it is tempting to move into a consideration of the
bases, in the language of poetry, for eye-ear synesthesia. In
many ways, the concept is itself misleading, for Wordsworth,
at any rate. We are dealing neither with the isolated, almost
ironic effect of a mixture of two conventional tropes (e.g.,
Coleridge: "Be the blind bard who on the Chian strand,/ By
those deep sounds possessed with inward light,/ Beheld the
Iliad and the Odyssey/ Rise to the swelling of the tuneful

sea") [38] nor with the violent Shelleyan interpenetration of sound and light occasioned by the interpenetration of tenor and vehicle in the metaphor; we are certainly always far removed from even an unsystematic disordering of the senses. In any event, these remarks are more concerned with language about sound than with strange reports about inner states; I should like only to consider momentarily the exemplary case of a rather attractive Romantic emblem. Carl Gustav Carus, friend of Goethe and imitator of Caspar David Friedrich, painted in 1823 a "Phantasie über die Musik." It shows the window of a chamber in a gothic building, looking out, at nightfall, on the moon rising over the sea, with a cathedral tower on the right; in the foreground is a bench, covered in dark blue drapery, with a harp resting on it. The harp fills most of the window—and the picture—and the moon shines through its strings. Subsequent commentators on the painting usually remarked that the moonlight "kissed" the strings, but the indoor scene is clearly a nocturnal version of the aeolian harp, with the moonlight playing the role of the wind.[39] To invoke synethesia in the reading of this picture would be, at very best, oblique. The light is as mythological a presence as the breeze that animates the poet who has become the instrument, in later versions of the theme. Carus's picture, in its hard-edged, emblematic manner, is a world apart from the painterly, atmospheric, diffuse scenes of indoor music at Petworth that Turner was doing at about the same time, in which the surface of the picture and the air in the room depicted both seem "filled," in an almost Wordsworthian way, with the sound of piano music.

Wordsworth's own metamorphoses of the aeolian harp figure follow interesting patterns. It will be remembered that the aeolian harp proper consists of strings of different diameters strung at different degrees of tensions across a flat, box-like sounding board so as to be tuned to unisons and octaves. Such an instrument, when set in an opened window, or suspended from a tree, generates full chords of the fundamental, up to the dominant seventh, as a function of the strength of the wind; that is, it does not play melodic lines nor does its fundamental pitch flatten, as in whistles and certain open flute pipes, when the wind's pressure decreases. Only the harmonics die down into the fundamental, and the over-all volume decreases. First described in Athanasius Kircher's musical encyclopedia in the seventeenth century, it became a sort of toy in the later decades of the eighteenth. Its appeal to the fancy is obvious: not only does the wind animating the strings combine the two genera of instrument, symbolic of the Apollonian and the Dionysian respectively in neoclassical tradition, but the aeolian harp comprises within itself the blending of instrumental sound and outdoor noise of wind which was becoming, in later eighteenth-century England, the imagination's authentic music.[40]

The aeolian harp image is far more profound and prevalent, I think, than has been previously noted. Even to sketch out its history here is impossible, for one should have to start with two distant and distinct topoi, the harp hung on the willows *super flumina Babylonis* as an indication of a refusal to perform even laments for a conqueror, and the *fistula* or pipe hung on the pine tree, in order to reconsecrate the music to Pan, and thus help define the pastoral genre, in Vergil's seventh eclogue. The instrument refused, and the other one hung up in what Erwin Panofsky described as a rustic *ex voto*,[41] fall together in Renaissance poetry as the instrument *aban-*

*doned;* it is an easy transition to the aeolian image, for the hand of the wind need only carelessly strike the neglected strings. There are many anticipations of this in Renaissance poetry, and the formal image is as frequent in German Romanticism as in England. (Indeed, the shift from instrument abandoned to aeolian harp is illustrated perfectly in such diverse passages as a major final speech in Grillparzer's *Sappho,* where the abandoned lyre, hanging on a column, sings in the wind; and the lyric "Pause" from *Die Schöne Müllerin,* where in a more homely context the same thing happens.)

The point is not that so many poets writing in English from James Thomson to Hart Crane make such different use of the aeolian harp image, but that it can appear in so many guises. Mörike writes a formal lyric about the aeolian harp, but Nietzsche, in *Ecce Homo,* uses it in an evolved form to describe how, while standing on a Venetian bridge, the sound of distant music over the canal blew through him as through the strings of an instrument, transforming everything he experienced. Emerson and Thoreau write poems manifestly directed to aeolian harps; but the latter, throughout his journals over many years, builds up an elaborate sequential prose-poem about what he calls his "telegraph-harp"—the aeolian harp effect (and, acoustically speaking, this is quite correct) of the wind blowing through telegraph wires along the railroad tracks, heard most clearly by putting one's ear to the resonating pole on which they are strung. Or take the following passage from *Walden:*

> Sometimes, on Sundays, I heard the bells, the Lincoln, Acton, Bedford, or Concord bell, when the wind was favorable, a faint, sweet and, as it were, natural melody, worth importing into the wilderness. At a sufficient dis-

tance over the woods this sound acquires a certain vibra-
tory hum, as if the pine needles were the strings of a
harp which is swept. All sound heard at the greatest possible distance produces one and the same effect, a vibration of the universal lyre, just as the intervening atmosphere makes a distant ridge of earth interesting to our
eyes by the azure tint it imparts to it. There came to me
in this case a melody which the air had strained, and
which had conversed with every leaf and needle of the
wood, that portion of the sound which the elements had
taken up and modulated and echoed from vale to vale.
The echo is, to some extent, an original sound, and
therein is the magic and charm of it. It is not merely a
repetition of what was worth repeating in the bell, but
partly the voice of the wood, the same trivial words and
notes sung by a wood-nymph.[42]

In one way, this is domesticated Wordsworth; but in the way
in which it moralizes the image and expands it into the "universal lyre," immediately adducing a pictorial analogue in
support of it, the passage is at once more Shelleyan and more
German.

Wordsworth's versions of the figure never reach the proportions of Coleridge's avowed use of it. An early, gothicized
parody shows up in "The Vale of Esthwaite";[43] at another extreme, the muse of "The White Doe of Rylstone," that invoca-
tion-figure of the Harp which is both what Wordsworth elsewhere calls "the romantic harp" and that of minstrelsy,
becomes aeolian at the end of the first canto, in an image at
first internalized and then remythologized again:

> Harp! we have been full long beguiled
> By vague thoughts, lured by fancies wild;
> To which, with no reluctant strings,

Thou hast attuned thy murmurings;
And now before this Pile we stand
In solitude, and utter peace:
But, Harp! thy murmurs may not cease—
A Spirit, with his angelic wings,
In soft and breeze-like visitings,
Has touched thee—and a Spirit's hand . . .[44]

The "vague thoughts" are the surrogate wind, at first; but the increasingly difficult imaginative tasks, as the poem unfolds, demand a more powerful voice from the aeolianized harp, and the doubling of "Spirit" and the "Spirit's hand" reinforces this need for augmented power.

Sometimes the aeolian harp figure can totally vanish within its naturalized form. The fifth of the *River Duddon Sonnets* begins with a characteristic moment in which an image of sound will awaken visual impressions: "Sole listener, Duddon! to the breeze that played / With thy clear voice, I caught the fitful sound / Wafted o'er sullen moss and craggy ground. . . ."[45] The breeze toys with the voice of the musical stream, playing *with* and almost *on* it; here the blending of music and noise occurs within the realm of natural noise itself, and the metaphorical musical voice here is naturalized even further by the breeze.

But perhaps the most problematic and revealing version of the image in Wordsworth comes from the Alfoxden notebook fragments. It should be quoted in its entirety; surely among the evocations of the ear as holding "A manifest communion with the heart," as being *inevitable*, this passage of all those sketches for *The Prelude* seems most fully realized:

There was a spot,
My favourite station when the winds were up
Three knots of fir-trees, small and circular,

Which with smooth space of open plain between
Stood single, for the delicate eye of taste
Too formally arrayed. Right opposite
The central clump I loved to stand and hear
The wind come on and touch the several groves
Each after each, and thence in the dark night
Elicit all proportions of sweet sounds
As from an instrument. "The strains are passed"
Thus often to myself I said, "the sounds
Even while they are approaching are gone by,
And now they are more distant, more and more.
O listen, listen how they wind away
Still heard they wind away, heard yet and yet,
While the lost touch they leave upon the sense
Is sweeter than whate'er was heard before,
And seems to say that they can never die." [46]

The instrument, activated by the wind, is a stringed one, and
the overformal arrangement of the trees, like the "birch-trees
risen in silver colonnade" in the sonnet from the *River Duddon* sequence just quoted, suggests an artifact. The wind-harp
music from the trees, dissolving into itself, is composed into
an animated emblem of the fleeting, the transitory; [47] sound is
heard (in the sense of "known" for which we often say "seen")
as process here. The extended use of verbal doublings, rang-
ing from the idiomatic "more and more" echoing and reecho-
ing the "more distant," through the "listen, listen" and the repeated "wind away" with the echoing senses of "blow,"
"twist," and almost "wend" (as of "way"), culminates in the
last "yet and yet" of lingering audibility. The penultimate
strain may indeed be the last accoustical one, echoed, at the
very end, by memory's playback. The archaic musical meaning of "touch" for "musical phrase or passage" is intertwined

with the tactile image, and reinforced by the parallel older, strictly musical sense of "sweet"; all these doublings and amplifications are finally echoed in the literal sense of "die" which outlasts, at the end, the figurative one. Echoes first "die," in Pope's "Ode for Music on St. Cecilia's Day," through adaptation of an earlier musical term: "The strains decay,/ And melt away,/ In a dying, dying fall." [48] The repetition is not only decorative but is meant to transfer the term to something like the famous Tennysonian usage, where the "flying-dying" rhyme is itself parallel to the animating, rising trumpet sound as opposed to the trailing, falling answer of the echoes. In the Wordworthian passage, it is the moment of experience itself, the transformed act of hearing which seems to become immortal.

Wordsworth's formal, public, and expository ode "On the Power of Sound" seems fully as interesting in its genre and rhetoric as in its doctrine; and in the light of the foregoing observations, the way in which both these aspects of the poem complete the metamorphosis of a neoclassical form seems an appropriate question with which to conclude. The ode poses critical problems which are not eased by the unduly high regard in which the poet himself held it: the same Vergilian phrase which he used as epigraph to the first printed version of the Immortality Ode appears in several MSS of the poem on sound: *Paulo majora canamus*,[49] the announcement of a new, prophetic strain at the opening of the Fourth Eclogue. On the other hand, the genesis of the poem (from some lines of a canceled aside from "The Triad") and its rather uncommanding structure (it grew from a more promising five strophes in its first draft to the published thirteen, and with the order quite changed) confirm one's suspicion. It is a poem

of the Will, despite the fact that Wordsworth deliberately
placed it at the close of the *Poems of the Imagination*. But
less so, in a way, than the 1806 poem on "The Power of
Music," which tries almost paradgimatically to mythologize a
street-corner fiddler as "An Orpheus! an Orpheus!" and which
organizes the urban landscape around him, as around the full
moon. All stop and watch him, and bend toward his playing
like leaning towers and trees; the only image of real power is
the final one, in which the urban street music is avowed to be
the fully authentic counterpart of the rural outdoor noise, and
the more trivial, literal counterpart of the murmurings of the
brook is heard for what it is:

> Now coaches and chariots! roar on like a stream;
> Here are twenty souls happy as souls in a dream:
> They are deaf to your murmurs—they care not for you,
> Nor what ye are flying, nor what ye pursue! [50]

The anapestic meter which this poem shares with "The Reverie of Poor Susan" is by no means accidental, nor is its
placement directly after it in the 1850 edition. Both the fiddler and the caged thrush have the power to *accost* in the
midst of the urban pressures that kill awareness, and in both
instances the power of the music is momentary.

The poem on music is secondary in many ways to "The
Reverie of Poor Susan"; the one on sound is anxiously conscious of the Immortality Ode at several places. Where it
boldly takes on a tradition in order to modulate it, the poem
is much more successful. I refer to its formal genre, the Augustan ode for music, as it descended from Dryden's two
great St. Cecilia's Day odes, composed a decade apart.[51]
Dryden's first poem, "A Song for St. Cecilia's Day," is doc-

trinal: it rehearses mythology about the creative and affective power of harmony, devoting successive strophes to particular instruments as representatives of particular modalities and affections; and it ends with the continuing presence of music, even beyond apocalypse, when music will ring down the curtain on the *theatrum mundi* by being the signal of the last trumpet. In "Alexander's Feast," the affective power of music is demonstrated dramatically, rather than expounded and orchestrally imitated in the accompaniment: an anecdote about Alexander and Timotheus is expanded into an elaborate cantata-text which has the musical treatment much more in mind than did the earlier one, but which confirms the convention by allowing successive strophes to embody various moods and modalities. The poems by Congreve, Tate, and most importantly, Pope, which follow Dryden, maintain the tradition of deliberately allowing for variations in the setting, solo, tutti, chorus, and so forth, and for the use of particular instrumental obbligati; they also tend to combine the two Dryden prototypes, combining the expository *laus musicae* and the quasi-operatic treatment of an Orphean myth. Pope's "Ode for Music on St. Cecilia's Day" is most important in this connection. It was held up, with Dryden's, as a model of the form; Christopher Smart, when he translated Pope's poem into Latin in 1746, prefaced it with some observations on the genre, almost predictably remarking that *"Dryden's* is the sublime and magnificent; but *Pope's* is the more elegant and correct." [52] More to the point, Martin Price has observed that Pope's use of Orpheus himself for a central figure, rather than Timotheus, is connected with the movement in Pope's ode "to the involvement in sensibility." [53] Certainly music's power comes to be that of expressing, rather than, in a strictly neo-

classic way, *eliciting* feelings, and in the echoic passage on
the death of Orpheus, a cliché of pastoral becomes put, with
its musical setting in mind, to expressive use:

> Yet ev'n in death Eurydice he sung,
> Eurydice still trembled on his tongue,
>   Eurydice the woods,
>   Eurydice the floods,
> Eurydice the rocks, and mountain hollows rung.[54]

Christopher Smart's own "Ode on St. Cecilia's Day," also
published along with his translation of Pope's, is a much
more self-conscious and ambitious poem, for it manifestly
turns the praise of music into the praise of English music and
English poetry, in the specific figures of Waller and Purcell.
It is a fully *literary* adaptation of the musical ode form, in
that it is by no means attentive to the exigencies of a prospec-
tive musical setting, and in that the convention it follows—
that of the Ode from Dryden to Pope—is modulated without
regard for the original function of the structure, rhetoric, and
mythology of the *laus musicae*. The most interesting sections
for a reader in mind of the Wordsworth ode are the third,
fourth, and fifth strophes. In the first of these, an astonishing
night-scene is unveiled, possibly based on an Orphean image
in one of Waller's own poems:

> In Penshurst's plains when Waller, sick with love,
> Has found some silent, solitary grove,
> Where the vague moon-beams pour a silver flood,
> Of trem'lous light athwart th'unshaven wood,
>   Within an hoary moss-grown cell,
> He lays his careless limbs without reserve,
> And strikes, impetuous strikes, each quer'lous nerve

Of his resounding shell.
In all the woods, in all the plains
Around a lively stillness reigns;
The deer approach the secret scene,
And weave their way thro' labyrinths green;
While Philomela learns the lay
And answers from the neighboring bay . . .[55]

In the pre-Keatsian silver of moonlight, the Ovidian nightingale story is inverted: it is the poet, the symbolic nightingale, who teaches the mere bird. The movement here is very much that of Robert Frost's "Never Again Would Birds' Song Be the Same" with its myth of the origins of nature's "voices" in the language and music of Eve's expressiveness. Smart's next two strophes are remarkable in their elaborate pictorial treatment of the story of Arion and the dolphin. Both he and Amphion are Orpheus-surrogates in Renaissance musical mythology, but the extended substitution of his story for those of Orpheus or Timotheus in the preceding major odes is introduced by the use of the river Medway, at the end of the Waller strophe, to waft the musical strains, as the wind might do, down to the sea. Arion is brought on theatrically thereafter.[56] It may be that Wordsworth's surprising use of Arion in his ode—rather than Amphion, builder of walls—derives from Smart.

But surely the most important stage in the untuning of the musical ode, in its transformation into a poem about language and feeling, and hence, about poetic tradition, comes with Collins. "The Passions: An Ode for Music," first performed, in one of the three musical settings it was to receive, in 1750, adapts the narrative format inherited from "Alexander's Feast" and the more purely historical and expository

pattern of the first Dryden ode in a different way from Pope
and Smart. The framing anecdote tells how, "When Music,
Heav'nly Maid, was young," in antiquity, the Passions themselves "Throng'd around her magic Cell" to hear her; but variously affected by her music, moved to the emotions they
themselves represented, fired up à la Alexander, they
"snatch'd her Instruments of Sound" in order to perform
themselves. What follows are the individual modal episodes,
in which Fear, Anger, Despair, Hope, Revenge, Pity, Jeal-
ousy, Love, Melancholy, Cheerfulness, Joy, and Mirth are all
momentarily represented as musicians. Each is afforded the
appropriate instrument, whether real or allegorical, so that
lyre and pipe mix with viol, trumpet, drum, and horn; the
shifting modality is underlined by the program for orchestra-
tion, as in all the odes. Most interesting are the episodes of
Hope and of Melancholy. Hope is associated with echoing:
"She call'd on Echo still thro' all the Song;/And where Her
sweetest theme She chose,/A soft responsive Voice was heard
at ev'ry Close." [57] It is the rhythms of rising and falling hope
that are suggested by the traditional pastoral figure of echoing landscape as nature applauding the poet; but by now we
are far from the representation of music, or even of sound,
and instead we are presented the arraying of the emotions on
an orchestral model.

Melancholy and her music are heard over distant water:

> And from her wild sequester'd Seat,
> In Notes by Distance made more sweet,
> Pour'd thro the mellow horn her pensive Soul:
>     And dashing soft from Rocks around,
>     Bubbling Runnels join'd the Sound;
> Thro' Glades and Glooms the mingled Measure stole,

Or oe'r some haunted Stream with fond Delay,
    Round an holy Calm diffusing,
    Love of Peace and lonely Musing,
In hollow Murmurs died away.[58]

Milton is here, not less in the confluence of music, darkness, and water from "Il Penseroso" than for the personification. The commonplace of distancing, as was observed earlier, is here; and an almost canonical instance of the expressive tone-sound *blending* is here as well. The mythology is almost parallel to Smart's anecdote of Waller informing the sound of the nightingale: it is Melancholy's aria with obbligato of *cor anglais* which gives its modality to the moving water resounding in the sublime landscape. The mingling is total and reciprocal, for the traditional authenticating force of the outdoor sound-scene is a necessary part of the personification itself.

Collins concludes with an encomium of "Caecilia's mingled World of Sound," [59] by which he means the entire spectrum of the passions and the orchestrated array of music's effects, the inventory of modes which invoke moods. He adapts the traditional ode which praises music by submitting itself to setting (and for England in the eighteenth century, this is no small sacrifice) for an exposition of what is not inherently musical, and his mythology only needs to be carried a step further into the realm of outdoor sound to lose manifest contact with concert music. Wordsworth's "On the Power of Sound" owes as much to Collins and to Smart as to Dryden and Pope; but in a larger sense, Collins's use of music as a metaphor for more general expressiveness underlies all English Romantic tradition.

Wordsworth's ode abandons the irregular "Pindaric" pattern, with what Smart called its "vehemence of sudden and unlook'd for transitions" even within the microcosm of its versification, for fourteen strophes of sixteen lines each, all on the same pattern. Certainly the "turns" and "counterturns" of the inner rhetoric are minimized by this, and the structure is both more arbitrary and, nevertheless, more expository than the suggestions of self-generated form in the irregular Pindaric or even in Wordsworthian blank verse. The poem opens with an address to the ear:

> Thy functions are ethereal,
> As if within thee dwelt a glancing mind,
> Organ of vision! And a Spirit aerial
> Informs the cell of Hearing, dark and blind . . .[60] (1–4)

But the ear is avowedly *le deuxième sens*—the dependence upon vision as a comparative and even a metaphorical base is unquestioned; nevertheless, the implicit contrast between the elements of *ether* and *air* (the "And" has almost the force of "but") invokes the latter as more concrete, more natural. Wordsworth continues:

> Intricate labyrinth, more dread for thought
> To enter than oracular cave;
> Strict passage, through which sighs are brought,
> And whispers for the heart, their slave . . .        (5–8)

and a catalogue of unpleasant sounds of pain and anguish concludes with "Hosannas pealing down the long-drawn aisle,/ And requiems answered by the pulse that beats/ Devoutly, in life's last retreats." The *auricular* cave which Blake envisoned as a great, spiral labyrinth leading upward (but collapsed, in its fallen state, into the constricting tiny windings of the *cochlea*) here is connected with the gothicized image of the cave of horrid sounds through the near-pun. And if groans and moans from Blair and Young are humanized in this passage, so are the images of sound-effects appearing in other Wordsworthian contexts.[61] Thus, the over-hanging echoes in the fan vaulting of King's Chapel, Cambridge, "that branching roof/Self-poised, and scooped into ten thousand cells,/Where light and shade repose, where music dwells/Lingering—and wandering on as loth to die" in one of the *Ecclesiatical Sonnets*,[62] are absorbed into the great corporeal expansion of the ear in this strophe.

The following ones continue to catalogue, on the model of musical odes but without any of the rhetoric of self-dramatization, the sounds of life. Echoes, the "Shadows/And Images of voice," are described as

> to hound and horn
> From rocky steep and rock-bestudded meadows
> Flung back, and, in the sky's blue caves, reborn—
> (34–37)

and paired with "a careless quire" which, in the convention of pastoral concert, would have been of birds:

> Happy milk-maids, one by one
> Scattering a ditty each to her desire,
> A liquid concert matchless by nice Art,
> A stream as if from one full heart.        (45–48)

With a shift of context, the last couplet could be Crashaw; the point about all these scattered fancies is that they keep pointing toward a primal presence and power behind the phenomena. Recapitulations of intensely musical moments in past poetry abound: "For the tired slave, Song lifts the languid oar,/And bids it aptly fall, with chime/That beautifies the fairest shore," and the musical oars of Cleopatra, Canute, and perhaps Marvell's Bermuda-bound pilgrims somehow blend with the naturalized music of water dripping from the blades of more domestic rowers. The "Lydian airs" of "L'Allegro" are specifically invoked. But almost at the center of the poem, the focus is manifestly shifted:

> Point not these mysteries to an Art
> Lodged above the starry pole;
> Pure modulations flowing from the heart
> Of divine Love, where Wisdom, Beauty, Truth
> With Order dwell, in endless youth?          (108–12)

—Not sounds, in short, but Sound.

The following strophes enact the search for the spirit of Sound, leaving the ear behind. With unambiguous echoes of Dryden's cadences, we follow "Orphean Insight" through "the first leagues of tutored passion," where

> Music deigned within this grosser sphere
> Her subtle essence to enfold,
> And voice a shell drew forth a tear
> Softer than Nature's self could mould.          (117–20)

We are led through the realms of medieval and Renaissance speculative music, through the mythologies of world order and healing and persuasion; "Hell to the lyre bowed low; the upper arch/Rejoiced that clamorous spell and magic verse/Her wan disasters could disperse." It is all the more remarkable how the ninth strophe, after a casual mention of Amphion, devotes itself totally to Arion and the dolphin, praising him as the musician who would "humanize the crea-

tures of the sea,/Where men were monsters." Wordsworth
would seem to be following Smart in his concentration on
what is usually a peripheral story, and to be thinking of the
Immortality Ode in his attention to the redemptive memo-
riousness of sound moving over water toward a final shore.
Certainly the Ovidian conclusion suggests this: "And he, with
his preserver, shine star-bright/In memory, through silent
night" (ll. 143–44).

Hard upon this comes the wilder myth of panic piping:
"the eyeballs of the leopards,/That in high triumph drew the
Lord of vines,/How did they sparkle to the cymbal's clang!"
And with a masterful shift of dynamic and tonality, the poem
moves out of the epochs of musical mythology into the Romantic world of sound: "To life, to *life* give back thine ear"
seems still part of the Dionysian revelry in the first half of the
strophe. But the movement away from the sound of music, in
the mythological sections, to the sound of sound is almost
programmatic for Wordsworth:

> Ye who are longing to be rid
> Of fable, though to truth subservient, hear
> The little sprinkling of cold earth that fell
> Echoed from the coffin-lid                    (154–57)

The whole eighteenth century had been listening for the
music of sound; Wordsworth had sought in many ways to escape the bondage of the ear to "laboured minstrelsies" of
musical language itself. In "Peter Bell," the continued pattern
of de-spooking the terrifying noises is part of a larger program of humanizing romance. On the top of Mount Snowdon,
the resounding of the bottom of consciousness occurs as a
complementary phase of the moment of vision. From time to
time Wordsworth plays with the music, if not the sound, of si-

lence.[63] But only in the sound ode does he try to abstract in a
systematic way a higher fiction.

The concept of "harmony" in its general sense flickers inter-
mittently, over the centuries, with an array of latent musical
meanings. Wordsworth wishes to free the "one pervading
spirit/Of tones and numbers" by which all is controlled from
some of the more deadened conventions; the ode's whole
movement from ear to music to a harmony beyond has been
to prepare for the splendid conclusion of the antepenultimate
strophe, with its reminders of the cadences of the Immortality
Ode:

> The heavens, whose aspect makes our minds as still
> As they themselves appear to be,
> Innumerable voices fill
> With everlasting harmony;
> The towering headlands, crowned with mist,
> Their feet among the billows, know
> That Ocean is a mighty harmonist;
> Thy pinions, universal Air,
> Ever waving to and fro,
> Are delegates of harmony, and bear
> Strains that support the seasons in their round;
> Stern Winter loves a dirge-like sound.          (181–92)

The final fiction of the ode will be that of the sound which
created light, and it signals a rondure in the poem from the
secondariness of the aural sense at the opening to the primacy, not of the ear, but to the disturbances of air to which it
responds. Sound pierces darkness, whereas light seems to
have no effect upon silence. It is sounds, rather than illumina-
tions, which seem to awaken us from sleep, and which can invade our dreams. Alarms release visions, and in poetic tradi-

tion the beginning of Pindar's first Pythian ode, its golden Apollonian lyre releasing a flurry of brilliant images, figures the sounds of beginnings, of creations. The final strophe of Wordsworth's ode returns to this:

> A Voice to Light gave Being;
> To Time, and Man his first-born chronicler;
> A Voice shall finish doubt and dim forseeing,
> And sweep away life's visionary stir          (209–12)

The model from Dryden, of music as order creating the world and music as the last trump undoing it, lies far behind this return. The Logos, as Sound, will outlast all the silences of eternity. Wordsworth's image of sound itself progresses through the crisis of the challenge of silence, the silence occasioned by switching culture off that the intermittences of nature may be audible. But at the end of the poem, again recapitulating the Immortality Ode, "the WORD, that shall not pass away" is restored to eternal life. A remythologizing of the music of the spheres, the *musica mundana* of ancient fiction, has been accomplished, *via, but not terminating in,* the fabulous power of what is, in the more domestic sense, mundane. Even the fancies of eighteenth-century poetry which celebrate this mundane sounding by calling it music are part of the fiction. And even the *musica mundana* of Rilke's *Ur-geräusch,* the music of one sense, or even of all senses, becoming another; even "the still, sad music of humanity" become, for the sound that lies as far behind language as it does beyond music, but phonetic shadows. If the largest shadow of all, that of the biblical fiction, looms over the conclusion, it is not one that the Wordsworth of 1828 would be in any position to avoid.

## Notes

1. Rainer Maria Rilke, "Primal Sound" (*Ur-geraüsch*), *Selected Works*, Vol. I, tr. G. Craig Houston (New York, 1967), pp. 51–56.

2. *Ibid.*, p. 53.

3. Warton's note on "The Ruines of Time," ll. 612–14, is given in the edition of Spenser by H. J. Todd (London, 1805), VII, 314.

4. Geoffrey H. Hartman, *Wordsworth's Poetry* (New Haven, 1964), pp. 91–115.

5. William Wordsworth, "On the Power of Sound" (composed 1828, published 1835), *The Poetical Works of William Wordsworth,* ed. E. de Selincourt and Helen Darbishire (Oxford, 1940–49), II, 324. (Hereafter cited as *PW*.)

6. Stephen Ullmann, *Principles of Semantics* (Glasgow, 1957), p. 280.

7. *PW*, II, 216.          8. *PW*, II, 122.

9. Ralph Waldo Emerson, "The Eye and Ear" (delivered 1837), *Early Lectures*, ed. Stephen E. Whicher *et al.* (Cambridge, Mass., 1964), p. 272.

10. For further discussion of these matters, see my *Images of Voice* (lecture given at Churchill College, Cambridge, 1968; published Cambridge, 1970); and "Spenser and the Mingled Measure," *English Literary Renaissance*, I (1971), 226–38.

11. See Arthur Loesser, *Men, Women and Pianos* (New York, 1954), 185–301, for some brilliant discussion of keyboard music in England during this period.

12. Novalis, quoted by Mario Praz, *The Romantic Agony* (Oxford, 1933), p. 14.

13. William Collins, "The Passions: An Ode for Music" (1747), ll. 59–61.

14. "Personal Talk," *PW*, IV, 74.

15. Samuel Taylor Coleridge, *Animae Poetae*, ed. E. H. Coleridge (Boston, 1895), pp. 35–36 (November 2, 1803).

16. Thomas Warton, Jr., "The Pleasures of Melancholy" (1747), ll. 10–12.

17. *Ibid.*. ll. 202–5.

18. Oliver Goldsmith, "The Deserted Village" (1770), ll. 43–46.

19. Thomas Gray, "The Progress of Poesy: A Pindaric Ode" (1754–68), ll. 68–72.

20. *PW*, II, 263.

21. "The Deserted Village", ll. 113–24. The treatment of sound in Joseph Warton's "The Enthusiast" is also of interest in this connection, particularly the sounds in the cave of Fancy (ll. 130–41 and other fanciful sounds at 170 ff.) as opposed to the urban noises which are opposed to it as being the sounds of *nature* (ll. 142–61).

22. The word probably comes from *Paradise Lost*, IV, 683, where the celestial voices are said to be "Sole, or responsive each to other's note."

23. Here again, see my "Spenser and the Mingled Measure."

24. Thomas Gray, "Ode on the Spring" (1742), ll. 5–7.

25. See Anton Pigler, *Barockthemen* (Budapest, 1956), II, 574, for documentation of this. The fancy that, in concerts like these, it is Love who is the *Kapellenmeister* is Heine's (*Neue Gedichte:* "Es erklingen alle Bäume").

26. *De Rerum Natura* 4. 544 ff. This passage is also interesting for the way in which it connects the music of the stream and the swans.

27. It was not only the famous couplets in "Cooper's Hill" which canonically connected the stream and the song for the Augustans; see, for example, the passage on prose style in "Democritus Junior to the Reader" from Burton's *Anatomy of Melancholy,* where the concepts of depth, surface, wandering, rushing, smoothness, etc., are naturally applied to language and thought. Also see Dr. Johnson's objection to Denham's famous lines.

28. John Dyer, "Grongar Hill" (1726), ll. 139–45.

29. *PW*, I, 41.        30. *PW*, IV, 73.        31. *PW*, I, 68.

32. *PW*, I, 69.        33. Samuel Johnson, "Life of Gray."

34. Loesser, *Men, Women and Pianos*, pp. 221–22.

35. *PW*, II, 212. A similar kind of doubling is that of "A volant tribe, etc." from the *Miscellaneous Sonnets*, XXXIV, ll. 13–14: "the intense tranquillity / Of silent hills, and more than silent sky." *PW*, III, 19.

36. William Wordsworth, *Guide to the Lakes* (1835), ed. Ernest de Selincourt (London, 1906), p. 95.

37. *PW*, II, 437.

38. Samuel Taylor Coleridge, "Fancy in Nubibus," *Poetical Works*, ed. E. H. Coleridge (Oxford, 1912), I, 435.

39. The painting is reproduced and discussed in Marianne Prause, *Carl Gustav Carus, Leben und Werk* (Berlin, 1968), p. 86. Also, see Hartman's discussion, *Wordsworth's Poetry*, pp. 182–83, of the musical moonlight in one of the Alfoxden fragments.

40. There are discussions of the aeolian harp in Geoffrey Grigson's *The Harp of Aeolus* (London, 1947), I, 32, and in Meyer Abrams, *The Mirror and the Lamp* (Oxford, 1953), pp. 51–52. Georges Kastner, *La Harpe d'Eole et Musique Cosmique* (Paris, 1856), is also extremely valuable for all manner of lore about the "Phenomènes Sonores de la Nature."

41. Erwin Panofsky, *Albrecht Dürer* (New York, 1948), I, 32.

42. Henry David Thoreau, *Walden*, ed. J. Lyndon Shanley (Princeton, 1971), p. 123. This passage is an adaptation of the journal entry for October 12, 1851, in all likelihood (see Thoreau, *Journal*, ed. Torrey and Allen [Boston, 1949], III, 67–68). The entries on the telegraph-harp start in September of 1851 and proceed for many years.

43. *PW*, I, 271. See Hartman, *Wordsworth's Poetry*, p. 355.

44. *PW*, III, 293.        45. *PW*, III, 248.

46. PW, II, 342.

47. This is also suggested by "Delicious as the gentlest breeze that sounds / Through that aerial fir-grove"—the aeolian fir-grove in "Home at Grasmere," *PW*, V, 427.

48. Alexander Pope, "Ode for Music on St. Cecilia's Day" (1713), ll. 19–21.

49. See de Selincourt's note, *PW*, II, 526.     50. *PW*, II, 219.

51. See my *The Untuning of the Sky* (New York, 1961), pp. 390–422, for a discussion of the St. Cecilia's Day ode convention, and Dryden's two poems in particular.

52. Christopher Smart, *Carmen Cl. Alexandri Pope in S. Caeciliam, etc.* (London, 1746). He pursues this further: "*Dryden* has the fire and spirit of *Pindar*, and *Pope* has the tenseness and purity of *Horace*."

53. Martin Price, *To the Palace of Wisdom* (New York, 1964), pp. 373–74.

54. Pope, "Ode for Music," ll. 113–17.     55. Smart, *Carmen*.

56. Smart in his introduction remarks that a Cambridge friend had originally suggested what we would now think to be Smart's great subject for such an ode, David playing before Saul. Smart, however, rejected it, remarking that "the chusing too high subjects has been the ruin of many a tolerable genius."

57. Collins, "The Passions," ll. 35–37.

58. "The Passions," ll. 59–68. A. S. P. Woodhouse, in "Collins and the Imagination," remarked that "*The Passions* is supposed to be descriptive of music, but in truth it is a series of pictures." See *Studies in English*, ed. M. W. Wallace (Toronto, 1931), p. 97. The problem seems to me to be one of linguistic, rather than pictorial, conventions.

59. "The Passions," l. 114.

60. *PW*, II, 323. Hereafter, only line numbers are cited.

61. Principal discussions of the sound ode have neglected the history of the treatment of sound in Wordsworth's poetry. Elizabeth

Sewell, in *The Orphic Voice* (New Haven, 1960), pp. 316–26, treats both "The Power of Music" and the ode as involving the theme of Orpheus in his relation to natural history. I find her analysis rather misleading. John Jones, in *The Egotistical Sublime* (2d ed., London, 1964), pp. 188–92, is interested in showing the emblematic relation of sound to poetic language. A consideration of Wordsworth's interest in echoes by John S. Martin, in *ELN*, V (1968), 186–92, does not mention the ode at all, nor is it very enlightening. Likewise, W. A. Heard, "Wordsworth's Treatment of Sound," *Transactions of the Wordsworth Society*, No. 6 (1884), pp. 40–57.

62. *PW*, III, 405. See also the following poem in the sequence: "The notes luxuriate, every stone is kissed / By sound, or ghost of sound, in mazy strife."

63. See, for example, the splendid passage in "Composed Upon an Evening of Extraordinary Spendour and Beauty" (*PW*, IV, 10–13):

> No sound is uttered,—but a deep
> And solemn harmony pervades
> The hollow vale from steep to steep,
> And penetrates the glades.
> Far-distant images draw night,
> Called forth by wondrous potency
> Of beamy radiance. . . .                    (21–27)

GEOFFREY H. HARTMAN

# REFLECTIONS ON THE EVENING STAR:

# AKENSIDE TO COLERIDGE

> to say of the evening star,
> The most ancient light in the most ancient sky
> That it is wholly an inner light, that it shines
> From the sleepy bosom of the real, re-creates,
> Searches a possible for its possibleness.
>
> (Wallace Stevens)
>
> The perished patterns murmur       (Emily Dickinson)

*For* most readers the charm of Akenside's "Ode to the Evening Star," a minorpiece of the 1740s,[1] resides in its first stanza, perhaps even in its first two lines:

> To-night retir'd, the queen of heaven
>     With young Endymion stays:
> And now to Hesper it is given
> Awhile to rule the vacant sky,
> Till she shall to her lamp supply
>     A stream of brighter rays.

The rising of the moon is delayed, in Akenside's version of the myth, because she is dallying with a human lover, the shepherd Endymion; there is something like a divine, erotic slowing of time, familiar from myths associated with Jove or the prevention of dawn; the theme of "staying" (l. 2) leads, moreover, into that of "supply" (l. 5), so that it is tempting to connect the moon's dalliance with her brightened lamp, her refurbished rising. Yet the myth does not flower into the form of an epyllion or little romance: it glimmers above the action like a distant star or constellated image. The poem remains a curious variant on addresses to the Evening Star. Hesper's brief reign suits perhaps the idea of the brief hymn whose prototype the eighteenth century found in a small poem attributed to Bion.[2]

Bion's influence can only be understood through some ideal of classic decorum, of silver mediocrity. His poem approximates the length of an epigram or what was considered as its modern form, the sonnet—and it is a juvenile sonnet Coleridge will hymn to *his* Evening Star in 1790.[3] But in Akenside a tension is felt between the compact form and its narrative elaboration. If his opening stanza is more condensed and suggestive than anything in Bion, the remainder of this poem of 78 lines (compared to Bion's eight) is devious and prolix. Akenside seems to have a problem with "development" or "manner of proceeding," not uncommon in eighteenth-century lyrics, and especially nature poems.

In the Romantic poets the nature lyric is as much about consciousness as about nature. Moreover, it is often about the *development* of consciousness; and this dynamic factor helps poets in the otherwise paradoxical task to plot, or narrate, nature. Akenside's problem may hinge, similarly, on finding a developmental pattern. Not for nature so much as for poetry: how can poetry, at this time in its life, be developed? Does it have a future or only a past? The course of the poem is so stylized that one thinks of the sorrows of the poet rather than of Olympia's mourning lover—the tears are tears of the muses, cultured pearls. The poet's concern seems to be with literary rather than personal continuity, or how the first bears on the second. Hesper is invoked as a link in a symbolic chain leading from loss to acceptance, and strongly suggesting the centrality of poetic sublimation.

## NEW LAMPS FOR OLD

In its simple form, patterned on Bion, the Hymn to the Evening Star makes Hesper a surrogate moon, a night-light guiding lover to beloved. But Akenside has "herald Hesper" (Keats) light the way to loss rather than to the beloved, for the star leads him to a second symbolic agent, the nightingale, which wakes memories of loss under the very moon that is the traditional sign of consummated love or restored presence. Ben Jonson's famous lyric from *Cynthia's Revels* (1601) with the refrain "Hesperus entreats thy light / Goddess excellently bright" and Milton's "Now came still Ev'ning on" (*Paradise Lost,* IV.598–609) follow the straight pattern and so illumine the deviousness of the later ode. Hesperus, in Milton, is to the absence of light as the nightingale is to that of sound: both are "wakeful" powers that bridge a dark moment and prepare hierarchically for the emergence of the moon as "Apparent Queen." Compared to the purity of Jonson's, Milton's, and Bion's sequence, Akenside's lyric is the night-ramble of a gloomy egotist.

The formal problem is made more intriguing by the fact
that the first three stanzas of the hymn, though prelusive, are
a detachable unit. Close in theme and length to Bion's lyric,
they constitute a small hailing that sets the scene (first
stanza), invokes the star (second stanza), and rounds the invocation with a vow (third stanza). Their internal structure is
equally cohesive. What the moon is to Endymion, Hesper is
to be for the poet: both condescend, the one for love-bright-
ness, the other for the poet's sake. This descendentalism exists, however, within a vivid sense of hierarchy. The latinate
diction, in fact, and the elaborate, even contrived syntax of
lines 9 to 12

> Oh listen to my suppliant song,
> If haply now the vocal sphere
> Can suffer thy delighted ear
>     To stoop to mortal sounds

sensitize the reader to the whole question of subordination.

The poem's formal development is closely linked to the tension that surrounds the concept of subordination. If the first
three stanzas are contortedly archaic in their evocation of sidereal hierarchy and the last three a moralizing frame aiming
at a similar kind of overview, the middle or narrative portion
of the ode depicts a reversal of influence. Philomel gradually
becomes a star-symbol replacing Hesper, as he the moon.
Though we begin in heaven, and stars stoop to conquer, as
we approach ritually the magic center or "green space" of the
nightingale (a centering movement we meet often in this type
of poem), power flows from earth to heaven. In stanza 7 the
nightingale's song "holds" the moon above the lovers in a repetition of the "staying" which began the ode, and in stanza 10

the breezes that attend the path of the nightingale's song re-
peat the star's attendance on Hesper (ll. 6–7):

> Hark, how through many a melting note
>      She now prolongs her lays:
> How sweetly down the void they float!
> The breeze their magic path attends:
> The stars shine out: the forest bends:
>      The wakeful heifers gaze.

This transfer of power, or reversal of earthly and starry
agents, was foreshadowed by syntactical and phonemic
stresses in the opening stanzas.[4]

"Far other vows must I prefer . . ." With these words, and
still paying formal tribute to Hesper, Akenside deviates from
Bion. He converts the Evening Star poem into something
psychic and strange, haunted by loss, memory, sublimation,
and the influence of poetic song. He leads us to a symmetrical
and cunning space:

> See the green space: on either hand
>      Inlarg'd it spreads around:
> See, in the midst she takes her stand. . .

both empty and full, natural yet ghostly. That narrow, clearly
framed, yet open space is not unlike poetry, especially when
based on the classical sense of centering. The very predomi-
nance of a prototype, the very fixation on theme or symbol, becomes the poet's way to a wilder symbolic action and an en-
larged vision of continuity.

## A PHENOMENOLOGICAL THEMATICS

The Evening Star poem is a fickle and minor genre. But its
brief span of life, mainly as an eighteenth-century idyllion,

belies the interest of a theme which poets occasionally renew and which is constantly merging with the larger question of continuity—personal or historical. The dual name of the star, Hesper (Vesper) and Phosphor (Venus), evening and morning star, and its "genial" (Venus-y or procreative) aspect make it symbolic of a continuity that persists within apparent loss. The epigram attributed to Plato and rendered by Shelley as

> Thou wert the morning star among the living
>> Ere thy fair light had fled;—
> Now, having died, thou art as Hesperus, giving
> New splendour to the dead [5]

is the very emblem of triumphant sublimation, of identity maintained in the realms of death.

In its broadest literary aspect, the starry theme becomes expressive of the problematics of *poesy*. Is there a true literary-historical continuity, a great chain of great poets, or how much vision (sublime style) can be saved? By 1750 the starry theme was in doubt; and while Blake in his deep and virtuoso way talks once more of poets "appearing" to him in the "poetical heavens," their succession is generally felt to be uncertain. Gray's "Stanzas to Mr. Bentley" (1752) expresses the sense of his age that poetry is in eclipse.

> But not to one in this benighted age
> Is that diviner inspiration given,
> That burns in Shakespear's or in Milton's page,
> The pomp and prodigality of heav'n.

This "not to one" may well echo Collins's "Ode on the Poetical Character," which assumes that each age has "one only one" significant poet and that his own age has not even him:

Heav'n, and *Fancy*, kindred Pow'rs,
Have now o'erturned th' inspiring Bow'rs,
Or curtain'd close such Scene from ev'ry future View.

Despite this cultural pessimism, hope does not die. Blake realized that the poets' loss of confidence was related to a wrong understanding of poetry's high seriousness. The divine makers of the previous era had raised poetry to the skies. Their strength had shown that Poetry and Divinity were "kindred pow'rs." But this did not mean poetry could compete with religion on religion's ground—as Milton had "inimitably" done. To burden it with divinity, to raise it to a sky preempted by the frozen forms of national religion, was to sink it under a weight Dr. Johnson's obstinate bass unwearily reiterated: "The good and evil of Eternity are too ponderous for the wings of wit. The mind sinks under them in passive helplessness, content with calm belief and humble admiration." The sidereal universe of religion, as he also said, could not be magnified.

In these circumstances, to bring an angel down could be more important than to raise a mortal to the skies. I will call this harrowing of the skies the descendental theme. So Milton enters Blake's left foot, and was already shown by Collins (in a complex image that goes up and down simultaneously) in the Eden of his own invention, and raising an "Evening Ear" from its ethereal dews toward a sphery music.[6]

Yet *poesy* is by no means a direct subject of evening star poems. The larger historical pathos is simply part of their aura. We begin, rather, with "the nightes dread,"[7] a power failure or dangerous interval, a moment when the light goes out. The evening star rises in that space, on that loss; and however strongly it rises there is often the fear of new withdrawal ("Soon, full soon, dost thou withdraw"[8]) and the dangerous sense that "sacred dew" or starry "influence" no longer prevails. To the descendental theme we can add, therefore, that of the dangerous, *interlunar* moment.

It is remarkable that in Blake's poem on the evening star the moon does not actually rise; but were it to rise it would just be a second star rather than a transcending presence. "Genius dies with its Possessor, and does not rise again until Another is born." There is a difference between Blake and Milton on this: Blake thinks of each great poet as a new and equal star.

Indeed, though Hesperus is traditionally the moon's precursor, it can be subversive of that "laboring" planet. As the most brilliant of the early stars it becomes for the expectant mind a singular mark. It seems absolute in its "steadfast" (if often brief) presence, and begins to stand for itself rather than for something to come. It expresses a power of feeling that is both solipsistic and unchanging, or so transcendently hopeful as not to be fulfilled by a temporal—chronologically easy—next stage. Its "intense lamp" does not die into another light: it narrows into itself, or sets unmodified in a kind of *liebestod.*[9]

With this we reach a difficult and subtle motif. As the moon of its own twilight zone, Hesperus tends to personify the threshold and evoke an enchanted spot of time in which a richly ominous signifier is all there is. The star-signifier appears as a sign accompanied by signs, or leading to other symbols rather than to a sign-transcending reality. Since man cannot live by signs alone, the evening star poem rouses our reality-hunger and perplexes the very idea of *development.*

In this it is like love itself, or desire. The star cannot be more than a sign, given the intensity of the desire invoking it. The poem feeds the sign, even fattens it: it wants it to be, if not more than a sign, then more of a sign. Yet the most successful poetry is still, so Shelley knew, "as darkness to a dying flame." The symbol remains a threshold; and the idea of development, of a waxing and waning that is also a ripening, a movement beyond mutability, remains moot. Darkness reenters the progression of interlunar moment, evening star, moonrise, at any point.

Why then, one might ask, do we need a starry paradigm at all? Could not any pseudo-progression serve? The reason why there is a star-symbolism is clarified by Los's struggle with his Spectre:

> Los reads the Stars of Albion! the Spectre reads the Voids
> Between the Stars; among the Arches of Albion's Tomb sublime. . . .

Plate 91 of *Jerusalem* shows Los decreating the sublime structures of traditional visionary poetry, which have been, in Blake's interpretation, a "Tomb sublime," that is, built upon, or in fearful reaction to, "the Voids." Los smites the Spectre, or his ingrained habits of perceiving, until

> all his pyramids were grains
> Of sand & his pillars: dust on the flys wing: & his starry Heavens; a moth of gold & silver mocking his anxious grasp.

What is foreseen here, though not attained—for Los remains "anxious," trembling before his new-found mortality as previously before phantoms—is a sublimity not based on subli-

mation. The stars, therefore, remain, but become as mortal
(or immortal) as men. They are "consumed" like erotic desire
and reborn out of its satisfaction:

> The stars consumd like a lamp blown out & in their
> stead behold
> The Expanding Eyes of Man behold the depths of won-
> drous worlds
> One Earth one sea beneath nor Erring Globes wander
> but Stars
> Of fire rise up nightly from the Ocean & one Sun
> Each morning like a New born Man issues with songs &
> Joy [10]

The most interesting Romantic lyrics do not begin in the
sky. They begin, nevertheless, with an interlunar moment created by the descendental "smiting" so powerfully stylized in
Blake. There is a downward displacement of the stars which
gives the impression of (1) sidereal darkness and (2) new
powers (stars) emerging from below. Poetry itself, at this point
in history, is generically associated with this downward displacement of skiey energies. Our phenomenological thematics, in other words, become poetical.

Let me give two examples of the starry theme no longer in
its thematic form, or not purely so. We are, for instance, only
subliminally aware on reading

> Tyger Tyger, burning bright,
> In the forests of the night

that usually stars burn this way and that this "descendental"
constellation, Tyger, presides over the moment after Hesper
has set, when "the lion glares thro' the dun forest." And while
there might seem to be no relation whatsoever between
Blake's lyric and Wordsworth's "Daffodils," the poet who

wanders "lonely as a cloud/That floats on high o'er vales and hills," could collide with a star. And that is, more or less, what happens: a moment of withdrawal, of Wordsworthian inwardness, is suddenly filled with the shock of *earthly* stars:

> When all at once I saw a crowd
> A host of golden daffodils. . .

The "golden" hint of these lines is elaborated by "As numerous as the stars that shine/And twinkle on the Milky Way," and the "flash" of the final stanza.[11]

The interlunar moment merges in Wordsworth with the themes of retirement, reflectiveness, and self-renewal. His flowery shock is the descendental obverse of the emotion of the sublime. In other poems, of course, up and down are more dizzyingly related—not only in the great passages from *The Prelude* (Mont Blanc, the Simplon Pass, Snowdon) but also in such evening poems as "Composed by the Side of Lake Grasmere" where the lake that yields a "vivid repetition of the stars" leads him into a curious surmise:

> Is it [the lake] a mirror, or the nether Sphere
> Opening to view the abyss in which she feeds
> Her own calm fires?

But it is not only the content of the surmise which interests here. If we try to go beyond thematics to poetics, the surmise becomes significant as a surmise, as part of a larger act of the poetic mind.

## WORDSWORTH (1) STAR AND SURMISE

The surmise comes from a sonnet composed when "clouds, lingering yet, extend in solid bars/Through the grey west." This lingering, a moment of suspense or interregnum, points to the interlunar rising of Hesperus. The brightest stars are already visible, intensified by the "mirror" of the lake. "And lo! these waters, steeled/ By breezeless air to smoothest polish, yield/ A vivid repetition of the stars." The word "steeled," which continues the metaphor "solid bars," echoes in the mind as "stilled"—"Tranquillity is here" (l. 14). Deeply internal, it repeats the wishful progress of the whole poem from martial to pastoral.

Yet no thematic continuity in Wordsworth is as remarkable as the poet's mind "in the act of finding/ What will suffice." Stillness, for that mind, is never loss: life should appear within loss, presence within absence. The evening sight is analogous, therefore, to the poet's morning vision of London from Westminster Bridge. The "lo" (l. 2) and "list" (l. 11) converge as gestures that skirt a desired epiphany. Yet, even as the mind searches for the sufficient, the twilight nature of the moment is fully respected. The very formality of the sonnet prevents the moment from merging into a next stage—it does not "die" into light. Time is almost suspended, like the clouds of the opening lines. The poem becomes a little sphere, restless within (since neither cloudland nor the battle-scarred earth suffices) but turning on its own axis, and furnished with its twilight, and tutelary, voice.

The image of clouds as bars already betrays the poet's desire for something firmer than cloud, for a *grounding* of eye or imagination. His descendental movement from sky to earth and even into earth is a movement toward both stillness (peace) and that ground. The more human field he reaches is, however, the Napoleonic battlefield, "earth's groaning field." The imagination moves away again, trying the nether sphere just as it had previously stepped among the stars. But the image of "calm fires" is counter-volcanic, and shows how precarious each speculation ("fancy") is: the middle-ground sought by Wordsworth, the twilight moment he respects, is always about to fade into starlight or fire.[12] To call earth's fires "calm" (sated) only emphasizes in its very boldness the restless journeying of his imagination toward a fold. So that the surmise ("Is it a mirror, or the nether Sphere . . .") is a restraint on that epiphanic movement, a "lingering" comparable to that of the clouds. The Wordsworthian imagination remains unpastured: it hungers for calm and finds no shepherd. Except Pan, at the every end, in the form of a piped-in, reedy voice, the opposite of panic.

WORDSWORTH (2) STAR AND SYMBOL

Before showing the deepest use, or displacement, of the evening star theme in Wordsworth, it is best to double back and consider poems where the theme is more explicitly present. Hesperus appears in two earlier poems, "Fair Star of Evening, Splendor of the West," written at Calais in August, 1802, and "It is No Spirit Which from Heaven Hath Flown," composed in 1803. Both exhibit that tension between *zoning* (the star seen as inhabiting its own zone separated by nature's or poetry's magic from various continua) and *zooming* (a sympathetic or ecstatic movement of identification) that we found in very subtle form in the Grasmere sonnet. The idea, for instance, of "the sky / He hath it to himself—'tis all his own" [13] so corresponds to Wordsworth's own homing instinct that his appropriation of an image he has helped to create threatens to destroy the separateness essential to it.

The poet zooms in on the star as his (and England's) encompassing symbol.

Both poems begin in the feeling of distance or exile. The earlier verses are written from Calais, with the poet looking westward toward his country during the fragile Peace of Amiens. The idea of an interregnum enters—however discreetly —if the political situation is kept in mind.[14] The star is "hanging" on the horizon's brink above the dusky spot which is England; and Wordsworth, though he sees the star and his country as twofold—one being the crown or bosom-jewel of the other—merges them finally into "one hope, one lot,/ One life, one glory."

The star seems to be a symbol yet participates so nearly in the imaginative essence of "real" England that symbol and reality coverage. Wordsworth knows that his imagination needs a "star" but he also knows it must be a "native star." It should encompass his own, human destiny from birth to setting. There is, on the one hand, a finely graded if descendental transformation of Hesperus from "Star of Evening" to "Star of my Country," and, on the other, an identifying movement which collapses distances and degrades the star into an emblem ("my Country's emblem . . . with laughter on her banners").

Wordsworth's later poem expresses a deeper or more general sense of exile. The distance is not that from Calais to Dover but an undefinable one from "my natural race"[15] to "some ground not [presently] mine." The star has transcended its zone by dominating the sky in broad daylight. It is so simply, so startlingly "there" that it at once incites and repels descendental or metamorphic myths (ll. 1–4). Wordsworth's need for a center or zoom, felt in the previous poem, culminates now in an almost hypnotic moment of enchanted stasis.

There is a further difference between the poems as acts of mind. The lyric of 1803 is more akin to experiences familiar to us from the great *Prelude* passages. Something startles sight by anticipating itself. Though the star is hoped for— indeed, one of hope's emblems—it defeats the perceptual or mythic apparatus prepared for its coming. It is there so naturally that it appears to be already *in its place* (cf. l. 13), that is, absolute, beyond temporal change. It has become a "fixed star" to imagination.

The poet, it is true, still talks of it as a sign or "admonition" (l. 5). But then the octave of this lengthened sonnet is clearly a sparring for time—for rebounding from a sublime or unexpected impression. The real "admonition" is to himself; and Wordsworth adverts to his own mind in the poem's second half, which no longer seeks to render the immediacy of an external image. It turns instead (cf. the tense change, from present to past) to what "wrought" within him. With "O most ambitious star" we reach, in fact, the symmetrical center (9–1–9) of the poem, its exact turning-point. This cry, star-oriented yet reflexive, turns us not from image to meaning—nowhere, and certainly not in Wordsworth, is imaging free of the interpretive consciousness—but from an objectifying mode that subsumes the subjective context, back to subjectivity. While Wordsworth's star-staring (ll. 1–8) elides the sense of time, now there is an "inquest"—an inward questing—into which time returns as time-for-reflection.

The final verses, presented as a "thought"—an illusion sustained consciously and *in* time—are actually an audacious return to first impressions, and quietly merge the idea of ground and heaven. Their subject is transcendence, but this is depicted as a *stepping*, and compared to the ghostly apparition of the soul in a place (i.e., heaven) not its own. Yet Wordsworth preserves, this time, a sense of distance: the soul is not of the place but appropriates it "strong her strength above."

WORDSWORTH (3) DEATH OF A STAR

Sieh, Sie erstand und schlief                                          (Rilke)

A signal transformation of the evening star theme is found in the Lucy poems. "Fair as a star when only one/ Is shining in the sky" is not, of course, a stingy compliment, but an allusion to Hesper which carries with it the suggestion of brief if intense emergence. Throughout the poems which have Lucy for subject the thought of her death blends curiously with that of her presence: she is a twilight or threshold figure that gleams upon the sight, then disappears. There is, almost simultaneously, emergence and discontinuity. As in Rilke's "Starker Stern," and in the later *Sonnets to Orpheus*, an image of setting overtakes that of dawning life:

> tausendfachen Aufgang überholend
> Mit dem reinen Untergang.

Though the erotic connotations are much stronger in Rilke, where Hesper is clearly Venus, in Wordsworth too the lover appears together with love's star. The guiding planet of "Strange Fits" is the "evening moon" rather than the evening star, yet it is already "sinking," and there occurs a ritual stepping and zoning similar to what guided Akenside's lover to a ghostly center. At the end of the lyric, in a reverse play of a familiar theme, both moon and Lucy enter on an "interlunar" phase, and it is only then that "thought" rises. The poem's curious use of both centering and descendental movements links it clearly enough to the idylls of Hesperus.

But Wordsworth's poem is as much about symbol as about star: in a sense, the symbol stars. We have, this time, an act of the mind finding what exceeds. The lover goes out of himself into star or moon: it is a mild case of ecstasy in which the distance between lover and Lucy—that precarious or psychic distance Hesper traditionally lights—is overcome by a deep, "symbolic" association of her with the moon. Lucy, to use a Renaissance term, is eternized, but unconsciously so. The evening moon not only leads to her but she becomes the moon, love's absorbing center. The narrative progressions of the poem make us feel the slope of things toward her until she is seen as their infinite threshold—and sets. When the moon drops it is as if a fixed had become a falling star; the distance between lover and Lucy is restored; the symbol proves fallible.

This purgation of the star-symbol is perfected in "A Slumber Did My Spirit Seal." Here is neither Lucy by name nor the visible image of a star. But she who is described in the first stanza, who rises on the poet's "slumber," is immortal as a star. Poet becomes Astrophil. She, however, who is described in the second stanza is ground not sky, yet "heaven" and "ground" subtly meet because she has merged with the rolling planet. The descendental theme is so subtly realized that the passage from stanza to stanza, which coincides with that from state to state, is a "stepping" not accompanied by open shock or disillusion. Because the rise and fall of the star-symbol occurs at a level "too deep for tears," there is no

such formal cry-ing as: "If Lucy should be dead!" or "The difference to me!"

The absence of rhetorical glitter does not mean, of course,
absence of structure. It means that Wordsworth has purified
*exclamation* even further than in "Strange Fits" and "She
Dwelt": he has killed the exclamation mark, in fact. Instead
of a reversal (↓) followed by point (.) to make (!) we have a
star turned asterisk:

> How went the Agile Kernel out
> Contusion of the Husk
> Nor Rip, nor wrinkle indicate
> But just an Asterisk.[16]

Stanza 1 implies the star ("The whole of Immortality / Secreted
in a star"), stanza 2 star as asterisk, or sign of an absence.
Lucy's essence and that of language coincide. If she is part
of a galaxy, it is Gutenberg's. Yet absence here has its own
presence, so that asterisk balances star. At last a poem without artificial center, a poem which does not overcondense
consciousness into symbol and symbol into star.

AN EXCURSUS ON THE ROMANTIC IMAGE

A voice, a mystery.                          (Wordsworth)

Wordsworth's revolt against the star-symbol has various
reasons: its trivialization in eighteenth-century poetry, a reli-
giously inspired prudence, etc. To conventionalize it we can
think of his distrust of personification, which it extends, or of
English poetry's recurrent bouts of conscience vis-à-vis pagan
myth. Yet we read Wordsworth unconscious much of the time
of his place in the history of ideas or the polemical history of

style. These histories, recovered, allow us to be articulate about his intentions but they describe his novelty rather than his originality. They remain external to his strong poetic presence.

Curiously strong, considering how little "glitter," or conventional texture, his poetry has. Many have suspected, therefore, that his imagery comes from a different loom. They have sought to discover the formula of its secret weave. It is equally inadequate, however—though far more interesting—to describe the diffusion of theme or image in Wordsworth, or the change from parallelistic to chiastic patterns in his metaphors. The only adequate rhetorical analysis is one that views his poems in terms of "mind in act," with the very temptation of symbolizing—that is, overcondensing, or turning contiguity (metonymy) into identity (metaphor)—as its subject.

This kind of rhetorical analysis does not deal with rhetoric but with rhetoricity, or word-consciousness. Speech, written or voiced, is only a special field within semiotics, defined as the study of signs in the context of signification generally. A poem may have a direct theme, subject, or reference, but it also contains, modifying these, an indication concerning the power and poverty of symbols. The older kind of rhetorical analysis (with its interest in stylistics or psycho-practical acts) was bound to emphasize the persuasive, quasi-visual figure, or such subliminal voicings as pseudo-morphemes. It can usefully point out, for example, a pun in line 11 of "It Is No Spirit" (the star "startles") or the pattern of reversal and transference in "A Slumber" (the speaker's slumber seems to have become the girl's as he wakes).

In poetry, however, we respond less to images or figures as

such than through them to the *image of a voice*. The newer
rhetorical analysis is caught up in this highly complex notion.
It does not automatically privilege voice over "dead speech"
(i.e., the written as such, what J. Derrida names *écriture*),
though it can do so, as when F. R. Leavis attacks Milton. We
know, however, that the nostalgia for an "inviolable voice" is
based quite consciously on the fact that such a voice is a fiction. It is always associated with prior loss or violation, as the
Philomel myth perfectly expresses.[17] Philomel sings in the interlunar moment, when there is silence—and silence is
pleased. Through the "wakeful descant" of poetry we become
conscious of the immensity of the detour leading from absence to presence, or from symbol to symbol rather than to
"the real thing."

What is Wordsworth's image of a voice? It might be said
that he seeks to avoid both "writing up"—the artifices of declamation, of raising speech to oratory; and "writing down"—
the appearance that verse is mere reflection, the mimesis of a
prior event, or speech-event. "Voicing" is clearly part of the
subject of the Lucy poems, and thus an older type of rhetorical reading will not suffice. As we have shown, exclamation is
more at issue than declamation. Voice becomes intratextual,
in the sense of merging with the text (*écriture*) rather than
seeking to transcend textuality by "opening" into an underlying or originative emotion.

As one moves, therefore, from "Strange Fits" to "A Slumber," not only does quoted speech disappear but something
happens to the intentionality of signs. In "Strange Fits" the
moon-sign is an omen, that is, it presages something greater
(lesser) to come. Voice enters as voice when the omen rides
the poet. The relation to voice is even stronger in "Three

Years" where Nature takes over in *propria sermone* at the very point at which children begin to speak articulately.[18] So that we hear Nature, and never Lucy: her life is tied to Nature's narrative. When Nature has finished speaking Lucy too is "finished." Nature's logos ("So Nature spoke, the work was done . . .") betrays. It promises life but produces death. Is the deeper thought here that speech always betrays—even this gentle, if still prophetic, mother-tongue?

The fully internalized speech of "A Slumber" does not cease to evoke a death, or the thought of a death. A representational element persists. Yet the poet's words neither anticipate a betrayal nor vicariously compensate for it. Their "pointed" or ominous quality is barely felt. There is no moon, no path, no precipitate symbol. They do not even give voice a chance to emerge as Voice.

We still feel, of course, how close the "idyll" of the first stanza is to a blind sublimity and the "elegy" of the second to a false sublimation. Yet they are shadows of moods only, reached through a purified form. The issue of loss and gain —of psychic balancing—has deepened measurably. If poetry still rises from loss, it has no magical (sublimating) or guilty (proleptic) relation to it. "A Slumber," a poem of enlightenment—and of the Enlightenment—removes superstition from poetic speech in a much deeper sense than expelling gaudy phrases and mythic personifications.

## THE MELODIOUS PLOT

Akenside's evening star lights him not to Olympia but from her tomb to Philomel's bower. One might take this as representing symbolically the very process of sublimation. A girl

dies, song is born. The myth of Philomel already founded
song on sorrow. Voice is intrinsically elegiac: Philomel's
bower a melodious bier.

But this would simplify both the myth and Akenside's
poem. The myth deals with loss of voice, not only with loss.
A mutilated tongue speaks again through the cunning of art.
In Akenside, moreover, the theme of voice precedes that of
loss: if the "suppliant song" should fail, there would be no
light for the poet. Loss of voice would mean loss of light. The
lyrist skirts that darkening of the voice. Philomel is a symbol,
primarily, for restored song rather than for restored love.

A "melodious plot," consequently, is both the aspired-to
center of the poet's quest and the form of its path. The star
must "suffer" the poet's song before it can grant a petition
that allows song and loss to merge in the "green space" of
memory. What moves us toward that full yet empty space,
that para-paradise, is what we find when we get there: voice,
our sense of its power and impotence. A memory-fiction of its
starry influence survives together with an awareness of its
present absence. This poet's poem helps us understand the
forces of nostalgic lyricism Wordsworth overcame.

Voice is the only epiphany in Akenside's ode, but it rever-
berates in the confines of an operatic set. We hear a frozen
music; such phrases as "the wakeful heifers gaze" are stagy
orphisms. Nothing remains of the logos-power of the word, of
its mimetic or re-creative virtue. What is evoked is a little
moony world far tighter it would seem than that generous intercourse of gods and men suggested by the opening verses.
How sterile this templar space when compared to the "wide
quietness" of "To Psyche" or "murmurous haunt" of "To a
Nightingale"! It is illumined by gaslight rather than by "a

light in sound." [19] Voice, or poetry in general, is worshipped
only as a fiction, as the fetish of a fiction even.

The tension between prophetic voice and fictive word becomes acute after Milton.[20] Not only is paradise understood
to be lost (i.e., understood to have been, or now always to be,
a fiction) but the great voice seems lost that knew itself as
logos: as participating in real influence. The *philomel moment* of English poetry is therefore the postprophetic moment,[21] when the theme of loss merges with that of voice—
when, in fact, a "lost voice" becomes the subject or moving
force of poetic song. "Shall we not hear thee in the storm? In
the noise of the mountain stream? When the feeble sons of
the wind come forth, and scarcely seen pass over the
desert?" [22]

The Ossianic poems overhear these wind-notes that try to
swell into a supreme fiction but remain curiously successive
and apart, wreaths in the Gaelic night. Macpherson's melic
vaporizer turns what light there is into motes of sound. One
voice spells another in a supposedly epic chain which remains a composite lyric. The chain has no real continuity because what memories pass over Ossian, as over a wind-harp,
are not ghosts of heroes so much as "sons of song." Their essence is vocative; their strength a fading power of vocifera-
tion. By a typical sublimation they die into song, or rather
into the spectral, ominously heightened voice of nature.
"When night comes on the hill; when the loud winds arise,
my ghost shall stand in the blast, and mourn the death of my
friends. The hunter shall hear from his booth. He shall fear
but love my voice!" [23]

This melic undermining of the theme of succession—this
substitution of voice for blood—is especially remarkable in

the *Songs of Selma*. A hero's life flourishes as briefly there as the evening star, and with strange delight in its setting. The poem begins with Ossian's address to Hesperus: the "fair-hair'd angel," as Blake will call it, lifts its "unshorn head" from the cloud, to observe the scene but a moment and to depart. "The waves come with joy around thee: they bathe thy lovely hair. Farewell, thou silent beam!" It goes, as it came, in strength; from this, perhaps, the poet's delight in its setting, and the upswing of the ensuing movement: "Let the light of Ossian's soul arise!"

That light is memory, matrix of epic art. Ossian's soul lights up with memories of dead friends, the heroes and bards who used to gather annually in Selma. The evening star has led us not to the moon, its bright epiphany, but to memory—these dying voices from the past. We become aware of a reversal and a twofold sequence. The star's "silent beam" leads to memory by distancing the raging sounds of day ("The murmur of the torrent comes from afar. Roaring waves climb the distant rock"); memory, however, recovers an inconsolable sound. "Colma left alone on the hill with all her voice of song!"

The interlunar moment now repeats itself as Ossianic lover-hero-bard invokes the silence, or the hidden moon, or absent friend. "Rise, moon! from behind thy clouds. Stars of the night arise! Lead me, some light, to the place, where my love rests. . . . But here I must sit alone, by the rock of the mossy stream. The stream and the wind roar aloud. I hear not the voice of my love." These voices are like ghosts, doomed to wander about ravening and unsatisfied. They cannot center on anything because nothing abides their question. "Thou dost smile, and depart," as Ossian says of the evening star.

The questioning voice alone, in its manifold, frustrated music of apostrophe, invocation, and exclamation, remains. This voice is heard as if afar, a passion to be memorialized but no longer owned. There is a kind of elegy in space itself, in our distance from the sublime of sound:

> The sons of song are gone to rest. My voice remains, like a blast, that roars, lonely, on a sea-surrounded rock, after the winds are laid. The dark moss whistles there; the distant mariner sees the waving trees! [24]

A voice without issue, a poetry without succession, is what meets us in the Ossianic fragments. They reflect the anxiety of English poetry as a whole. Macpherson's forgery is strangely true because the original voice he claimed to discover is so lonely, so discontinuous with the origin it posits. The poetry of this new Homer discloses "the westwardness of everything." [25] Deep no longer responds to deep and each hill repeats a lonely sound. The pseudo-psalmodic landscape before us actually spells the end of that "responsive" poetry Christopher Smart sought to revive at exactly the same historical moment.

Now too the poet's self-image changes radically. He sees himself as an aeolian harp, "self-sounding in the night." [26] Macpherson is acclaimed as a Northern Homer, an autochthonous poet springing from the peculiar genius of his region. Or, more sophisticated, poets understand that all origins are forged origins. For Blake they are part of the "mystery" caricatured in his mock-Eastern style, which multiplies births and creates an extraordinary mélange of genealogical fictions. The impossibility of succession leads to a clearer facing of the burden of originality on all poets, which a return to pseudo-

origins evades. Blake's evening star, therefore, rises upon the
twilight of English and classicizing poetry with the energy of
dawn: it is, already, the morning star:

> Thou fair-hair'd angel of the evening,
> Now, while the sun rests on the mountains, light
> Thy bright torch of love; thy radiant crown
> Put on. . . .

### COLERIDGE AND THE MORNING STAR

> Tell also of the false Tongue! vegetated
> Beneath your land of shadows, of its sacrifices and
> Its offerings                                    (Blake)

My subject has not been a theme, or even thematics, but
poetry—poetry as it impinges on those who seek to continue
it. The drama begins, as always, in a darkling moment. There
is the shadow of a prior greatness, or the discovery of a distance from a creating source. That shadow is always there,
but the manifest voice of achievement from Spenser to Milton
had made of England classic ground and put the glory on
each successor poet.[27]

The burden of creativity became both ineluctable and as
heavy as the pack Christian wore. After Milton, poetry joins
or even rivals divinity in pressing its claim on the artist.
Moreover, as soon as greatness is acknowledged, it raises the
question of succession. A theological element enters; a reflection on who is—or could be—worthy to continue the line. In
these circumstances literary criticism can take the form of a
theologico-poetical examination of the pretender. Is he apos-
tolic? The question need not be imposed from the outside: in-

deed, it generally comes from within the visionary poet, and leads to self-doubt as easily as to self-justification. The poet's struggle with his vocation is not always overt or dramatic; only with Collins, Smart, and the great Romantics does it become religious in intensity and direct their voice. What is at stake is, in fact, the erection of a voice. "Would to God all the Lord's people were prophets." [28]

Like drama generally, this one can have two endings: a happy and an unhappy. Keats's poetry is representative of the former. His "To a Nightingale," with its finely repeated darkling moment and green space, is a fulfillment of Akenside's "To the Evening Star." A belated poet rejoices in the symbols and accouterments of his tradition. They fill his verses with a presence rarely as frigid as Akenside's. But Coleridge is representative of the sadder ending. He is afflicted by secondariness as by a curse: his relation to writing of all kinds is more embarrassed than that of Keats and more devious than that of Akenside. His imagination sees itself as inherently "secondary"—not only because it follows great precursors in poetry or philosophy (though that is a factor) but chiefly because of the one precursor, the "primary Imagination . . . living power and prime agent of all human perception . . . repetition in the finite mind of the eternal act of creation in the infinite I AM." His religious sensibility, conspiring with a burdened personal situation, makes him feel at a hopeless remove from originality.

That Coleridge was deeply disturbed by the priority of others—and of the Other—is hardly in question. Too much in his life and writings reflects it. It can be argued that he was, in his way, as "counterfeit" a poet as Macpherson and Chatterton. He had done better, perhaps, to invent new ori-

gins, as they did, rather than to be echo and imitate imita-
tions in a perverse sacrifice to divine primacy. His poetry
shows to what extent he *shrinks* into creation, like Blake's Ur-
izen.[29]

But we are not engaged here in a biography that would ex-
pose the *contre-faisant* to real creation Coleridge practiced.
The one biographical detail relevant to this study is that he
had to contend not only with an inherited sublime that
"counterfeited infinity" (see "Religious Musings" and "The
Destiny of Nations") but also with "sounds less deep and
loud," with the new voice of feeling in Wordsworth. The latter meets him at the very threshold of his liberation from sublimity.

Some of his early poems—the "To the Nightingale" and
"Aeolian Harp" of 1795 in particular—are clearly moving in a
Wordsworthian direction, as is Southey in his *English Ec-
logues* (1797). But then "the giant Wordsworth—God bless
him" preempts them all. Coleridge soon entails his portion of
poetic genius on this contemporary giant. Though "Frost at
Midnight" and "To the Nightingale" (the latter as revised for
*Lyrical Ballads*) repay Wordsworth's influence by leading
into "Tintern Abbey," such dialogue between the poets (Coleridge's truest "conversation") lasts but a year. It breaks off
when the poets separate in Germany, with Coleridge going
off to study at Göttingen. To the priority of Wordsworth,
Germany eventually adds that of Kant, Schelling, and the
Schlegels in philosophy and criticism.

Of course, such nova as "Kubla Khan" and "The Ancient
Mariner" may make the question of originality seem a blind
alley. It is true, nevertheless, that the "Ancyent Marinere"

was written "in imitation of the *style* as well as of the spirit of the elder poets" and that the gloss added by Coleridge at a later date antiques the poem even more as well as putting its author at curious remove from his own work. The gloss—that cool, continuous trot—frames a precipitous rime. The burden of originality, in this original poem, is relieved by a (repeated) return to fake eld.

A psychological analysis of the conditions that removed Coleridge's literary impotence is not our concern, however. Enough if we understand how problematic imaginative writing was for him. It was, at once, inherently dependent or secondary, yet virtually primary or participating in the divine "I AM." His bravest poems tend to recant themselves. The pattern is obvious in "The Aeolian Harp," yet elsewhere too, if more subtly, he worships the whirlwind or puts a finger on his mouth like Job.

A test-case for this sacrificial or self-counterfeiting movement (when originality was in his reach) is the "Hymn before Sunrise, in the Vale of Chamouni." Coleridge falsifies his experience in two ways. He had been on Scafell, not in Chamouny. This transposition to a traditionally sublime spot occurred despite Wordsworth, or perhaps because of him. It is difficult to work out the relation, but Coleridge, in this poem, could have celebrated a native mountain in Wordsworthian style before Wordsworth (*The Prelude*'s account of Snowdon was unwritten or still in manuscript). There is also his notorious use of a minor German poetess, Frederike Brun. He quietly incorporates essential lines from her short "Chamonix beym Sonnenaufgang." This double shift, from England to France in locality, and from English to German

(Klopstockian) verse in features of style and experience, is surely a kind of flight from native origins, or from whatever Wordsworth exemplified.[30]

Even were we to accept the Hymn's egregious sublimity, it would remain a strange production. The style, as Wordsworth charged, is "mock sublime," a turgid almost parodistic development of Miltonic hymns to Creation. The impression is that Klopstock has been the model rather than an English visionary. Add to this that the poem turns on the old conceit of making silence speak—that its essential subject is presence or absence of Voice—and you have a signal case of Coleridge speaking with a tongue not his own, or adopting a counterfeit logos. "Bowed low/ In adoration" he ventriloquizes nature, and sacrifices his genius and the *genius loci* to the tritest forms of sublime ejaculation.

This is not the whole story, however. The poem's first section (to about line 37) bears traces of inward record and a powerful grasp of myth-making. The only conventional thing about it is the desensualizing movement from visible to invisible. This is imposed on a remarkable *situation*. The poem begins with the near-mythic contrast of the "white" mountain (Blanc) shrouded in black, and the silent mountain rising from a sounding base. We feel the contending elements and approach Manichaeanism. For a moment only—but still for that moment—we understand Abel's cry in "The Wanderings of Cain": "The Lord is God of the living only, the dead have another God."

The Manichaean contrasts disappear into the conventional paradoxes of sublime rhetoric which characterize the later portions of the Hymn. (A "mighty voice" both calls the torrents "from night and utter death/ From dark and icy caverns" and stops them "at once amid their maddest plunge," reverting them to "silent cataracts.") What does not disappear is the horror of stasis implicit in the opening moments. "Hast thou a charm to stay the morning-star . . . ?" Dread of stillness combines with dread of blackness. The mountain, co-herald of the dawn because of its snowy height, seems to be in league with darkness. It is a passing impression; yet that there was this *charm*, this bewitchment of time, is conveyed by a pattern of stills that, as in "The Ancient Mariner," can suddenly freeze the image of motion. It is as if time were subject to sudden arrest—to an embolism felt in the poem's development as a whole, which is really a nondevelopment, or a passionate rhetorical goad to make the soul "rise" together with obstructed dawn.

In *this* darkling and enchanted moment it is morning that almost fails to rise. "Nightes dread" is now associated with dawn's delay. As a slowing of time it is, moreover, the opposite of erotic; [31] the "bald awful head," the "dread mountain form," etc., suggest if anything a scene of sacrifice. It is also significant that when the mountain is linked to the morning star a second time (ll. 30 ff.), the diction swells distinctly toward the Miltonic and repeats the nightmare resonance of the opening verses. Is the mountain or the poet's soul the true subject of these lines?

> And thou, O silent Mountain, sole and bare
> O blacker than the darkness all the night
>> (original version)

> Thou first and chief, sole sovereign of the Vale!
> O struggling with the darkness all the night
>> (later version)

And who is being contended for in this cosmic battle?

> And visited all night by troops of stars
> Or when they climb the sky or when they sink. . . .

This place, then, soul or mountain, is a virtual Prince of Darkness. The visiting "troops of stars" could be the Satanic "Stars of Night" (*Paradise Lost*, V.745) or a sustaining, heavenly host.[32] We are on the verge of a "wild allegory"; [33] but nothing really is clear except that the soul, in trying to "wake" or "rise," meets quasi-demonic forces. "Rising" gets confused with "rising up"—perhaps through a montage of the image of the morning star with the myth of Lucifer.

What more can be said? In this deeply religious, or mythopoeic, situation, continuity of self (in time) is threatened, and there is need for a rite, and specifically a rite of passage.[34] The morning star must be freed to continue its rising course: a progress leading toward dawn must be restored. The mountain too must "rise," for the sable charm invests it as well. But to free mountain or morning star is tantamount to finding some lost intermediary between darkness and dawn, some symbolic form, at least a voice. The darkness is a darkness of mediations. And in this darkness, even constituting it, is the poet's struggle to extricate a religious rather than demonic mediation. The image of Lucifer as Prince of the Air, Prince of Darkness, has merged with that of the mountain as "great hierarch" and "dread ambassador"; yet the image of Lucifer as morning star is also there, and blends with a mountain described as "Companion of the morning-star at dawn." The poet's soul, in this hymn, tries to call the one and not the other. "O which one, is it each one?" [35]

At the end, it is unsure who prevails. The mountain's mediation seems to lift the weight of that "dark, substantial, black" which oppressed air and soul in the beginning, but the supposed upward lumbering of its voice ("tell thou the silent sky," etc.) merely differentiates a silence which reaches, as in Pascal, the stars. Coleridge leaves us with a depressing sense of hierarchy, measured by the contrast between his bowed head and the "bald awful head" of "stupendous" Blanc. His "Instructions to a Mountain" would sound ludicrous if they were not despairing. They suggest the opposite of Shelley's "Thou hast a voice, great Mountain, to repeal/ Large codes of fraud and woe," for they effectively make the mountain into the rock of institutionalized religion, complete with frigidly hieratic spheres. In a sense, then, the debased (Urizenic) Lucifer has triumphed because indistinguishable from the religious code. The true morning star never rises.[36]

Only at one point is there something like a genuine release from the "ebon mass." It is not unlike what the mariner feels after the spell begins to break and the albatross falls off; and it involves quiet gazing rather than rhetorical shouting. Struggling against the charm, the poet views the mountain as a wedge that pierces the surrounding blackness. Then, as if recanting, he thinks the blackness away as a "crystal shrine" which is the mountain's home. Finally he desubstantializes it completely when through rapt gazing Mont Blanc vanishes from consciousness only to reappear blending subliminally— like a "beguiling melody"—into thought. Several stills, then, or re-visions relax the hold of a spell that almost paralyzed the soul. This spell becomes the "trance" of prayer and a "beguiling" thought-music. Its power continues to echo as the stills move quasi-cinematically into the unitive swell of mountain and mind.

The most curious of these still ecstasies [37] in Coleridge is also one of the earliest. A sonnet of 1790 shows the lover absorbed in the evening star:

> On thee full oft with fixèd eye I gaze
> Till I, methinks, all spirit seem to grow.

By a sacrificial sleight of mind he then identifies the star with the beloved woman, so that, in effect, gazing is all there is—until his spirit should join hers in the star's "kindred orb":

> Must she not be, as is thy placid sphere
> Serenely brilliant? Whilst to gaze a while
> Be all my wish 'mid Fancy's high career
> E'en till she quit this scene of earthly toil;
> Then Hope perchance might fondly sigh to join
> Her spirit in thy kindred orb, O Star benign!

I am not convinced of the star's benignity. Anti-erotic, it leads to death not love, or to a life beyond life. Nothing is lost by this sublimation except all. Having is replaced by hoping in a fatal movement that confirms Blake's "O Sunflower." Coleridge does not hope to have, he hopes that *then* he may hope. He does not seem to know his life has been stolen—as he knows, at least, in his mountain poem. There he recognizes the charm and tries to break a heliotropic (or melantropic) trance by recovering a sense of his own presence amid the ghostliness. But though he resists the charm it gets the better of him. The desire for sublimation is too strong and his soul passes into "the mighty Vision" and so "swells" to heaven. This dilation is sublimation still. The mountain's presence is no more benign than the star's.

"Ghost of a mountain—the forms seizing my Body as I

passed & became realities—I, a Ghost, till I had recon-
quered my substance." This notebook entry, recorded first in
November, 1799, is repeated in September, 1802, at the time,
probably, of composing the "Hymn before Sunrise." The ghostliness he describes also befell the Ancient Mariner. It takes
away the sense of easy personal presence while intensifying
the presence of otherness. Emptied of personality he must
stand on this very emptiness against impinging surreality. It is
his only "ground" (the question of ground being further subverted by locating the action on a shifty sea). One can understand why the "coal-ridge" of this massive mountain became
a place for Coleridge's struggle to ground the self. A late and
beautiful letter recapitulates his whole spiritual history as it
impinges on the Hymn:

> . . . from my very childhood I have been accustomed to
> *abstract* and as it were unrealize whatever of more than
> common interest my eyes dwelt on; and then by a sort of
> transfusion and transmission of my consciousness to iden-
> tify myself with the Object—and I have often thought
> . . . that if ever I should feel once again the genial
> warmth and stir of the poetic impulse, and refer to my
> own experiences, I should venture on a yet stranger &
> wilder Allegory than of yore—that I would *allegorize*
> myself, as a Rock with it's summit just raised above the
> surface of some Bay or Strait in the Arctic Sea,
>
> While yet the stern and solitary Night
> Brook'd no alternate Sway—
>
> all around me fixed and firm, methought as my own Sub-
> stance, and near me lofty Masses, that might have
> seemed to "hold the Moon and Stars in fee" and often in

such wild play with meteoric lights, or with the quiet
Shine from above . . . that it was a pride and a place of
Healing to lie, as in an Apostle's Shadow, within the
Eclipse and deep substance-seeming Gloom of "these
dread Ambassadors from Earth to Heaven, Great Hier-
archs"! and tho' obscured yet to think myself obscured
by consubstantial Forms, based in the same Foundation
as my own. I grieved not to serve them—yea, lovingly
and with gladsomeness I abased myself in their presence:
for they are my Brothers, I said.[38]

So the Valley of Chamouny is truly a "Valley of Wonders."
But does the poet succeed in "reconquering" his "substance"
there? (How much play with that grounding word in the
above letter! ) It is hard to say, from the Hymn, whether loss
of self or loss of voice was more important. Yet writing the
Hymn meant recovering a voice. In the Hymn as in the Rime,
release from the curse—that dread stillness, or paralysis of
motion—is obtained by the ability to pray. And prayer is interpreted in both poems as praise:

> O happy living things! no tongue
> Their beauty might declare. . . .

The weight of the Albatross (like the air's "ebon mass") is re-
moved, together with the stone from the tongue.
   Yet voice remains uneasy, both in the Hymn and in the
Rime. Praise mutes itself in the act:

> O happy living things! *no tongue*
> Their beauty might declare:
> A spring of love gushed from my heart
> And I blessed them *unaware*

There is too great a contrast between the compulsive speech of the Mariner and this first, tongueless moment. The Hymn, similarly, is hardly an "unaware" blessing: its one moment of sweet unconsciousness (ll. 17–23) does not compensate us for the forced sublimity of the rest.

Praise, according to the Psalmist, is a "sacrifice of thanksgiving." It substitutes for, or sublimates, the rite of blood-sacrifice. The Hymn on Mont Blanc is written against this background of sublimation. The exact pressure put on Coleridge —the offering demanded of him by the dread form—we shall never know. Coleridge's "Sca'fell Letter" shows him as "overawed," but there was nothing necessarily mysterious. He felt, that much is certain, a loss of substance, a passivity both shaming and sublime [39]—and he recovers himself, at least in the Hymn, by the will of his voice; more precisely, by the willed imitation of a sublime voice.

I will not deny that the inferred human situation is more impressive than the Hymn produced by it. But that is because, in Coleridge, poetry remains so closely linked to sublimation. Sublimation always sacrifices to an origin stronger than itself. If it did not cherish or dread this origin—this "hiding-place" of power—it would not shroud it from sight by displacement or falsification:

> Never mortal saw
> The cradle of the strong one,
> Never mortal heard
> The gathering of his voice,
> The deep-murmured charm. . . .[40]

Such "wildly-silent" scenes [41] are not infrequent in Coleridge. He is often, in fancy, near an origin where a "great

Spirit" with "plastic sweep"—the wind or voice of the opening of Genesis—moves on the still darkness. But he is, at the
same time, so removed from this primal scene that it becomes
a "stilly murmur" which "tells of silence." The voice redeeming that silence, or vexed into being by it, can be as cold as
the eye of Ancient Mariner or moon. "Green vales and icy
cliffs, all join my Hymn." Its "sunny domes" are accompanied
by "caves of ice." In the end what predominates are the
strange soteriological images, the "secret ministry of frost,"
the rock "in wild play . . . with the quiet Shine from above,"
or others calm yet glittering: the "mild splendor," for instance, of a "serenely brilliant" star, which summons the poet
at evening to accept his death-in-life.


AFTERTHOUGHT

> The Imagination is always at the end of an era.
>
> (Wallace Stevens)

These reflections must finally turn back on themselves. Is
their objective really "objective"? Are we, should we be, aiming at positive literary history? Or have we found a kind of
history-writing compatible with its subject-matter: poetry?

The theme of the evening star, as a point of departure, is
not objective, but neither is it arbitrary. I have described
elsewhere the idea of a Westering of the poetical spirit, and
the fear of a decline in poetical energy which accompanied it.
Others too, notably W. J. Bate and Harold Bloom, have put
forward a thesis on the belatedness of English poetry.[42]
While it is notoriously difficult to explain the birth or rebirth
of a symbol, I suspect that, after the Renaissance, the com-

plex evening-consciousness of English poets reached toward the Hesper/Lucifer theme as toward a limit.

What was limited by the theme? The fear of discontinuity, of a break in personal or cultural development; but also a vatic overestimation of poetry which, putting too great a burden on the artist, made this break more likely. Vaticination remains in evening star poetry, yet is diminished in a special way. Symbol or substitute (Hesper/Philomel in Akenside) tends to become more important than the epiphanic source (the moon). A prophetic background supports a purely symbolic foreground. The aura of the symbol is reduced even as its autonomy is strengthened. It is ironic that, by the time of Stevens, "the philosophy of symbols" (as Yeats called it) confronts the poet with a new discontinuity: the symbols, or romantic relics, are so attenuated by common use that their ground (sky?) is lost. They become starry junk, and the poem is a device to dump them, to let the moon rise as moon, free of

> the moon and moon
> The yellow moon of words about the nightingale
> In measureless measures. . . .[43]

Perhaps it was the masque, with its courtly center and operatic machinery, which first encouraged a translation of prophecy into "descendental" picture. Ben Jonson's masques, for instance, can be elaborate night-pieces converging on queen-moon or *roi-soleil*. Royal center, epiphanic allegory, and pictorial hinge go together.[44] A star-god or genius of some kind "descends" to point out his representative on earth, or do obeisance. In *Pleasure Reconciled to Virtue* (1619) the center explicitly descends westward: King James and Prince

Charles are linked to the "bright race of Hesperus," which de-
limits their royal aura yet still discloses, epiphanically, an origin. To call James "the glory of the West" evokes a consciously Hesperian ideology with consequences for later
English poetry.[45] In Hesperian verse, the epiphanic figure

> Sitting like a goddess bright
> In the center of her light [46]

diffuses into various, equally mortal or westering, presences:

> The Rainbow comes and goes,
> And lovely is the Rose,
> The Moon doth with delight
> Look round her when the heavens are bare;
> Waters on a starry night
> Are beautiful and fair;
> The sunshine is a glorious birth. . . .[47]

From Ben Jonson to Wordsworth, and from masque to ode,
is too abrupt a jump. But it illumines an important difference
between epochs, bridged in part by our previous, historically
oriented sketch: a difference in structure of sensibility or
mode of representation. Wordsworth's mind, in the above
stanza, loses itself only fractionally in the moon-moment. Its
delight in other images is even more restrained: they remain
as intransitive as the verbs, and alternate deliberately between sky and earth. Sight is segmented by them; and the se-
rial impression they leave is of Wordsworth counting his
blessings or storing them against the dying of all light. He is
restrained because he is reflective; he is reflective because he
is perplexed at nature's losing its immediacy. But the image
of the moon challenges his restraint. With it the verses almost

leap from perplexity into vision: the poet too would throw off all shadow, like heaven its clouds.

Yet the visionary personification that rises in him is simply the act of seeing—natural seeing—magnified. A personified moon makes the eyes of man personal again. Sight hovers on the edge of visionariness without passing over: "when the heavens are bare" is not an apocalyptic notation. Wordsworth's restraint is, as always, a restraint of vision. Though his eye leaps up, he subdues the star-symbol.

The evening star is, typically, like this Rainbow, Rose, Moon. A Hesperian image, it both rouses and chastens the prophetic soul. A fixed yet fugitive sign, its virtue is virtuality. It signals at most a continuation of the line. Through its binominal character, moreover, Hesper/Lucifer points at once beyond and toward itself. Always setting, yet always steadfast, it repeats in small the strange survival of poetry within the lights and shadows of historical circumstance.

## NOTES

1. This is the accepted date, though it is speculative. The poem first appeared in the posthumous edition of Akenside's *Poems* (1772).

2. See *The Greek Bucolic Poets*, ed. J. M. Edmonds (Loeb Classical Library, New York, 1928), pp. 410–13.

3. See *The Poems of Samuel Taylor Coleridge*, ed. E. H. Coleridge (Oxford University Press Standard Authors), p. 16. In the 2d (1797) edition of his *Poems on Various Subjects* Coleridge surmised that "if the Sonnet were comprized in less than fourteen lines, it would become a serious epigram."

4. The preposition "to" in st. 1 foregrounds itself so strongly that, to subordinate it, one is tempted to read it on the pattern of "to-

night" (i.e., proclitically) and so bring it closer to the bonded prep-osition "sub" in *supply, suppliant* (a near pun, anticipating the re-versal mentioned above) and even *suffer*. Cf. the syntax of st. 6; also the "prefer" of l. 19 which makes "vows" both its direct and indirect object. It draws attention once more not only to the prep-ositional but also to the syntactical bonding of one verse-line with another. All this fosters a sense of the discontinuous or precarious path followed by the verses' "feet." It is interesting that in Chris-topher Smart's *Song to David* (1763) the problem of hierarchy, subordination (hypotaxis), and prepositional-syntactical bonding reaches an acute stage.

5. Cf. Tennyson, *In Memoriam*, 121, "Sweet Hesper-Phosphor, double name . . ."

6. See Blake, *Milton*, and Collins, "Ode on the Poetical Charac-ter."

7. Spenser, "Epithalamium," l. 290.

8. Blake, "To the Evening Star." "Full soon" could mean both "very soon" and "soon full" (having reached its ripest or intensest point).

9. Shelley, "To a Skylark," ll. 21–25. This describes the morning star; Shelley wrote an expressively bad poem to the evening star in 1811 (see *The Complete Works*, ed. T. Hutchinson, p. 870) and uses Plato's verses (cited above, p. 90) as an epigraph for "Ado-nais." His most famous evocation of Hesperus-Lucifer is in "The Triumph of Life," ll. 412–20. On the importance to Shelley of the evening–morning star theme, cf. W. B. Yeats, "The Philosophy of Shelley's Poetry," in *Ideas of Good and Evil* (1903). To gain a complete "phenomenological thematics" it would be necessary, of course, to consider the evening star theme in relation to that of the moon, the night, other stars, birds (nightingale / lark), star flowers, the hymeneal theme (cf. Catullus, "Vesper adest"), etc.

10. See the ending of "Night the Ninth" in the *Four Zoas*.

11. Like "golden," these lines were added in 1815. Cf. "She Was a Phantom of Delight," whose first stanza is clearly indebted to the

evening star motif, and whose rhythm is similar. For a large-scale speculation on sky-earth imagery in "Daffodils," see Frederick Garber, *Wordsworth and the Poetry of Encounter* (Urbana, 1971), pp. 152 ff.

12. For an interpretation of Wordsworth's "middle-ground" parallel to mine, and to which I am indebted, see Paul De Man, "Symbolic Landscape in Wordsworth and Yeats," *In Defense of Reading*, eds. R. A. Brower and R. Poirier (New York, 1963).

13. "It Is No Spirit," ll. 7–8.

14. Also perhaps Wordsworth's marital situation. He had gone to France to see Annette Vallon and his daughter prior to marrying Mary (in October, 1802). There is also the poet's general sensitivity to "floating," or images of suspended animation, or even the word "hung."

15. For "race," a probable pun, cf. Psalms 19:5.

16. This and the following quotation are from *The Complete Poems of Emily Dickinson*, ed. T. H. Johnson, poems 1135 and 1616. See also Eleanor Wilner, "The Poetics of Emily Dickinson," *ELH*, XXXVIII (1971), 138–40.

17. Cf. T. S. Eliot, *The Waste Land*, ll. 97 ff.

18. I am indebted for this insight to my student Frances Ferguson.

19. Coleridge, "The Aeolian Harp" (1795), l. 28. The line was not in the original published version, but entered the text in 1828.

20. For the role Milton as Voice played in Wordsworth, and the Romantics generally, see Leslie Brisman, *A Second Will* (Cornell University Press, forthcoming), ch. 5. For "Voice" after Wordsworth, cf. Thomas Whitaker's "Voices in the Open" (lecture at the 1970 English Institute) and John Hollander's *Images of Voice* (Cambridge, 1970), as well as his essay in this volume.

21. See Angus Fletcher, *The Prophetic Moment* (Chicago, 1971).

22. "Fingal," in James Macpherson, *The Poems of Ossian*. Cf. the role of voice (the wind's and that of—originally—Lucy Gray) in Coleridge's "Dejection: An Ode."

23. Macpherson, *Songs of Selma*.

24. Last lines of *Songs of Selma*.

25. Wallace Stevens, "Our Stars Come from Ireland," in *The Auroras of Autumn*.

26. Michael Bruce, "Lochleven," in *Poems on Several Occasions* (Edinburgh, 1782).

27. For the general thesis cf. Harold Bloom, "Coleridge: The Anxiety of Influence," in this volume; W. J. Bate, *The Burden of the Past and the English Poet* (Cambridge, Mass., 1970); and G. H. Hartman, *Beyond Formalism* (New Haven, 1970), pp. 270 ff. and 367 ff.

28. Numbers 11:29, and Plate 1 of Blake's *Milton*.

29. Norman Fruman, in ch. 6 of *Coleridge, the Damaged Archangel* (New York, 1971), shows the young poet systematically "vamping" the mediocre poetry of his time. On this "substitution of conventionality for originality" and the closeness in Coleridge of "self-construction" and "self-annihilation," see M. G. Cooke, "*Quisque Sui Faber:* Coleridge in the *Biographia Literaria*," *Philological Quarterly*, L (1971), 208–29.

30. The psychological background is extremely complex: he was deeply identified, by this time, with Wordsworth and indeed the entire Wordsworth "family," as the Verse Letter to Sara Hutchinson (later "Dejection") of the previous April shows. His Scafell experience was also recorded in (prose) letters to Sara. Bowles's "Coombe Ellen" and "Saint Michael's Mount" may have been in his mind, but in a negative way—his letter to Sotheby of September 10, 1802, leads into a mention of the Scafell-Chamouny Hymn via criticisms of Bowles's "second Volume" (*Poems,* by the Reverend Wm. Lisle Bowles, Vol. II, 1801) which contained these poems.

31. Fruman has interesting remarks on Coleridge's use of "hope" in an implicitly sexual sense (*Coleridge*, pp. 425 ff.). Sara Hutchinson is always in his thought at this time (see note 30 above), and

the attempt to "rise" out of a nightmare moment of trance or passivity could have involved sensual "Hopes & Fears."

32. "Stay" in "Hast thou a charm to stay the morning star / In his steep course" could be ambiguous and reflect the double image of the mountain-darkness as (1) preventing and (2) supporting the star.

33. See the letter quoted below, pp. 119–20.

34. Cf. Angus Fletcher on "liminal anxiety" in Coleridge, below, pp. 140 ff.

35. G. M. Hopkins "Carrion Comfort," 1. 13.

36. Cf. Harold Bloom, *Shelley's Mythmaking* (New Haven, 1959), pp. 15–19.

37. Cf. "To the Nightingale," ll. 12–14; "This Lime-Tree Bower My Prison," ll. 38 ff.; and passages mainly from the *Notebooks* which tell how gazing produced a "phantom-feeling" by abstracting or "unrealizing" objects. See *The Notebooks of Samuel Taylor Coleridge* (New York, 1961), II, 2495, 2546; also the letter quoted below, p. 119.

38. *Collected Letters of Samuel Taylor Coleridge,* ed. E. L. Griggs (Oxford, 1956–), IV, 974–75.

39. There seem to have been two Scafell letters, now extant only in Sara Hutchinson's transcript (Griggs, *Collected Letters,* II, 834–45). The second one (no. 451 in Griggs) begins strangely with Coleridge mentioning his "criminal" (for a family man) addiction to recklessness when descending mountains, then describing a narrow escape. "I lay in a state of almost prophetic Trance & Delight—& blessed God aloud, for the powers of Reason & the Will, which remaining no Danger can overpower us! O God, I exclaimed aloud —how calm, how blessed am I now / I know not how to proceed, how to return / but I am calm & fearless & confident / if this Reality were a Dream, if I were asleep, what agonies had I suffered! what screams!—When the Reason & the Will are away, what remains to us but Darkness & Dimness & a bewildering Shame, and

Pain that is utterly Lord over us, or fantastic Pleasure." This experience of mingled fear and exaltation may have something of the
conventional "sublime" in it; but it confirms that there was a
*trance* and a deep moment of wakeful, rather than sleep-bound,
passivity. It also suggests that, however exalted the trance, Coleridge feared it could lead (by the "streamy nature" of consciousness?) into painful sexual thoughts. The only explicit trace, in the
Hymn, of this shame at passivity is its formal turn: "Awake my
soul! not only passive praise / Thou owest . . ."

40. "On a Cataract. Improved from Stolberg" (1799?). Both of the
F. L. Stolberg lyrics translated by Coleridge—"Der Felsenstrom"
and "Bei William Tell's Geburtsstätte"—are about places of origin.

41. The quotations in this paragraph come from "To the Rev.
W. L. Bowles," "The Aeolian Harp," "Hymn before Sunrise, in
the Vale of Chamouni," and "Kubla Khan."

42. That there may be a subjective or pseudo-historical element in
the thesis does not disqualify it, unless we erect it into actual history: all art, it can be argued, seen from the point of view of
"imagination," is a *second* rather than a *first*—haunted, that is, by
being mere copy, re-creation, or afterglow. If poetry since the Renaissance (and at times in the Renaissance) felt itself approaching an
evening stage, it could mean that poets judged their work more absolutely: either as coinciding with, or failing, Imagination. For the
thesis, cf. W. J. Bate, *The Burden of the Past and the English
Poet;* Harold Bloom, *Yeats* (New York, 1970), and, forthcoming,
*The Anxiety of Influence: A Theory of Poetry;* also G. H. Hartman, "Blake and the Progress of Poesy" and "Romantic Poetry and
the Genius Loci," in *Beyond Formalism.*

43. Wallace Stevens, "Autumn Refrain." Cf. "Man on the Dump."

44. On the relation between vision and representation in the
masque, see Angus Fletcher, *The Transcendental Masque: An
Essay on Milton's Comus* (Ithaca, 1972), pp. 8–18.

45. Tudor myth, which exalted Elizabeth as "that bright *Occiden-
tal* star" (Dedicatory Epistle to the King James Bible) and com-

pared James to "the radiant Cymbeline / Which shines here in the west" (*Cymbeline*, V.v.474–77), helped to convert the theme of a *translatio imperii* into that of a *translatio artis*.

46. Milton, "Arcades," ll. 18–19. This queen-moon, it may be added, is also a "western star," since "Arcades" is based on the conceit of finding a new Arcady in the West—that is, in England. Keats's "Endymion" stands to the theme of the moon as Shelley's "Adonais" to that of the evening star: my essay breaks off before those luxurious revivals.

47. Wordsworth, "Ode: Intimations of Immortality," stanza 2.

ANGUS FLETCHER

# "POSITIVE NEGATION": THRESHOLD, SEQUENCE,
# AND PERSONIFICATION IN COLERIDGE

"*It* was, I think, in the month of August, but certainly in the summer season, and certainly in the year 1807, that I first saw this illustrious man, the largest and most spacious intellect, the subtlest and the most comprehensive, in my judgment, that has yet existed amongst men." Thus, in an article written some twenty-seven years later, Thomas De Quincey recalled his first encounter with Coleridge. The encounter was somewhat uncanny. Coleridge, one might say, *appeared* to his young admirer.

> I had received directions for finding out the house where Coleridge was visiting; and, in riding down a main street of Bridgewater, I noticed a gateway corresponding to the description given me. Under this was standing, and gazing about him, a man . . . . his eyes were large and soft in their expression; and it was from the peculiar appear-

ance of haze or dreaminess, which mixed with their light,
that I recognized my object. This was Coleridge. I exam-
ined him steadfastly for a minute or more; and it struck
me that he saw neither myself nor any other object in the
street. He was in deep reverie; for I had dismounted,
made two or three trifling arrangements at an inn door,
and advanced close to him, before he had apparently become conscious of my presence. The sound of my voice,
announcing my own name, first awoke him: he started,
and, for a moment, seemed at a loss to understand my
purpose or his situation; for he repeated rapidly a number of words which had no relation to either of us. There
was no *mauvaise honte* in his manner, but simple perplexity, and an apparent difficulty in recovering his position amongst daylight realities. This little scene over, he
received me with a kindness of manner so marked it
might be called gracious.[1]

Coleridge appeared to De Quincey in the hovering stance of
"a solitary haunted by vast conceptions in which he cannot
participate," Hartman's romantic "hero of consciousness."[2]
He stood on the threshold between a building and a street, a
palace and a highway, a temple and a labyrinth. This threshold is an edge at which simultaneous participation in the sacred and the profane becomes available to the hero of consciousness.

THRESHOLDS: A SPENSERIAN ORIGIN

The gateway is a sacred *via transitionae* in all cultures: in
our materialist world there are myths of carrying brides over
doorsteps, though we no longer break oatcakes over the
heads of newlyweds. Thresholds, which are dangerous, have

an ancient, rigorous mythography and rite. The Romans consecrated a god of gates, Janus, whose bifrontal face looked opposite ways, in and out of the city, blessing or cursing the passer in his entrance to or exit from the city.

Janus was also a god of beginnings, which suggests that, in any advanced civilization, a genuine beginning always starts from somewhere. Within culture, it would seem, there are no beginnings *ex nihilo*. The scene of the origin is a fountain, a *templum*, a ground made sacred because it is the iconic double of the world conceived as sacred space and therefore, as so frequently in the ancient civilizations, a space formally demarcated by a sacred limit, the so-called *mundus*—the world-wall. Within culture, also, deaths and endings seem to belong to what lies outside the sacred inner-space, an outside archetypally structured as "the labyrinth."

Ancient religious traditions descend and enter into English poetics largely through the imagery of a dialectical opposition between temple and labyrinth.[3] The Romantic fascination with these two great images of life seems to gain its power from the hybrid nature of classical and Christian mythography, as a Christian Humanist combination. The temple and labyrinth are the paradigmatic mythic structures for biblical, as much as classical, historicity and prophecy. The hybridization of pagan and Christian myth is, at least in this area, entirely conventional.

If temple and labyrinth provide the models of sacred stillness and profane movement, the threshold is the model of the transitional phase that links these two fundamental modes of being. Mythographically thresholds take many forms: Homer's Cave of the Nymphs, Vergil's twin Gates of Horn and Ivory, Dante's Limbo—or, leaping into the modern era,

Wordsworthian "spots of time," Conrad's shadow line, For-
ster's Caves of Marabar. While epic tradition supplies conventional models of the threshold, these conventions are always
subject to deliberate poetic blurring, and this shift from the
distinct limen to the indistinct serves a double purpose. On
the one hand, poets, like painters, may delight in the softening of outline because it permits an intensification of medium:
thus Turner's mastery of the indistinct expresses a technical
interest in medium which is remarkably parallel to that of his
near-contemporary, Coleridge.[4] On the other hand, and this
is perhaps the fundamental and more substantial point, poets
have wished to subtilize, to dissolve, to fragment, to blur the
hard material edge, because poetry hunts down the soul, with
its obscure passions, feelings, other-than-cognitive symbolic
forms. Spenser, for example, places doormen at the gates of
his various temples; Milton stations various guardians of the
gates: angels watch over Eden, Heaven, and Hell (including
the counterwatch of Sin and Death). Such porters actively
frame their universes. Yet despite this hard and obvious util-
ity of suggesting the security force watching over mythic borders, few poets of major stature remain long interested in the
material aspect of the threshold. If not always before, at least
with the Renaissance there is a poetic commitment to a
blurred psychologized threshold. Earlier authors like Vergil
and Apuleius appeal to the Renaissance poets partly because
this psychological element had been so strong in their earlier
rites of passage.

    Spenser's thresholds are often occurrences in the minds of
his protagonists, changes of mind, rather than transitions of
body or thing. At his most powerful, as at the end of Book III
of *The Faerie Queene*, Spenser may accommodate a physical

and mental crossover, so that the two merge in one single, un-broken psychosomatic drama. Scudamour cannot pass the threshold of Busirane's castle-prison, because his "mind" will not permit the passage, but Britomart can pass over, and when she does, as with her other marvelous psychological break-throughs, she achieves for Spenser an originating shift within English romantic sensibility. She enacts the exchange of psychic energies.

From Spenser, Milton learns the iconographies of mental shift. Milton takes the mind to be the locus of the symbolic threshold, and he begins his career (after saluting Shake-speare, Donne, and the other Metaphysicals) with shorter works on various rites of passage, among them the "Ode on the Morning of Christ's Nativity," *Comus,* and "Lycidas." The later epic works dramatize cosmic threshold-scenes, but the same sense of dawning animates even the prose works of Milton—his *Areopagitica* breathes light as the form or medium of truth. Milton places dramatic action at the cosmic threshold. For English romantic rites of passage he is a most vocal prophet.

Where this prophetic voicing becomes problematic, how-ever, is not in the discrimination of our romantic interest in it: that we recognize. But threshold becomes a more elusive concept when we stress, as such, the prophetic speech that marks its liminal apprehension. Here both sight and sound tend to create a sense of time, and time is enigmatic.

BETWEENNESS AND TIME

In poetry, as in the Scriptures, one notes at once the tem-poral aspect of the threshold. Measures of the precise amount of natural light (or artificial light, if you take *The Invisible Man* as the contemporary model) specify the experiencing of a shift from one period to another. The archetypal liminal scene occurs at dawn or dusk (Baudelaire's two *crépuscules*), at the end of a departing year or the start of a new year (January), the end or beginning of an era, a millennium perhaps. Whatever the magnitude of the joined time-frames, however, there seems to be no reason why thresholdness, which its chief modern theorist, Heidegger, would call "betweenness" —*das Zwischen*—could not minimally refer to a crossing from one instant to another. Montaigne, in *Repentance*, when he says "I do not portray being, I portray passing," is assuming the possibility of instantaneous change—"from minute to minute," he says, "my history needs to be adapted to the moment. I may presently change." Indeed, in high Coleridgean fashion, he can conceive that since all things in the world are in constant motion, "stability itself is nothing but a more languid motion."

Montaigne is the philosopher of modern poetry, and the one thinker whom we at once associate with the Shakespearean (and by an extrapolation, with the Coleridgean) enterprise. Montaigne records the way things more and more seem to be staggering with "natural drunkenness." Remarkably, while more extension-conscious than even Descartes himself, Montaigne can speak to Shakespeare because he shares the sense of the dramatic confusions wrought upon us by the "petty pace" of diurnal time.

The slow Cartesian scientific development of a system opposed to Montaigne, the "elimination of time" which Whitrow has shown descending earlier from Archimedes, flowering with Descartes, and culminating with Einstein's "geometrization" of all time and space, makes war upon the poet's sense of time as lived duration, lived succession. "Physics endeavours in principle to make do with space-like concepts alone, and strives to express with their aid all relations having the form of laws." [5] Here "space-like" means, or may be translated to mean, "dimensional." Einstein is not monogamously wedded to space—the great fiddle-player allows time into the cosmic system as long as it can be "space-*like*." The wars of space and time in modern science are no more monolithic than any other wars fought since the Renaissance. Yet time took refuge, after Descartes and Locke, in the arms of the poets.

Time, of course, had never even seemed neatly or conveniently dimensional. Dimensionally, in terms of measurement, despite natural clocks like the human pulse or the moon and artificial clocks like hour-glasses, time had always been mysterious, which Saint Augustine admitted in Book XI of the *Confessions*. To take only one Augustinian paradox of temporal nondimensionality: "In other words we cannot rightly say that time *is*, except by reason of its impending state of *not* being" (i.e., its falling away into the disappeared past, out of an empty future that is not yet). Rather in the manner of Hamlet, Augustine has just made his famous aside: "What, then, is time? I know well what it is, provided that nobody asks me."

Augustine's epistemological jest reminds us that it has never been difficult for Western man to perceive time as the model of nothingness, with space the model of somethingness. Time in our world displays an instantaneity so perfect in its slippery transit—its slither from one temporal fix to another —that there is nothing to mark, let alone measure, its being,

its at-homeness. Like the doomed brother and sister of Coleridge's "Time Real and Imaginary," time's arrow dissolves finally before us into nothingness, as it flies forever outward toward the infinitely going-away horizon we call "space." Time
as the creator and destroyer of space is relatively easy for us
to imagine. Time, as becoming, is then whatever is not space.
Yet the heart only painfully accepts this divorce.

Coleridge, whose heart is so full, if sometimes only of its
own emptiness, its desire to be filled, seems fully aware that
the betweenness of time-as-moment, pure thresholdness, barren liminality, at least in what Einstein would call a "space-
like" way, must be a nothingness. Between the temple and
labyrinth there must be a crossing which, viewed from the
perspective of time, does not stand, stay, hold, or persist. Yet
the poet craves persistence and duration—like Spenser and
Milton, Coleridge would dilate the prophetic moment; unlike
them he takes opium, with what effects of temporal dilation
we can only surmise. So he is caught in a psychosomatic paradox: though the threshold is temporally nonexistent, a phan-
tom-place, the passage across this no-man's-land seems to be
more intense, experientially, than life either inside or outside
the temple, inside or outside the labyrinth. The threshold un-
makes the dialectic of inside and outside, replacing it by an
unmediating passage between. Its motto: Readiness is all.

The intensity of the rite of passage, or simply, of Montaigne's "passing," seems with Coleridge to raise an accompanying liminal anxiety—the existential vertigo that led Herbert Read to associate Coleridge and Kierkegaard. This
anxiety characteristically feels like a border-crossing emotion.
It manifests itself as uncertainty, as fear approaching paranoia, the fear that life processes will be blocked, that one will

be arrested, pressed down, or suffocated in the manner of
Poe's heroes (with whom Coleridge shares the terror of suffo-
cation). As one approaches the border, this anxiety rises; as
one crosses it successfully, the anxiety recedes. While anxiety
may also be "free floating," here it tends to focus on the bor-
der-scene itself, the moment of crossing the border, with its
guards. The moment is finally a dramatic event, as one's actual experience at borders will testify, and in the final stages
of this present essay I will consider one aspect of the dramatic nature of the threshold experience, its personifying tendency. Nevertheless, the special, painful uncertainty of
thresholdness should first, in a theoretical account, give rise
to a connected problem, the problem of sequence, and to this
we must now turn in our search for the Coleridgean readiness.

## SEQUENCE

In the present context, "sequence" means the process and
the promise that something will follow something else. Spatially, sequence means the *successive* placement of events
which, when they occur "in sequence," will display a one-af-
ter-the-otherness. If events occur "in rapid sequence," they
come right next to each other. This neighborly aspect of sequence does not necessarily mean that events will always follow one next to the other in a crowded way, each event as it
were jammed right up against its neighbor and "predecessor."
Predecessors and precursors get linked to their successors, if
anything, because there is a strung-out, stretched relation
from earlier to later. A sequence is like a line; it has length.
Tempted as we may be to argue that two points or events

may make a sequence, we perhaps should question whether sequences do not need to be constructed out of three or more points. The initial statement might be made that a sequence is not likely to be a *straight* line or shortest distance between two points. Common experience suggests that sequences are wavy lines, strung out like the linked chains of logical sorites.[6]

Words like "line" and "string" imply a necessarily spatial or "rhopalic" definition of sequence, and yet sequence can also mean what follows logically, and here space is ideal. This logical concatenation might, for example, be represented by the theoretical circles of Boolean algebra or the thickness of lines and points in geometry, that is, a thickness known by its own theoretical absence. Logical space is the space which, "In the beginning," was occupied by the Logos of St. John. Although the readiest terms by which we understand sequence are spatial, there is a question as to what kind of space sequences may be occupying if, as so often in the thought of Coleridge, they are sequences with logical, theoretical, or visionary form.

There is a yet further difficulty, which almost defines the problem of sequence so far as it relates to Coleridge: the fact that serious concern with "what follows" will have to entertain a temporal factor, whether science wishes so or not. Can a poet imagine a sequence that is devoid of any passing of time, when the poem shifts from space to space, point to point, as long as there are more than two points in the diagram? From this question arises the Sisyphian labor of modern philosophy, whether a Jamesian, Bergsonian, Husserlian, or any other phenomenological attempt, to define the role of time-consciousness in the grasp of logical wholes. Under this

structure of analysis, our phrase "next door" would have to be
replaced by "and then" or simply by "afterwards." In spite of
the fact that, in dealing with sequence, we begin spatially, we
end on a note of temporal description. God alone has the
power to be absolutely timeless. All His acts occur at once.
To begin with, "The Infinite I Am" names an entirely spatial
mode of being, set off against man's relativistic temporal nature.

The Fourth Gospel counters the utter timelessness of God.
To this text Coleridge intended to devote a critical study
(which, in effect, he sketched in *The Confessions of an Inquiring Spirit*). Paradoxically, St. John's doctrine of the Logos
is the most powerful philosophic machine within Christian
culture for the counterattack against the logical annihilation
of time. The Incarnate Word is a theoretical notion of man-
in-time, and thus Coleridge mythologizes The Word when he
reads the Fourth Gospel.

Time and the Logos are, no doubt, violently yoked together. Coleridge, the diachronic thinker, believes in the Johannine Incarnation, *even though* the mystique of The Word
sometimes shifts ideas of sequence into a mystique of stillness, which is stated as a numerological mystery leading to
the static number symbolism of Revelation. In such static
symbolism a sequence "follows" because each element of it is
like a natural number, the larger numbers "following" because they contain the smaller numbers. Numerology, if not
number theory, suggests a timeless ontology.

Yet the *poetics* of number accept, and do not, under pressure from logic, reject man's time-bound duration. Augustine's
*De Musica* conceived poetry as the art of right proportioning
(*bene modulandi*), and ultimately as the mirror or *speculum*

of the world—an apparently stabilizing, if not static, symbolic system. But poetry moves, and verses turn, as Augustine knew well (the first five books of *De Musica* discuss rhythm and meter). Poets use spatial terms to control changes in time. They spend their lives measuring lines of poetry—we still study metrics—and Coleridge was a notable metrical experimenter, like almost all metaphysical poets in the English tradition. We may conclude that the poetic pursuit of the logos demands a measuring and time-feeling poetic activity. This runs counter to the *contemplation* of number, as the unchanging pattern of the logos, and instead embraces an incarnational notion of the poet as a living, moving, breathing, uttering prophet. Incarnation brings the logos into the world as a living, and dying, man—the Son of Man. It temporalizes and historicizes number.

PATER ON RELATIVISM: A DIGRESSION

The Coleridgean homing on the Fourth Gospel reminds us further that incarnation is a relativistic concept and that, with it in mind, the philosophic poet can introduce relativity —in the form of causal conditions—into the otherwise absolute and timeless mysteries of a Platonic system. It was Walter Pater, the next great English critical theorist after Coleridge, who saw this problem most clearly. His essay *Coleridge* observed by way of introduction to his subject that "modern thought is distinguished from ancient by its cultivation of the 'relative' spirit in place of the 'absolute.' Ancient philosophy sought to arrest every object in an eternal outline, to fix thought in a necessary formula, and the varieties of life in a classification by 'kinds,' or *genera*. To the modern spirit nothing is, or can be rightly known, except relatively and under conditions." [7] Then follows an exquisite description of the delicacy of true scientific observation, which reveals "types of life evanescing into each other by inexpressible refinements of change." We are listening to the doctrine of Impressionism in its most exact refinement. Coleridge, we expect, will be its chief relativistic progenitor.

Yet Pater proceeds to argue the converse: he finds Coleridge the defender, in a lost cause, of the older absolutism. As the greatest English critical impressionist, Pater could make the point. Perhaps today he would speak differently if, like us, he had access to Coleridge's *Notebooks*. Yet he almost seems disingenuous. Pater seems blind to the real Coleridge who appears to us in so many ways the first hero of critical relativism in English literature. When Pater says that "the literary life of Coleridge was a disinterested struggle against the relative spirit," we may wonder if the follower has not falsified his paternity. Pater to the contrary, there is plenty of "the excitement of the literary sense" in Coleridge, and is this sense not relativistic? But what really matters is the framework in which Pater placed his precursor: the conflict between the absolute and relative spirits.

This digression will have reminded the reader that the deep Coleridgean interest in the incarnation of genius amounts to a concern for the activity of man, inspired man, *in time*. Genius for Coleridge is nothing if not relative, and this includes a causal dimension of temporal sequence. Sequence attains relativistic form when it is allowed to show its causal enlinkedness. If sequences of events are "causal sequences," their temporal nature is hedged by those conditional limits which can only be known to Pater's spirit of relative perceptions.

Poets, of course, have always shared with storytellers the knowledge that mythic time is not an absolute and causally blank dimension. Mythmakers know that if you tell a story confidently, no matter how strange its materials, sequence as a causally relativistic set of conditions will begin to arise all by itself. Sequence will arise from the metonymic next-door placement of event after event. The reader imports a hidden causality, though none be present on the surface. If, in a story, one event is told after another, a causal conditionality is very hard *not* to imagine. The imagination, in short, manufactures causes. *Post hoc, ergo propter hoc* is one principle of myth.

What distinguishes Coleridge from Pater is then not a priority of absolute over relative spirit, but rather a different attitude—which Pater did not sufficiently discriminate—toward sequence. Pater displays a synchronous method, while Coleridge is heroically diachronic in his relativisms. Coleridge begins his poetic career wishing to preserve the mythmaker's "story line," because its implicit metaphysic reaffirms his sense of diachronic order. He wants this exactly in proportion to his immense anxiety about its being possible.

SEQUENCE AND SURVIVAL

Coleridge appears to have suffered from the particular fear that sequence might not organize his world. This is not to say that his lifelong interest in, and study of, logic, is a mere defense-mechanism against a malaise which logic should have had the magic power to undo. Nor, necessarily, that his fascination with logical sequence implies the paranoia which Freud supposed might underlie philosophic thought in general. We need not go so far. We can, however, observe that Coleridge appears comforted and reassured by the contemplation of "method," as various recent students of his life and work have shown. His criticism adopts Method as a liturgical ideal; for him method is the expression, and the experience, of grace as it appears in this life. Conversely, like Hamlet he is terrified lest events simply may not follow. His work can be conceived as an intensely interested struggle against this fear.

The great sequences of this struggle are to be found in works of prose, not verse. Prose articulates sequence in grammatical form. The theoretical center for Coleridge is the prose treatise contained in the Essays of *The Friend,* where the critic develops his theory of method. Most perfectly exemplified by Shakespeare, method implies, as a kind of providential order, that the mind keeps moving and shaping simultaneously the conditions of its movement. Thus, in methodical sequence the poet may wander narratively or dramatically with great range, yet will always project the sense of over-all design, a sort of implicit city-plan for his own development in the myth. Shakespeare the model author achieves a balance, since "without continuous transition there can be no method," while "without a preconception there can be no transition with continuity." Method is survival through and beyond continuous uncertain eventualities, achieved because its progression is vital, the reverse of "dead arrangement." Method is inevitably somewhat dramatic and unafraid in spite of the underlying fear that one will lose one's way. Or, more bluntly, method is the expression of courage in the presence

of that fear. The literary model of a superordinate structure
built on this courageous plan is the whole Shakespearean
canon, which for Coleridge has the precise status of a Bible.
The model of a subordinate structure of methodical sequence
will be the dramatic texture of the poems and plays of Shakespeare, whose genius carries the action careering forward,
while judgment continually checks the "Fiery-Four-in-Hand."

The second great document in the Coleridgean pursuit of
method is the *Biographia*. Whereas the *Essays on Method* describes the wayward yet ordered sequence of thought that
gives Shakespearean drama its "implicit metaphysic," the *Biographia* is more ingenious and ambitious. It does not just describe. It embodies. It enacts, while it narrates, the series of
learnings that went into the final providence of the poet's
own critical and poetic life. In a way Coleridge one-ups
Wordsworth, since his own *Prelude*—the *Biographia*—is
written in prose, whereas Wordsworth exploited the method-
making powers of the medium of prose only to the extent that
prose modulates his blank verse. One other clue to the
method underlying the *Biographia* is its epic structure and its
final settling upon an agon between Wordsworth and the author, in the concluding chapters. The critical analysis of
Wordsworth's theory and practice is not just criticism; it is,
more adequately considered, a conceptual myth of the confrontation of two great, jarring, fraternal intellects. Method
appears in the *Biographia,* therefore, secondarily in the analysis of mind and imagination as such, and primarily in the
dramatic impersonation of that analysis as Coleridge wrestles
with his essential adversary, Wordsworth. The critique enacts
the biography, and does so methodically, because this is a *literary* biography. In a sense the critique is Shakespearean,

since it personifies the critical issues at stake. The *Biographia*, like its double, *The Prelude*, is a myth of imaginative life-style.

This life-style has two possible poles, one of which might be called operatic. It leads to the plan for the impossible *Magnum Opus*. Its chief yearning is sublimity and unbounded power over vast domains. The Magnum Opus mania drove Coleridge to plot endless impossible projects, most of which envisage the ultimate transformation of some vast labyrinthine body of inchoate materials into an equally vast, but now perfectly lucid and structured, temple of ideal order. With intuitive grace and genius, Coleridge managed to dictate the *Biographia* and to write a number of other extended prose works, so that, in spite of himself, especially through the *Biographia*, he achieved his desired scope—largely because in that and other works he escaped his compulsions, and just played.

The other polarity of life-style implicit in Coleridge's "method" is an obverse one, the reduction to the infinitely small, to the instantaneous threshold, where anxiety and uncertainty produce an ideal *reduction* of the *magnum opus* to an *opus minimum*. As Coleridge himself was fond of saying, extremes meet, and here the compulsion to overwhelm with sublimity meets the compulsion to pass lightly over the threshold.

The poetics of threshold require an inversion of the ideal of epic containment, such that the poet now strives for lyric concision, *to act for* the epic scope of his vision. The ideal poem depends in this inverted aesthetic on an art of perfect exclusion. The tradition is thus one of brevity, wit, and metaphysical conceit, of the kind that increasingly fascinated Coleridge

as he grew older and more deeply pursued the poetry of
Donne, Herbert, Crashaw, and others from his favorite century, the seventeenth. No earlier models, however, could
quite predict the varieties of threshold-poem which Coleridge
was to achieve.

## EMOTIONS AT THE THRESHOLD

To get at this range we need an instrument, the emotive
spectrum, which can measure the sense of threshold itself. If
readiness is the stance within the doorway, then an attitude
of confidence or courage is the ideal mode of readiness. This
contrasts with the labyrinth, where the natural emotive state
is terror or a generalized anxiety; or perhaps, if life is a Spenserian Wood of Error, then the feeling there is a specifically
competitive anxiety, to which Marvell draws attention: "How
vainly men themselves amaze/ To win the palm, the oak, or
bays." Conversely in the temple (or garden) one need not
fear, though upon first entering from the labyrinth, one may
experience an irrelevant, leftover fear. This is opposed to the
controlled sense of trial which often the hero is ritually and
penitentially, though not experientially, led through, before
his final triumph within the structure of the temple. In the
temple, at last, one learns confidence; one's faith triumphs.

At the threshold—between temple and maze—there is a
possible range of normal threshold-feelings: anxiety, readiness, blind hope. This continuum measures the degrees of
dread, and it refers specifically to a range of feelings aroused
by the *sacer*, the taboo, the holy. For if within the temple the
holy seems triumphant, in the labyrinth the holy is either lost
or irrelevant, whereas at the threshold these differences are

exactly what is put into question. The threshold tries the sense of the holy.

Thresholds in Coleridge range widely in the degree of confidence or fear they may generate. "Frost at Midnight," with its emphasis on silence and ministry, identifies the ritual transition with the "secret ministry" of frost hanging up its silent icicles, "Quietly shining in the quiet Moon." Poised, the poet —in his threshold *persona*—may bless the child, asleep in his arms, and while meditating on the "stranger," the film of flame glowing in the fire, he prophesies a hopeful future for the child; he sees the child poised also, but on the threshold of a happier life than what the poet had known when he was a child. "Fears in Solitude" balances liminal feelings, so that it suspends war and human conflict within the scales of "Love, and the thoughts that yearn for human kind." "This Lime-Tree Bower My Prison" suspends the poet on the edge of a perfect templum, yet there is a double threat implicit in his suspended state: the bower, as in Spenser, imprisons, while the beloved friends depart from it, leaving the poet alone. Their leaving him has the effect of making the bower a Goldengrove; the poet still utters a hope: "Henceforth I shall know/ That Nature ne'er deserts the wise and pure"—but friends may leave other friends, quite innocently, though accidentally, alone.

The danger in being optimistic about Coleridge's visions of threshold is quite simple: it is absurdly wrong for him, in general. The typical case, for example "The Ancient Mariner," is infused with terror. This is a holy dread, not useful caution. The poem is an exercise in what Hartman has called the "spectral confrontations" which are the essential moments of liminal experience.[8] The Mariner's tale is set against the

framing doorway before the marriage feast—the basic threshold, of house and home—but its myth sweeps us and the
Mariner along the corridors of death and time in a terror-
driven sequence of liminal passages, as the ship becomes the
first vessel to "burst" into the silent sea of transformational
rites. Similarly, in "Kubla Khan," there may be a "sunny pleas-
ure-dome" for optimists to dwell on, but the finality of the
poem is a meditation on the terrors of prophetic vision as it
confronts theological ultimates and the naïve simplicity of
templar rituals ("Weave a circle round him thrice"), leaving
us in some doubt as to how much poison there is in the milk
of Paradise. "Christabel," in another direction, romanticizes
erotic anxiety at the moment of most fearsome sexual initia-
tion. Perceived conventionally, the poem is a gothic tale, full
of graveyard atmosphere. Within the convention, one notes
the importance of the metric invention, to the hesitancy implied by the theme of demonic eros. But "Christabel" denies
the catharsis of its gothic convention. It almost immediately
insists on the sacred separation of castle and forest. Christabel reaches her fatal crossover, having brought Geraldine
back to the Castle with her.

> Christabel with might and main
> Lifted her up, a weary weight,
> Over the threshold of the gate,

and from this moment the poem scarcely pauses in the explo-
ration of the transit between dream and wake, control and
abandon, eros and death, taboo and free sexuality, through a
vicious regress of antinomies.

"Christabel" fascinated its early readers especially because
it foresaw the world of Victorian inhibition. Isolating sexual

boundaries and metamorphoses, it also isolated a growing sexual anxiety. It anticipated the Tennysonian eros. For many years Coleridge insisted that he would finish the poem, but it may be that he hesitated, not because no story could be machined to follow upon Parts I and II, but because the two parts had already adequately set forth their real tenor, the threshold phenomenon itself, and to move along from their unfinished liminality would have been to destroy their perfect readiness by a useful, but merely conventional, narrative ending.

There are times, of course, when Coleridge openly confronts terror as a pure state, that is, as nightmare. In "The Pains of Sleep" the "wide blessing" of deep sleep is subverted by an interim condition of labyrinthine dreams: "For aye entempesting anew / The unfathomable hell within, / The horror of their deeds to view, / To know and loathe, yet wish and do!" As one reflects on these terrible moments in the poet's visionary life, one values more deeply his attachment to the moon, which sustains him in a most extraordinary way, not least because the moon is a primary natural clock older than any chronometric device.

PRAYER AND THE JOURNEYING MOON

The moon has always been known to poets for its changes, its continuous waxing and waning. With Coleridge the moon, among many meanings, enjoys status as an angelic messenger of the possibility of safe crossing, and safe standing at the threshold. As angelic messenger, the moon brings news to the poet by reflecting the sun's light, and other messages depend upon that primary mirroring. Reflected, moonlight is benign,

the opposite of that lurid sunset-red Visconti used everywhere in his film "The Damned," which in its original version
is called "The Twilight of the Gods." Female, or androgy-
nous, the moon brings happier messages of confident augury.
Thus the marginal gloss upon the moon in "The Ancient Mariner": "In his loneliness and fixedness he yearneth towards the
journeying Moon, and the stars that still sojourn, yet still
move onward; and everywhere the blue sky belongs to them,
and is their appointed rest, and their native country and their
own natural homes, which they enter unannounced, as lords
that are certainly expected and yet there is a silent joy at
their arrival."

The journeying moon is the harbinger of the return of the
hero of consciousness. The celestial bodies are like lords "certainly expected," the prodigal sons of heaven. Coleridge, I
suppose, wanted to create a myth of expectation. He praised
Shakespeare for achieving plots which work, not through sur-
prise, but through fulfilled expectation. His own criticism is
more alive than most, mainly because it stands poised and
ready to notice, to respond where there is no standard response. He can observe the most delicate verbal, especially
syntactic, shifts. Coleridge is the poet-critic of expectancy.
Perhaps in order to intensify this method of response, he
shifts, in later years, to a mode of poetry quite unlike that
practiced in "The Ancient Mariner" or "Christabel," a poetry,
even so, which derives partly from those early poems. As
Coleridge the poet becomes increasingly liminal, he seeks poetic prayer—praying being the liturgical form of crossing
over once again. The climax of "Mariner" occurs when the
Mariner prays—this climax is to become the modal pattern in
several later poems, where, however, there is little narrative.

Coleridge finally seeks an entente with George Herbert, and especially with the poem "Prayer." Generally *The Temple* creates a structuring dramatic scene of prayer, but in that one lyric the maximum expectancy is reached through a total annihilation of all verbs. No single predominant turn of thought forces itself upon the reader, because the poet allows no constricting verb to push the reader here, there, or anywhere. Verbless, the poem and its reader kneel down, waiting, devoted. Herbert has a formalist importance for Coleridge which Donne, whom he so admires, could never have, for *The Temple* explores the pressures preventing prayer, as much as its amenities and glories. Studying Herbert (and Donne too, one must grant), Coleridge would appear to have sharpened his own skills in addressing the absolute. That, not Pater's notion of "tracking of all questions, critical or practical, to first principles," is the problem solved by *The Temple* and then by Coleridge's later poems. He has to address himself to a frightening sacredness—his "deity."

## "LIMBO" AND THE METAPHYSICAL MODE

It is a systematic consequence, therefore, when the finest poems of threshold, "Limbo" and "Ne Plus Ultra," derive from a Herbertian poetic and state the limits of the powers of prayer. "Ne Plus Ultra" is directly imitated from "Prayer," and it too lacks any verb, with the same liminal intensification accruing to it as a result of a syntactic stillness. Yet Coleridge is not easy or very calm in this stillness; it threatens, with short, weighted, magical phrases that portend storms of spirit and destiny. Like Herbert, Coleridge is rather more dramatic than lyrical as he adopts the attitude of prayer. Bate has observed further that "in the better verse of Coleridge from 1817 until his death we find a denseness of thought embodied in an odd, original imagery, frequently homely, occasionally even grotesque." [9] This reborn Metaphysical wit manages such "amalgamation or fusion under pressure" that its philosophical words and phrases become "almost substances for him, thick with emotion and meaning. In these poems, with their dense reflectiveness, their odd, often crowded metaphor, their allusion to the technical vocabulary and conceptualizations of Philosophy, Coleridge creates a mode of poetry entirely his own."

Perhaps the finest example is "Limbo," thought to have been written in the same period as the *Biographia*. "Limbo," more complex in form than its companion piece, "Ne Plus Ultra," is a strange mixture of personification, dramatic monologue, and visionary fugue. Its most prominent feature is a dramatic or melodramatic attitude, while its iconography is variously allusive, including echoes of Dante, Milton, perhaps Shakespeare (Hamlet calls the Ghost "old mole"), more probably Henry Vaughan's "Night" and its portrait of Nicodemus (who could be the model for Coleridge's Human Time). The sense of varied poetic origins reveals the essential Coleridge. He is eclectic, yet single-voiced. Nor does the poem assert a doctrinal or dogmatic view of human salvation. The poet seems mainly interested in the transition between this world and the next. A hesitancy throughout conveys anxiety over the liminal condition itself, rather than a theological debate.

Despite this evanescence of doctrine, however, "Limbo" attempts to define an indefinable, ultimate limit, which the poet calls "positive negation." In so doing he justifies his bizarre method of metaphysical wit and prayer: he personifies a bulk of nothingness. His declamatory style, solidifying horror and anxiety, recovers the primitive, or primary, sources of poetic animation. If to personify is to give soul to an idea or thing, then here the poetry is gaining soul through personification.

Coleridge, we are informed, designed his shorter pieces and then read them in such a way that "the verses seem as if *played* to the ear upon some unseen instrument. And the poet's manner of reciting is similar. It is not rhetorical, but musical; so very near recitative, that for any one else to attempt it would be ridiculous, and yet it is perfectly miraculous with what exquisite searching he elicits and makes sensible every particular of the meaning, not leaving a shadow of the feeling, the mood, the degree, untouched." [10] This searching, inflecting recitative expresses the animation of the personifying process.

### PERSONIFICATION AND NEGATIVITY

A new or renewed Renaissance mode of personification would seem to be the main yield of the poetry of threshold. The need to renew personification was inherited directly from most eighteenth-century verse except the greatest. During that period the older, conventional personified abstractions slowly froze to death, and now poets had to bring the statues back to life. Frank Manuel, like Hartman in his studies of genius, has shown that the Preromantics could reanimate a daemonic universe in the mode of "the new allegory." [11] From another point of view personifications could come alive again because there were once again adequate conditions of rumination. As Michel Foucault has said, the celebratory religions of an earlier time now gave place to "an empty milieu—that of idleness and remorse, in which the heart of man is abandoned to its own anxiety, in which the passions surrender time to unconcern or to repetition in which, finally, madness can function freely." [12] Madness is complete personification. Poets need not, though some in fact did, descend into this generative void.

Yet the conditions of madness and a renewed animism still demand the appropriate poetic forms, which Coleridge had to invent. As Huizinga has remarked, personification is a kind of mental play, and this ludic strain is strong in Coleridge's make-up.[13] Formally, we can say that personification is the figurative emergent of the liminal scene. In the temple there appear to be personified abstractions hard at work, virtues and noble essences, while labyrinths are stocked by an equal and opposite number of vices and personified negations—the lions of the Marquess of Bath. Yet these polar opposites perhaps only gain animate life, if they have it, from their participation in the process of passage. Personifications come alive the moment there is psychological breakthrough, with an accompanying liberation of utterance, which in its radical form is a first deep breath. Poetry seeking a fresh animation is poetry seeking to throw off the "smothering weight" of the "Dejection" Ode. Such a poetry must breathe, showing life coming or going away, as in "Limbo."

This breathing may be explained in part, if we reckon with the inner nature of personification. An active, vital, person-making figure must not be a moral cliché. It must not be a machine in a materialist sense. It cannot simply parody the *daimon*. It must be a "real ghost," like the spectral presence of a drug experience or a nightmare or daydream. Hartman has finely observed: "In fact, whenever the question of persona arises in a radical way, whenever self-choosing, self-identification, becomes a more than personal, indeed, prophetic, decision—which happens when the poet feels himself alien to the genius of country or age and determined to assume an adversary role—poetry renews itself by its contact with what may seem to be archaic forces." [14] *This* personifying author will find himself listening, as well as looking, for phantoms.

Above all the phantom must not exist. It must resist existence. To envision and realize the phantom person poetically the poet must empty his imagery of piety and sense, allowing in their place some measure of daemonic possession. The one necessary poetic act will be to utter, to speak, nothingness. To achieve this defining negativity, the poem "Limbo" typically seeks to *posit* negation as the ultimate daemon. By asserting the life of this final nothingness, the poet has reinvented the Ghost of *Hamlet,* the Witches of *Macbeth,* the daemonic powers that abandon Antony, Hermione's statue that comes alive in *The Winter's Tale.* This is a dramatic reinvention; it enghosts and embodies the persons of a play.

The logic of personification requires a phantom nihilism and a return to the heart of drama. This achievement in the later Coleridge depends upon the liminal scene, which permits the greatest experiential intensity at the very moment when the rite of passage denies or reduces the extensity of either the temple or the labyrinth. Drama gets its personifying nothingness—its phantoms—from the making of continuous threshold-scenes. Because the Elizabethan period had so fully subscribed to the norms of drama, its free use of personification—unlike most eighteenth-century personification—goes quite unnoticed. But there is scarcely a line in a Shakespeare sonnet that does not breathe this language of the personified force. Coleridge, in turning to the theme of nothingness, was trying to get back some of that Renaissance utterancy and dramatic presence. Half-brother to Hamlet, he almost succeeded.

## THE DRAMATIC PERSONIFICATION

The dramatic or, perhaps more accurately, the melodramatic aspect of the personified "positive negation" must fit a general theory of figurative language. Of late much has been written about the precise differences between metaphor and metonymy. It should by now be clear that the problem of sequence is also a problem of figurative series.

In the modern era, when not only music, but all the arts, have tried to hold their balance while experiencing the loss of tonal center, poets and novelists have testified to the complete loss of cadence within the figurative structures provided by traditional poetics. Atonalism and even aleatory procedures are natural, in an era such as ours. But before its radical breakdowns had occurred, poets could still employ the ancient figurative structures, by bending them.

Such was the Coleridgean scene, where the figurative aspect of threshold and sequence was traditional enough. For the temple and its "timeless" hypotactic structures of sacred being, there was the normal and normative use of part/whole relations, figured in *synecdoche*. For the labyrinth and its unrelieved parataxis the norms were bound to be *metonymic*, as they are in the modern novel, where life is represented in the naturalistic maze of meaningless eventuality. For the threshold the norms were, as the term itself forces us to believe, *metaphoric*. This was the great Romantic rediscovery.

Metaphor has always been the figure of threshold, of passing over. Its symbolic function has always been transfer, transference, metamorphosis, shifting across, through, and over. Metaphor is a semantic process of balancing at the threshold. Metaphor draws the edge of the limen with surgical exactness. When we ally metaphor and the dramatic, we accept the momentary adoption of *an other self*, which the mask of dramatic *persona* makes possible. Significant human integers—men as unique creatures with endowments of a yet universal nature—demand metaphor, because metaphor provides the freedom (not the chaos) of a momentary masking.

The person-making, personifying, gestures of the dramatic poet thus sink down, or fall, to the level of nothingness and ghosts, because at that level of the *ex nihilo* there is a test of the "too, too solid flesh" of man. If a ghost can exist, then so can the hero. If his father has a ghost, Hamlet can avenge (and destroy) him, and *be* Hamlet. Hamlet must personify his father, as it were, in order to be himself. Admiring Shakespeare and identifying with Hamlet, Coleridge brought the study of figurative language into the modern context, by giving it a psycholinguistic basis. This modern grasp of the metaphoric—which Johnson vaguely anticipated in *The Life of Cowley*—seems to require an awareness of the experiential element in the *discordia concors*, an anxiety and liminal trembling which is the experience of living through a metaphor. I have envisaged this tremor as the emergence of a personification, at a threshold. Perhaps these too are "only metaphors." [15] If so, they may illuminate the ludic view of theory-building. Coleridge was in nothing so modern as in his theoretical playfulness.

His instincts naturally led him to center his critical theories
on the career of Shakespeare, that is, upon a dramatic or dra-
matistic center. In part this was bardolatry. But Coleridge
had a cosmopolitan range of thought, and in his critical
theory of method the dramatic (if not always the drama) has
fundamental force. For him the drama is the saving test by
which men are discovered in their personhood through dialogue.[16] Essaying a poetry and a critique of the liminal moment, he took up arms against the excessive mass of problems
which the modern critic knows only too well—our sea of in-
formation. Coleridge wanted to find an All that could be One,
believed he found it in the final personification—the Trinity
—and failed, if he did fail, because he no more than any
other man could prevent life's perverse atomism. If he failed
to control the world with his personifying eloquence, we
should grant him that person and metaphor are the utterance
of the gateway, and most men do not want to be standing in
gateways. They would rather be inside, or out in the street.

## Notes

1. *Recollections of the Lakes and the Lake Poets,* ed. David
Wright (Penguin ed., 1970), pp. 43–44.

2. Geoffrey H. Hartman, "Reflections on Romanticism in France,"
*Studies in Romanticism,* IX (Fall, 1970), No. 4, 245.

3. Angus Fletcher, *The Prophetic Moment: An Essay on Spenser*
(Chicago, 1971), pp. 11–56.

4. Lawrence Gowing, *Turner: Imagination and Reality* (New York,
1966), p. 13, quotes Hazlitt: "We here allude particularly to
Turner, the ablest landscape-painter now living, whose pictures
are, however, too much abstractions of aerial perspective, and representations not properly of the objects of nature as of the medium

through which they were seen. They are the triumph of the knowledge of the artist and of the power of the pencil over the barrenness of the subject. They are pictures of the elements of air, earth and water. The artist delights to go back to the first chaos of the world, or to that state of things, when the waters were separated from the dry land, and light from darkness, but as yet no living thing nor tree bearing fruit was seen on the face of the earth. All is without form and void. Someone said of his landscapes that they were *pictures of nothing and very like*" (Hazlitt's italics). Gowing tells a parallel anecdote: "After Mr. Lenox of New York had received a picture which heralded the later style, Turner met C. R. Leslie who had bought it for him:

'Well, and how does he like the picture?'
'He thinks it indistinct.'
'You should tell him that indistinctness is my forte.'"

Hazlitt and Turner assert the need to de-create, to undo, to unmake elemental nature, when the artist wishes to rediscover pure medium.

5. G. J. Whitrow, *The Natural Philosophy of Time* (New York, 1961), p. 3.

6. In his profoundly Coleridgean essay, *The Doors of Perception* (Penguin ed.), Aldous Huxley draws an analogue between the "living hieroglyphics" of flowing drapery and the "implicit philosophy" of the Coleridgean "knowledge of the intrinsic significance of every existent": in Watteau's painting there is "a silken wilderness of countless tiny pleats and wrinkles, with an incessant modulation—inner uncertainty rendered with the perfect assurance of a master hand—of tone into tone, of one indeterminate colour into another" (p. 28).

7. Walter Pater, *Appreciations: With an Essay on Style* (London, 1944), p. 65.

8. Geoffrey H. Hartman, *Beyond Formalism* (New Haven, 1971), p. 334. See also Hartman, "History-Writing as Answerable Style," *New Literary History*, II (1970), No. 1, 73–83.

9. Walter Jackson Bate, *Coleridge* (New York, 1970), p. 176.

10. Henry Nelson Coleridge, in the *Quarterly Review* (1934), quoted from the anthology ed. by J. de G. Jackson, *Coleridge* (London, 1971), p. 627.

11. Frank Manuel, *The Eighteenth Century Confronts the Gods* (Cambridge, Mass., 1959), and Hartman, *Beyond Formalism.*

12. Michel Foucault, *Madness and Civilization* (Signet ed.), p. 176.

13. Johan Huizinga, *Homo Ludens* (Boston, 1950), pp. 136–45. A similar view underlies much of the commentary by Edgar Wind in his *Pagan Mysteries in the Renaissance* and the recent, encyclopedic treatise of D. C. Allen, *Mysteriously Meant: The Rediscovery of Pagan Symbolism and Allegorical Interpretation in the Renaissance* (Baltimore, 1970).

14. Hartman, *Beyond Formalism,* p. 335.

15. See Paul De Man, *Blindness and Insight: Essays on the Rhetoric of Contemporary Criticism* (New York, 1971).

16. In connection with ideas of threshold and personification, I have been helped particularly by three essays, Heinrich Ott's "Hermeneutics and Personhood," and Owen Barfield's "Imagination and Inspiration," collected in S. R. Hopper and D. L. Miller, *Interpretation: The Poetry of Meaning* (New York, 1967), and Hartman, "History-Writing as Answerable Style" (see above, note 8). For the related problem of what he calls "stationing," see James Bunn, "Keats's *Ode to Psyche* and the Transformation of Mental Landscape," *ELH,* XXXVII (1970), No. 4, 581–94.

MICHAEL G. COOKE

# THE MANIPULATION OF SPACE IN
# COLERIDGE'S POETRY

*Even* a moderate inquiry into the study of space and time discloses the fact—so objectionable to Wyndham Lewis [1]—that time, while twinned with space, always gets the lion's share of attention. It has been deemed active, independent, substantive, and has been called "the mind of Space," [2] leaving the latter at best the dignity of a passive instrument. Time makes things happen and become; space is only where things happen or are. As J. T. Fraser puts it:

> Time . . . seemed to be a constituent of all human knowledge, experience and mode[s] of expression; an entity intimately connected with the functions of the mind; and a fundamental feature of the universe. No other properties of reality, such as space or space-time, seemed to bear the same pertinence to the basic concerns of man as did the idea of time. In short, it appeared . . .

that time must and should occupy the center of man's intellectual and emotive interest.[3]

The very people who exhibit the "spatializing instinct," [4] including Wyndham Lewis himself, fall into the solecism of not seeing space for the objects it accommodates. Thus James Joyce, while he avows an apprehension of "the ruin of all space," conjures up only "shattered glass and toppling masonry," that is, the destruction of objects in space.

The paucity of poetic theories of space does not, however, preclude a direct rather than a discursive sense of it, such as we can recognize, as it were from the beginning, in the Christian myth of creation. And that sense, from the beginning, has been of space as convenient to set up in, whether one set up a cave or a civilization, but difficult and perhaps treacherous where one was not set up; or again as alien, and verging on the hostile, because its two primary features, vacancy and formlessness, seem so inaccessibly ahumanistic. Now one of the products of the Romantic concern with nature and questioning of the forms of society is, I suggest, a heightened sense of space, not only in the acknowledgment of its primary qualities, but also in the renewed awareness of how these qualities, vacancy and formlessness, invade the very objects that should be safeguards in relation to space. Thus, while objects do not necessarily disappear, their vital being is taken away; they cease to be serviceable to the spirit or mind, and become "objects . . . essentially dead."

Thus the dissolution of objects, to consciousness if not in fact, is the first upshot of the rowboat episode in *The Prelude*:

> o'er my thoughts
> There hung a darkness, call it solitude

Or blank desertion. No familiar shapes
Remained, no pleasant images of trees,
Of sea or sky, no colours of green fields;
But huge and mighty forms, that do not live
Like living men, moved slowly through the mind
By day, and were a trouble to my dreams. (I.393–400)

Though pregnant with ultimate good, the moment is stark and dreadful, its solitude tantamount to being lost in space. Again in Book V of *The Prelude* the threat of primordial space informs the dream of the Arab, and it recurs in various contexts and intensities right up to the start of Book XIV, where it is definitively resolved. Another sort of realization of space occurs in "Mont Blanc," as Shelley is fixed in the vale by a metaphysical condition rather than by any athletic deficiency; being mortal and finite, he cannot approach the peak. Still another realization of space appears in the "Ode to the Nightingale," where the absolute barrier between Keats and the nightingale is space, or his mortal powerlessness in space, rather than "the near meadows, . . . the still stream,/ [and] . . . the hill-side. . . ." In all these cases we are dealing with a spiritual or mythogenic, as opposed to a scientific, conception of space; in other words, that conception which has space containing, rather than anything definite and secure, virtually nothing but the self.

The sense of space, related to an anxious sense of exposure and the danger of being lost, pulses through Coleridge's poetry. Again and again his mind runs to a stage where one finds oneself without props: one puts a foot down, and the earth is not there. One is given over to elemental powers, in a physical subjection that is full of metaphysical and moral intimations. Or one experiences a bitter solitude which is only compounded by the presence of other men, in an unnatural denial of the Coleridgean dictum that "man is truly altered by the co-existence of other men." [5] Perhaps the paradigm for this situation is Satan's fall, including his destination in hell as a place that proves tantamount to no place. In the case of Coleridge, the moral and cosmological framework appears on the whole obliquely, and we must deal with his confrontation of geographical randomness, with his involvement in the potential confusion—the restitution to chaos—of whatever we may know and have, and ultimately with his attempt, since escape seems improbable, to rationalize space, or at best to ward off its threatening implications. This question of space lends a special resonance to the almost Shelleyan eagerness for a sacred retreat [6] we recognize in his work. And it is the presupposition over against which Coleridge seeks so variously, and on balance so vainly, to come to formal imaginative terms with the material world, to elaborate a grammar of redemption.

"Dura Navis," Coleridge seems to insist, is not just an early but a juvenile poem. He declares that it boasts no "line that any clever schoolboy might not have written," and is willing to dismiss it as a *"Putting of Thought into Verse."* The thought at first seems arrested in pious love of home and pompous adolescence, but it does take on a special affectiveness, when taken in relation to the evidence we see of perverse energy and a threatened dislocation. It is because of this threat that Coleridge does not seek merely to cool the delusive hopes of "heated Fancy"; he drowns them overwhelmingly, transferring to the waves the ambition of the venturous youth, but vesting in the waves all the power vainly wished by him:

> Hast thou foreseen the Storm's impending rage,
> When to the Clouds the Waves ambitious rise,

And seem with Heaven a doubtful war to wage,
Whilst total darkness overspreads the skies;
Save when the lightnings darting winged Fate
Quick bursting from the pitchy clouds between
In forked Terror, and destructive state
Shall shew with double gloom the horrid scene?

The overtones of Satanic desperation in "Waves ambitious"
and the "doubtful war" only worsen the dizzy shift from the
planned horizontal movement of the ship to a seemingly endless upheaval, just as the bursts of lightning worsen the horror and the gloom. The poem goes on to single out the youth
and pitch him into "the wild tempestuous sea," and thence, a
Jonah with no hope of redemption, into "some monster's
belly." The thought here, like many of the phrases, may seem
shopworn enough, and yet the effect of the congregated
clichés is, by virtue of their almost obsessive character, to be-
tray a genuine anxiety.

The metaphor of the voyage upon an unknown ocean can
be illustrated literally by itself, and the opening stanzas of
"Dura Navis" accordingly have a predominantly physical
quality. But the poem gives evidence of an inner drive or
emotion that transcends at once the merely momentary power
of physical circumstance and the merely formal piety of its
surface. The intense dread [7] of the lines is fundamentally a
matter of spirit; and the poem establishes the sort of continuity from physical to meta-physical levels of experience that
indicates at least the analogizing intellect at work. The transference of the youth's ambition onto the waves is reiterated in
the human, naval warfare that mirrors the elemental war between sea and sky. Physical and social upheavals correspond,
and there prevails a general unnaturalness that reaches its
peak, once again, in terms of an individual experience. The

youth who in the physical scheme might have ended up in some monster's belly appears himself to become a social monster with the forecast of ineluctable cannibalism: "Lo! Hunger *drives* thee to th' inhuman feast."

Granting that "Dura Navis" has a physical, almost palpable quality, one cannot but be struck by the fact that it is essentially unlocalized, or *placeless*. The "native land" whose blessings it would seem designed to promote remains itself unlocalized and abstract. The poem's physicality is ultimately surreal, or at least grotesque. Moreover, the reminiscence and evolution of certain key ideas (incontinent ambition, dislodgment, war, devouring) through various states of experience suggest a primary mode of perceiving and understanding. One is then tempted to conclude that the poem is expressing, and not just discussing, an experience of placelessness. And this, I would propose, is the experience of space as space, out into which one is flung, and in which one is violated or lost.

It may be useful to recall that Coleridge, apart from his *sotto voce* boast to Thomas Poole that in a philosophical vein he had "completely extricated the notions of Time, and Space" (*Letters*, II, 706), did at least adumbrate a practical perception or experience of space. In this perception a state of *"feeling"* seems paramount; Coleridge, struggling to explicate the "Coarctation of ✕ Time into ‡ Space," offers this: "One might express it by the Horizontalizing of the Perpendicular but this was not the *feeling*" (*Notebooks*, I, 1823). Just the year before, in 1803, he had tried to convey the same notion to Southey:

> There is a state of mind, wholly unnoticed as far as I know, by any Physical or Metaphysical Writer hitherto, & which yet is necessary to the explanation of some of

the most important phaenomena of Sleep & Disease / it is a transmutation of the *succession of Time* into the *juxtaposition of Space*, by which the smallest Impulses, if quickly and regularly recurrent *aggregate* themselves—& attain a kind of visual magnitude with a correspondent Intensity of general Feeling.

(*Letters,* II, 974)

However tentative the experience remains, Coleridge is basically insisting not only on feeling but on willing it. He brings about the coarctation, or the transmutation, and the idea of disease should not blind us to the gain in magnitude and in feeling. It would almost seem that Coleridge is exploiting the shelter of sleep or disease to guarantee himself the kind of space which assures him an "absence of resistance" (*Letters,* IV, 852). What he means by this "absence" emerges sharply in his notebook discussion of motion:

. . . my idea of *motion*—namely, that it is presence & absence rapidly alternating, so as that the fits of absence exist continuously in the Feeling, & the Fits of Presence vice versa continuedly in the Eye / Of course, I am speaking of Motion psychologically, not physically— What it is in us, not what the supposed mundane Cause may be.—I believe, that what we call *motion* is our consciousness of motion, arising from the interruption of motion = the acting of the Soul resisted ./. Free unresisted action (the going forth of the Soul) Life without Consciousness, properly infinite, i.e. unlimited—for whatever resists, limits, & vice versa / This is (psychologically speaking) SPACE. The sense of resistance or limitation TIME—& MOTION is a Synthesis of the Two. The closest approach of Time to Space forms co-existent Multitude.

(*Notebooks,* I, 1771)

It is noteworthy that he retains the action of the soul but gives up consciousness; for the paradox of the finite being seeking freedom, the free being depending on the finite is very much to the point for the understanding of Coleridge and space. As "Reflections on Having Left a Place of Retirement" as well as "The Eolian Harp" will show, Coleridge can desire comprehensive or universal competence—perhaps even the lordship that is the gift of the imagination—and at the same time need a protected nook or dell. Moreover, he conceived of a barren and blighting space, within and without. Here in illustration is a famous passage from the *Notebooks:*

> inward desolations—
> an horror of great darkness
> great things that on the ocean
> counterfeit infinity.                    (*Notebooks,* I, 273)

Or again we may consider Coleridge's defense of Plato in terms of its benefits to man as a being in space:

> One excellence of the Doctrine of Plato, or of the Plotino-platonic Philosophy, is that it never suffers, much less causes or even occasions, its Disciples to forget themselves, lost and scattered in sensible Objects disjoined or as disjoined from themselves.
>
> (*Notebooks,* III, 3935)

The consummation of this experience of space occurs in "Limbo," but it is a consummation slowly prepared, and should not be taken for a belated revelation. Images and features of "Dura Navis"—lightning, storm, irresistible and confused force, darkness—continually wheel together in Coleridge's work, suggesting as a key term of Coleridge's preoccupation with space "the chaotic ocean"; this is the rubric under which "The Ancient Mariner" would come. An alternative set of images, with suggestive overlapping in the case of lightning and darkness, for example, may be put under the heading of "the unrelieved plain," the path that offers no rest, and no destination, and yet admits of no diversion. Thus Coleridge, in the poem "On Receiving an Account That His Only Sister's Death Was Inevitable," evinces helpless bewilderment in the confession that he feels himself "Fated to rove thro' Life's wide cheerless plain."

Recognition of such categories as the chaotic ocean and the unrelieved plain may, it is hoped, stand without a parade of excerpts; but perhaps a few illustrations will pass muster, if they pass quickly. Coleridge's alacrity in invoking these categories can be discerned in the poem on "Pain," which ought also to recall his description of pain as a "trembling on through sands and swamps of Evil, & bodily grievance" [8] (*Letters*, I, 648–49). His capacity, à la De Quincey, to discover or infuse terror into everyday, if not comic travail appears in "Devonshire Roads," a mock-furious tour de force from which there spins a sense of physical discomfort becoming spiritual disorientation, and indeed hell, since Milton's hell is stubbornly invoked.

Finally, Coleridge's gravitating toward situations that support his preoccupation with chaotic ocean or unrelieved plain evidences itself in the "Lines Written at Shurton Bars." Actually this poem initially depresses the terror of the ocean by focusing on the spectator instead of the sufferer; but the spectator's pathological glee brings that terror back, compounded.

In his "black soul-jaundiced fit," for he is the spectator, Coleridge favored the bleak solitude of the lighthouse tower and thought it sweet

> A sad gloom-pamper'd Man to sit,
> And listen to the roar:
> When mountain surges bellowing deep
> With an uncouth monster-leap
> Plung'd foaming to the shore.
> Then by the lightning's blaze to mark
> Some toiling tempest-shatter'd bark;
> Her vain distress-guns hear;
> And when a second sheet of light
> Flash'd o'er the blackness of the night—
> To see *no* vessel there!

Both practically and morally this stands as the worst the chaotic ocean can do; the sufferers are effectively annihilated, and as a sort of sinister service to the speaker's merciless craving for sensation. The poem, rather Coleridge himself, pulls away from the moment and its strange taste in sweets, simply by declaring that he is redeemed (ll. 61 f.). Whether we take this declaration at face value or not, it remains clear that Coleridge is portraying a cruelty which stems from isolation and cursedness; the speaker is not just a doer but a quintessential victim of evil. "Lines Written at Shurton Bars," like all intemperate dependence on force, is an oblique confession of Coleridge's own sense of helplessness, projected outward as a momentary illusion of power, yes, but reflecting more deeply the consciousness of being quite insignificant and ineffectual.

A naturalistic atmosphere occasionally surrounds Coleridge's fearful depiction of space; this is most notable in "An

Effusion at Evening," where the "savage Hunter" awakes amid thunder and lurid lightning and is "aghast" to hear "the rushing Whirlwind's Sweep"

> in climes beyond the western Main
> Where boundless spreads the wildly-silent Plain.

Sometimes a neutral dementia is expressed in images of the chaotic ocean or unrelieved plain; the grief-unbalanced girl in "The Old Man of the Alps" utters "Sighs which chasms of icy vales outbreathe,/ Sent from the dark, imprison'd floods beneath" (ll. 81–82), and before her death (which significantly coincides with a fierce storm and darkness) is said to have "roam'd, without a purpose, all alone,/ Thro' high grey vales unknowing and unknown" (ll. 87–88). But in works as various as "The Destiny of Nations," "Lines to a Friend in Answer to a Melancholy Letter," and "The Wanderings of Cain," a moral bearing is insisted on. This is typical. It is the bringing home of its fearful definition of human being that gives space such power for Coleridge.

Rather than the pathology that marks the "Lines Written at Shurton Bars," righteous indignation in "Lines to a Friend" moves Coleridge to punish the "sanguinary Despot" with space; Fortune will "hurl" him

> from his height,
> Unwept to wander in some savage isle.

> There shiv'ring sad beneath the tempest's frown
> Round his tir'd limbs to wrap his purple vest;
> And mix'd with nails and beads, an equal jest!
> Barter for food, the jewels of his crown.

In like manner "The Destiny of Nations" sees immorality in terms of storms and foul darkness, and the world before morality and civilization as a frightfully inhuman state:

> And first a landscape rose
> More wild and waste and desolate than where
> The white bear, drifting on a field of ice,
> Howls to her sundered cubs with piteous rage [9]

And savage agony.

"The Wanderings of Cain" clearly brings out the fact that Coleridge is using space morally, and humanistically, to portray a man's influence, or lack of influence, over his own destiny, and to convey the consequences of wanting, or losing, a viable sense of the coexistence of other men. It is the mark of the extremity of Cain's sin, weariness, and grief that he longs for absolute space, with all its vacancy and formlessness: "O that a man might live without the breath of his nostrils. So I might abide in darkness, and blackness, and an empty space!" Of course Cain is not invoking Coleridge's free soul as against finite consciousness, but rather that extreme of deprivation which would remove consciousness altogether, and perhaps also poetry. What the poetry does give is, however, little short of total deprivation. Cain and Enos arriving at a looked-for clearing find that

> The scene around was desolate; as far as the eye could reach it was desolate. . . . There was no spring, no summer, no autumn: and the winter's snow, that would have been lovely, fell not on these hot rocks and scorching sands.

The poignant interjection that the snow, as variety and relief, would have been lovely upsets a common interpretation of the snow image, almost making most men's poison one man's meat. And it only heightens loss when things that might sustain or stimulate human experience are reduced to a "rude mimicry" in the landscape. When the ghost of Abel is shown with "skin . . . like the white sands beneath their feet," the link between ghost and landscape suggests, first, that Cain himself is always in the presence of his evil deed, and, second, that the earth he endures on is itself, in a way, a tormented specter.

"The Wanderings of Cain" is culturally the most evocative of Coleridge's treatments of man cast into space, and morally the most decisive; for a moment it also bids fair to be the most elaborate, offering an alternative or anti-system to life, under the dominion of the Manichaean "God of the dead." What the laws and powers of this God may have been we cannot learn, but perhaps such details matter less than the fact that Coleridge, as in the "Lines Written at Shurton Bars," conceives of a plausible footing in inimical space. Even apart from the God of the dead, "The Wanderings of Cain" suggests in its trio of characters something like an inverted trinity, where Abel "threw himself on his face upon the sand . . . , and Cain and Enos sate beside him; the child by his right hand, and Cain by his left." But it is an absurdist trinity, made up of a petulant ghost as God, a moral cripple as the Holy Spirit, and a powerless child (sitting on the right hand) as redeemer and Christ.

It is in "Limbo" that the hypostasis of terrifying space occurs, but as the awareness rather than the experience of "positive Negation." Let me not minimize the ramifications of the poem's peculiar consciousness for Coleridge—his dread of the "shrinking" and ultimately "annihilating" power of limbo and its adumbrations in "space." Yet Coleridge is not *immediately* involved in anything more than a philosophical canvasing of the weird metaphysics of limbo. Its power and terror are conceptual, instead of truly spiritual, known rather than undergone. Indeed, the mind that is so exquisitely aware of limbo seems to move easily to our earth and to the heavens, and to dwell as knowingly and cogently on the relation of the two as on the uniqueness of limbo itself. The lines on Human Time, arising so readily out of the description of limbo, turn with decisive serenity into other realms and moods. Coleridge is introducing a purely affirmative aegis.

The direction of thought seems unsettled at first, but its ultimate bearing is not difficult to chart. Coleridge makes a negative statement ("unmeaning . . . moonlight . . . on the dial of the day"), then offers an exception ("But that is lovely") to introduce a positive note which he soon reverses ("But he is blind"), only at last to come up with another qualification ("Yet having moonward turn'd his face"), whereby the lines are set resolutely on a positive plane. The adverbial phrase, "by chance," may make the harmony and near identification between the Old Man and the Moon mysterious, but not dubious; [10] something certain and good is happening, without calculation to be sure, but also without mistake. Here is the passage in context:

> Lank Space, and scytheless Time with branny hands
> Barren and soundless as the measuring sands,
> Not mark'd by flit of Shades,—unmeaning they
> As moonlight on the dial of the day!

But that is lovely—looks like Human Time,
An Old Man with a steady look sublime,
That stops his earthly task to watch the skies;
But he is blind—a Statue hath such eyes;—
Yet having moonward turn'd his face by chance,
Gazes the orb with moon-like countenance,
With scant white hairs, with foretop bald and high,
He gazes still,—his eyeless face all eye;—
As 'twere an organ full of silent sight
His whole face seemeth to rejoice in light!
Lip touching lip, all moveless, bust and limb—
He seems to gaze at that which seems to gaze on him!

The lines do make limbo seem worse, but by contrast. If at
first the Old Man or Human Time seems to have disabilities,
presently each one is reassessed and stamped good. He is
after all not blind, inasmuch as his whole face becomes full of
silent sight; in like manner the statue association is revised to
suggest, in "bust and limb," the immobility of entranced contemplation, a sublime focus of the "steady look sublime"
which characterizes him from the start. Above all, his interest
in the skies, again evinced as a seemingly casual given, grows
deliberate and strong ("he gazes still"), and is vitally recipro-
cated at last. It seems reasonable to conclude, from this spontaneous outwelling in the poem, that man, who is aware of
and threatened by limbo, is mindful of heaven, and heaven of
him. Perhaps "Limbo," especially as the final lines describe a
stark negation, remains Coleridge's most harrowing depiction
of the terrors of ahuman space. But the notion of something
"lovely" is viable in this poem, as opposed to the privative
speculation on "lovely" snow in "The Wanderings of Cain."
The terrors of "Limbo" are possible only because the means

of solace and redemption in it, human time and an answerable sky, take nothing but a despairingly potential form.

But Coleridge's preoccupation with space was not left till the eleventh hour without an essay at psychic and moral stability. His position was always too acute for that. Poem after poem manifests one or another element of the answer that, as far as I can see, never became definitive or whole. The teenaged poem "Life" invokes, as an answer to "torpid woe" on the "extensive plain," a sort of progressive, infinite incorporation of Knowledge as Wisdom. The poem is more earnest than effective, but it merits citation as a crude signpost. The sonnet "To the Rev. W. L. Bowles" works better in its own terms, as the allusion, though wanton enough, lends some imaginable substance to Coleridge's claim that his "wavy and tumultuous" mind was as "the formless deep," till Bowles's "lays" with "plastic sweep" induced some semblance of clarity and shape.

These constitute perfunctory illustrations of Coleridge's efforts to cope with the models of the chaotic ocean and unrelieved plain by which his mind habitually expressed itself. Certain poems of faith or love as resolutions of the issue also appear perfunctory, or at least baselessly assertive,[11] or contain without resolving into unity "many a various mood." [12] But two systematic, though not necessarily convincing, answers do develop in Coleridge's works: in poems that explore the mystery of poetic inspiration, where the chaotic ocean serves as an emblem of artistic power if not its responsive raw material; [13] and in poems that propose a continuity or at least compatibility between the secure dell and the now not unrelieved plain, exhibiting a view of things that is simultaneously concave and convex. In these poems, we discover not only a new position but a new manner of handling the subject. Coleridge will not let himself be worsted, and brings his outstanding artistic resources, of structure, vocabulary, perspective, and personal voice, to the service of his presiding choice.

"Reflections on Having Left a Place of Retirement" starts with a sort of contemplative and grateful description of "The Valley of Seclusion," swells into a rather ecstatic recognition of what seems "the whole World" beyond, and proceeds to reflect in mirror-image order on the respective attractions of the world and of the dear dell. The poem would be nostalgic if its wish for the happy place were not finally religious, idealized, millennial. What it does, actually, is combine the lover of pastoral retirement and the champion of high, urgent causes, what is "quiet" and what is "sublime," "feelings . . . delicate" and "honorable toil" or action, "Myrtles" and "mild sea-air." [14] Of the dell the poem seems to say: it was a luxury to be there; but meeting the whole world it makes the unqualified confession: "It was a luxury,—to be!" The distinction between dell and world vanishes, for the man Coleridge projects, as the world calls up a higher and ampler form of the virtue enjoyed in the dell.

Something is amiss, though, in the poem; the more closely we look into its articulation of this rare resolution, the more problematical it comes to seem. The shadow of a curse trails across both dell and wide world. This is recognizable at once in the way Coleridge, having sallied into the domain of action, insists on disparaging what he has left and been. "Was it right," he asks,

> That I should dream away the entrusted hours
> On rose-leaf beds, pampering the coward heart
> With feelings all too delicate for use?

And in picking up the sort of correspondence between peculiar and general states which organizes the poem, he inveighs
against "Pity's vision-weaving tribe" who nurse "in some delicious solitude/ Their slothful loves and dainty sympathies!"

The negative side of the treatment of the world is less
explicit, but more pervasive, having gotten into the very
stream of description. Once Coleridge has made it past the
stony mount and perilous toil of the transitional area, he
gives us ostensibly a "goodly scene" and a whole world saturated with sanctity. But the picture is strangely recalcitrant
to the thesis:

> *Here* the bleak mount,
> The bare bleak mountain speckled thin with sheep;
> Grey clouds, that shadowing spot the sunny fields;
> And river, now with bushy rocks o'er-brow'd,
> Now winding bright and full, with naked banks;
> And seats, and lawns, the Abbey and the wood,
> And cots, and hamlets, and faint city-spire;
> The Channel *there,* the Islands and white sails,
> Dim coasts, and cloud-like hills, and shoreless Ocean—
> It seem'd like Omnipresence!

Certainly just about everything is cited, but we may wonder
whether it is proper to identify the presence of everything
with Omnipresence. No explicit power of emotion or of intellect is enlisted to make the "all" into a "whole." We seem to
have "an immense heap of *little* things" suffering from a lack
of "something *great*" to unify them (*Letters,* I, 349). In addition, the language betrays a strain of anxiety if not hostility
as regards the parts of this supposed Omnipresence. The reit-
eration of "bleak" and the intensifying "bare" set an ominous
tone at once, and find support in the penury of "speckled

thin" and "naked banks," in the impending trouble of "grey clouds" that "spot" (in one sense, blemish) "the sunny fields," as well as in the overbrowing rocks. Whatever is "here" appears qualified in this way, or else neutral; and what is "there," we cannot but note, appears faint or dim.[15]

At one pitch of response, the poem is credible and moving as a harmony of the disparate "here" and "there"; but at another pitch of response, which it invites, it comes dangerously close to being neither. In some sense the poem ends by betraying the acuteness of Coleridge's situation in relation to space, with its vacillation between claustro- and agoraphobia.

A similar sense that Coleridge's bias toward unity is at best teetering on a point of satisfaction develops out of "Fears in Solitude" and "This Lime-Tree Bower My Prison." "Fears in Solitude" repeats the spatial characteristics of the "Reflections," with the good of the "spirit-healing nook" made ampler and livelier by the large "prospect." But the querulousness that cannot be quite repressed in the "Reflections" breaks forth in a veritable jeremiad, an unbridled expression of fears in solitude. War, which in "Dura Navis" is depicted as a heightened chaos, competes with the "burst of prospect" to define things outside the nook, and the poem but ill digests its consciousness of chaos:

> What uproar and what strife . . .
> This way or that way . . .
> Invasion, and the thunder and the shout,
> And all the crash of onset; fear and rage,
> And undetermined conflict. . . .

By the image of the gust that "roared" in the distant tree without so much as bowing "the delicate grass" in his "low dell," Coleridge can persuade us that war is not everywhere. But his aim is to suggest a radiation, outward from the dell, of "Love, and the thoughts that yearn for human kind." It does not quite work. The proportions of the poem, with so much eager space given to lament and denunciation, rather suggest that something, or someone, is contaminated with fear and rage in the dell.

The instability or vulnerability of mood which mars Coleridge's solutions to the problem of space virtually disappears in "This Lime-Tree Bower My Prison." It is not a poem with "no hint of negative emotions," [16] but its very first utterance, "Well! they are gone, and here must I remain," resounds with a composure in loss and an assurance in resignation that control its amplitudes to the end. Even so, a skeptic might well see it that Coleridge is having his cake and eating it too. He blithely treats as identical in substance and value the matter of speculation, perception, and memory (ll. 5–42); [17] accordingly, what seems like deprivation is but an opportunity to conjure up experience—the poem comprises his experience, with all its precision and lucidity, as it were lavished on others. The reflection that

> 'Tis well to be bereft of promis'd good,
> That we may lift the soul, and contemplate
> With lively joy the joys we cannot share

does not quite ring true. Coleridge is more than sharing the joys. He is creating or re-creating them. Furthermore, the site of deprivation, the "prison," is a bower wherein he actually enjoys experiences not available to the others, and not bestowed on them.

The physical scope of the poem, from bower to wide wide

Heaven and sea and (by grace of imagination) vacant wastes, is also deceptive. For unlike "Reflections" or "Fears in Solitude," "This Lime-Tree Bower My Prison" asks nobody to leave the "centre" which Coleridge so continually reveres; they merely sally out to its circumference, and Coleridge himself is not even exposed to a random intimation of unprotected space. Much may be made of this fact; it is the basis on which Coleridge, though ostensibly dealing with spatial issues, can infuse time into the poem, using memory and imagination to possess indefinitely things met and lost in space.[18] The abrupt introduction of time ("I have lost/ Beauties and feelings") advises us that the poem will observe a dual concern with place and time, the latter becoming increasingly critical as the topical response to space (characteristic of "Reflections," say) gives way to an imaginative one.

We can see how perfectly Coleridge has exorcized the demon of space in the suppression of any anxious overtone in the Miltonic echo with which the poem closes:

> when the last rook
> Beat its straight path along the dusky air
> Homewards, I blest it! deeming its black wing
> (Now a dim speck, now vanishing in light)
> Had cross'd the mighty Orb's dilated glory,
> While thou stood gazing. . . .[19]

Here is an ominous prelapsarian moment—Satan athwart the Sun—rendered harmless, indeed invested with "a charm," and casually if subtly endowed with a blessing of consciousness not provided in the original Paradise: this "Adam" observes the passage, and knows it portends no evil. The world is less than Paradise, no doubt; it has in it loss and clumsy

wives. But it is briefly more as well, a "paradise within" that
emerges in the modes of implied sodality and imaginative expansion.

A further manifestation of Coleridge's will and need to
come to terms with space may be found in his images of
creativity, where in effect he is not exploiting but celebrating
the artistic gift. Again, though, the resolution he achieves
seems doubtful. Only once does he offer a picture of unqualified resolution, and it is vicarious. In "To William Wordsworth" aspiration (Coleridge's) and experience (Wordsworth's) fuse as one. Wordsworth's mastery is such as
Coleridge has wished, present in solitude no less than in the
wide world:

> In vales and glens
> Native or outland, lakes and famous hills!
> Or on the lonely high-road, when the stars
> Were rising; or by secret mountain-stream,
> The guides and the companions of thy way.

Not only does Wordsworth negate the unrelieved plain, he
negates the alien void and the chaotic ocean, his

> various strain
> Driven as in surges now beneath the stars,
> . . . now a tranquil sea,
> Outspread and bright, yet swelling to the moon.

Clearly the upheaval of "Dura Navis" is occurring to express,
rather than overthrow, one's innermost power and being. This
kind of composition of elemental power not insignificantly
causes Coleridge to accord Wordsworth "one visible space" of
his own, as something he has and is not subject to. "Kubla

Khan," we may say, stands as Coleridge's bid to discover and
lay claim to such a space; the poet is the only person in the
poem who has no space or place,[20] and this, though it could
make him infinite, seems rather to leave him indefinite ("If I
could . . ."). Coleridge, to assume his identity as poet, must
duplicate the politico-physical fiat of Kubla Khan, but make
it essential and universal where it is only local; and he must
duplicate the terrific spontaneous power of nature as something self-realizing and permanent, and not marked by a
wasting precipitancy. It may be argued that he manages this,
but it seems sounder to say he knows what he needs to do; he
is describing and not strictly fulfilling his obligations as poet.
The success of the poem is reproductive, rather than purely
creative—the centipede, however lucid and eloquent, is up-
side down in the ditch.

Part of the doubtfulness of the poem springs, I think, from
the fact that Coleridge is a member of the audience in whom
the possessed poet inspires fear. The more powerful and intrinsic the storm of inspiration he describes, the more ambiguous the response he seems to make. The lines "To Matilda
Betham from a Stranger" have "poetic feelings" not *as* but *in*
a storm. They "pay homage" to the storm, but take on only as
much storminess as mighty oaks exhibit in their "fluttering
leaves." Hence all is well. But in the "Monody on the Death
of Chatterton" the storm of "Inspiration's eager hour" is both
without and within, and Coleridge conveys its danger no less
than its power:

> Here, far from men, amid this pathless grove,
> In solemn thought the Minstrel wont to rove. . . .
> These wilds, these caverns roaming o'er
> Round which the screaming sea-gulls soar,

> With wild unequal steps he pass'd along,
> Oft pouring on the winds a broken song:
> Anon, upon some rough rock's fearful brow
> Would pause abrupt—and gaze upon the waves below.

Certainly this is not "Cortez" upon a peak. Chatterton, in a problematical position both socially and spiritually, so stands as to denote either dominance or desperation. He is here at the mid-point between his greatest capability and disaster; and we may note that for both states Coleridge resorts to the image of the ocean. The happy moment shows both poet and poetry through an ocean metaphor; while

> The members flowing strong
> In eddies whirl, in surges throng,
> Exulting in the spirits genial throe
> In tides of power his life-blood seems to flow.

Though Chatterton collapses, the metaphor persists, even as its activity is perverted: "the black tide of Death" rolls "through every freezing vein" (l. 102). It is as though power, by its nature, exhausts and undoes itself. In fact, "Constancy to an Ideal Object" somberly limns the illusoriness of power, with key terms like "westward," "wintry," "maze," and "viewless" importing an aimless drift toward death.

> The woodman winding westward up the glen
> At wintry dawn where o'er the sheeptrack's maze
> The viewless snow-mist weaves a glist'ning haze,

sees

> An image with a glory round its head;
> The enamoured rustic worships its fair hues,
> Nor knows he makes the shadow, he pursues!

If "France: An Ode" shows Coleridge in ecstatic fearlessness of sea or storm (ll. 99–102), "The Night-Scene" spells out relentlessly what unrelieved plain such blasts of passion have for their aftermath and reality: "the mighty columns were but sand,/ And lazy snakes trail o'er the level ruins."

One is struck with the persistence and permutations of Coleridge's concern with space. Yet it is a persistence without a clear pattern: "Limbo" includes, indeed generates, a redeeming image out of its very extremity, and by the same token "Reflections on Having Left a Place of Retirement" bears its own strange self-denial. One must recognize the issue as cardinal for Coleridge; it is at once the proof and the arena of his anxiety concerning "the fearful nakedness of [man's] brief existence within this vast cosmos, his helplessness, his need." [21] Perhaps it first crystallizes on the night Coleridge spent huddled and forlorn in the fields (*Letters*, I, 353); certainly it survives analysis, ecstasy, cosy retreats, and wide domain, continually posing the question: where am I? And what, and—if there's no knowing—who am I?

It is striking, perhaps, that the poem which best comes to terms with the trauma of space, "This Lime-Tree Bower My Prison," does so by temporalizing the issue. One is reminded of Paul De Man's astute observation that the allegorizing of geographical sites in Wordsworth, who copes fairly successfully with space, "always corresponds to the unveiling of an authentically temporal destiny." [22] Coleridge, by contrast, has relatively few poems that deal substantively with time, and of the major Romantic poets, as opposed to philosophers, seems least given to myths or theories of time.

I would stop short of calling Coleridge the poet of moods and moments, but certainly as regards his handling of space some such bias appears, in the teeth of his desire for the implied permanence of total reconciliation and unity. "The Ancient Mariner," the one work which offers a sustained unfolding action, thereby shows better than any other the difficulty Coleridge experiences in devising an action sufficient at once to symbolize *and to resolve* the problem of space. Just as the ceremony of the narration is irreconcilable with that of the wedding feast, so the inescapable moral is not just inadequate to, but incongruous with, the inescapable experience of the poem. "The Ancient Mariner," like "Christabel," makes peculiarly human presumptions about the point and use of physical law, moral law, and the customary structures of religion and civilization. But where the penetrating presence of evil challenges these presumptions in "Christabel"—but only challenges them, since everyone from the narrator to Geraldine herself affirms the primacy of the good—in "The Ancient Mariner" something that bears no logical or natural relation to "morality," that is, randomness, weirdly shares dominion with it. The ocean *mise en scène* is very much to the point, the anomalous incidents very much in keeping with Coleridge's sensitivity to the ocean's potential for chaos.[23] The ocean world obviously can be brought back to land, and seems even to spawn in the tides of memory and imagination. But only separation or usurpation of territory takes place. It will not suffice either to moralize the poem [24] or to charge it with "incoherence" and the "absence of a moral or intellectual core," [25] in that both views treat it as if formal coherence and morality must stand as the essential principle of response. The moral question does of course represent more than an "obtrusion." [26] The Mariner himself wishes there to be a moral, but if we remember that his situation is at best erratic and at worst arbitrarily bleak before the Albatross puts in an appearance, the Franciscan conclusion seems clearly eccentric. Its value, I would suggest, is to be measured by reference to the third ceremony in the poem,[27] that of ordinary (the marriage feast is special) social and religious observance detailing man's relation to man and to God (ll. 601 f.). The world defined by this ceremony is moral and, indeed, consolingly "sweet," but it only holds off the throes of space through which the Mariner has gone.

Coleridge at times, as in "Religious Musings," "Hymn before Sunrise," and "France: An Ode," asserts that he enjoys a state of unity in space, but when he passes from assertion to demonstration the issue seems doubtful. The variety and perhaps compulsiveness of his attempts to order space may suggest a problem in, and not just for, the mind. Thus the Ancient Mariner, while eager to espouse a sustaining Franciscan morality, cannot free himself from the knowledge of random space. In the final analysis, Coleridge's *magnum opus* brings space home, within the Mariner, who in his own compelling way brings it home to others.

## Notes

1. *Time and Western Man* (Boston, 1957), *passim*.

2. *Ibid.*, p. xi.

3. J. T. Fraser, *The Voices of Time* (New York, 1966), p. xviii.

4. Lewis, *Time and Western Man*, pp. 429 f.

5. *Collected Letters of Samuel Taylor Coleridge*, ed. Earl Leslie Griggs, 4 vols. (Oxford, 1956–59), II, 1197.

6. On this subject see Francis Scarfe, "Coleridge's Nightscapes," *Etudes Anglaises*, XVIII (1965), 31 f. and 38. It will be profitable,

too, to consider this essay in conjunction with Kathleen Coburn's "Coleridge and Restraint," *University of Toronto Quarterly*, XXXVIII (1969), 233–48.

7. The form of this dread is not cited, but Coleridge's confession that "Dread" had haunted and undone him continually throughout his life has a distinct bearing here (*The Notebooks of Samuel Taylor Coleridge*, ed. Kathleen Coburn [New York and London, 1957], II, 2398).

8. The poem on "Pain" internalizes this metaphor, and translates it from the plain to the ocean (which are often interchanged, or combined): "Seas of pain seem waving through each limb." Despite the severing and multiplying of the waves through the singling out of "each limb," the chaos of the ocean seems abated here; at the same time this does not lessen but intensify the idea of helplessness and perverted nature we get with the storm: the pace of the waves conveys endlessness, instead of order, and what is endless is oceanic pain.

9. The image of the lost child touches deep in Coleridge's memory and imagination. In "Dejection: An Ode" it is tempered somewhat by the child's being "not far from home." This, however, holds good in the reader's mind, not in the child's. Her "bitter grief and fear," even her hopeful "screams," might seem the inaudible antiphon to the utterances of the ursine mother.

10. Walter Jackson Bate in part bases his uniformly grim interpretation of "Limbo" on a negative construction of this phrase; see his *Coleridge* (New York, 1968), p. 178.

11. Consider, e.g., "Religious Musings," ll. 68–73, 94–104, 124–26, 144–52, 236–57, 266 f., or, again, "Ver Perpetuum," or "Lines Written at Shurton Bars."

12. "To the Rev. George Coleridge."

13. Certain poems, including "Ode to the Departing Year" (st. 7) and "Lines Composed while Climbing . . . Brockley Coomb," simply treat the ocean as a protective boundary, eliminating the threat it poses as an alien field and making all England a safe retreat.

"Lines Written in an Album at Elbingerode," one hastens to note here, candidly avows Coleridge's recourse to patriotism for psychic assurance.

14. Given Coleridge's sense of the chaotic ocean, this latter phrase enjoys a special resonance, as it both recalls and negates the ocean's potential storminess and fearsomeness. A similar reverberation may be discerned in the "placid lightning" so esteemed by Coleridge in the poem "To the Autumnal Moon." Rather than being "flabby," as Francis Scarfe maintains ("Coleridge's Nightscapes," p. 28), the epithet is finely strung and keyed to make us aware of an unexpected graciousness rather than the usual minatoriness in the moon's "lightning."

15. Richard Haven, in his *Patterns of Consciousness: An Essay on Coleridge* (Amherst, Mass., 1969), notes the loss of distinctness, but sees it as the means of merging everything "into one totality" (p. 52). The trouble is that the loss of objective character leaves omnipresence as a proportionately subjective state. Coleridge, I think, wants it otherwise, wants a "widening perspective" to lead "to a sort of cosmic view" (A. Gerard, "The Systolic Rhythm: The Structure of Coleridge's Conversation Poems," *Essays in Criticism*, X [1960], 310).

16. Scarfe, "Coleridge's Nightscapes," p. 28.

17. In the same way, a collective—nearly undifferentiated—vision and a highly particularized vision merge into one another, as do the present and the past. Consider, for example, the passage where Coleridge notes

> Much that *has sooth'd* me. Pale beneath the blaze
> Hung *the transparent foliage;* and I *watch'd*
> *Some* broad and sunny leaf, and lov'd to see
> The shadow of *the* leaf and stem above
> Dappling its sunshine! And *that* walnut tree
> Was richly ting'd. . . .
> . . . and though *now* the bat
> *Wheels* silent by. . . .

(Italics added.)

18. He is working in the *"Space"* that we have in "memory," perhaps (Lewis, *Time and Western Man*, p. 420); but this avoids the issue of space as such. As Haven points out, the opening which Coleridge finally settled on involves the reader "in contemplation, in reverie" (*Patterns*, pp. 66–67).

19. Coleridge's love of home combines with the sympathy he always felt for the less favored creatures (Coburn, "Coleridge and Restraint," p. 238) to strengthen an air of grace in the lines.

20. Elizabeth Schneider sees him as "half-present" (*Coleridge, Opium and Kubla Khan* [New York, 1966], p. 287).

21. Bate, *Coleridge*, p. 190.

22. "The Rhetoric of Temporality," in *Interpretation: Theogy and Practice*, ed. Charles S. Singleton (Baltimore, 1969), p. 190.

23. The personal or psychological valences of "The Ancient Mariner" are effectively presented by George Whalley, "The Mariner and the Albatross," *University of Toronto Quarterly*, XVI (1947), 381–98.

24. As does Robert Penn Warren in his celebrated reading, *The Rime of the Ancient Mariner, with an Essay* (New York, 1946).

25. I. A. Richards, in his introduction to *The Portable Coleridge* (New York, 1961), p. 34.

26. A succinct and judicious statement of the problem involved here is to be found in J. D. Boulger's introduction to *Twentieth-Century Interpretations of The Ancient Mariner* (Englewood Cliffs, N.J., 1969), pp. 9–11. On the whole Professor Boulger seems to espouse "imaginative process" (p. 11) and again a "central religious parable" (p. 13) as crucial to understanding the poem, where I would set either in an antinomical relationship with ahumanistic space.

27. I have already spoken of the other two: the narration itself, and the marriage feast in the background.

THOMAS MCFARLAND

# THE ORIGIN AND SIGNIFICANCE
# OF COLERIDGE'S THEORY OF
# SECONDARY IMAGINATION

*Coleridge* refers to the secondary imagination only once in his writings. The place is, of course, the end of the thirteenth chapter of the *Biographia Literaria:*

> The IMAGINATION then, I consider either as primary, or secondary. The primary IMAGINATION I hold to be the living Power and prime Agent of all human Perception, and as a repetition in the finite mind of the eternal act of creation in the infinite I AM. The secondary Imagination I consider as an echo of the former, co-existing with the conscious will, yet still as identical with the primary in the *kind* of its agency, and differing only in *degree,* and in the *mode* of its operation. It dissolves, diffuses, dissipates, in order to recreate; or where this process is rendered impossible, yet still at all events it struggles to

idealize and to unify. It is essentially *vital,* even as all objects (*as* objects) are essentially fixed and dead.

FANCY, on the contrary, has no other counters to play with, but fixities and definites. The Fancy is indeed no other than a mode of Memory emancipated from the order of time and space; while it is blended with, and modified by that empirical phenomenon of the will, which we express by the word CHOICE. But equally with the ordinary memory the Fancy must receive all its materials ready made from the law of association.[1]

It is probably fair to say that this is both one of the most famous passages in all of English prose and one of the least satisfactorily understood. Up until about the middle of this century or shortly afterward, indeed, scholars usually approached it with an almost reverential regard, at the same time that a feeble and redundant gloss was all they could supply by way of commentary.

Where there was not merely ritualistic citation, there was apt to be a certain disgruntlement. To cite a single instance, W. J. Bate, in 1950, said that "this rather artificial distinction between 'primary' and 'secondary' imagination is not among Coleridge's more lucid contributions to aesthetics":

The passage [he continues] may be regarded as simply a cryptic phrasing of what one may discover in other ways to be Coleridge's general theory of the imagination. . . . Whatever its meaning, Coleridge does not dwell upon it elsewhere. As it now stands, it is neither clear nor particularly helpful.[2]

It is easy to sympathize with such objections. Not only is there no preparation for the threefold distinction of Chapter Thirteen in Coleridge's previous writings, there is none even in the *Biographia*. In Chapter Four of that work Coleridge states his conviction that "fancy and imagination" are "two distinct and widely different faculties," illustrates the difference by the examples of Cowley and Milton, and says that it is his object "to investigate the seminal principle" of the distinction.[3] Nowhere is there any mention of, or preparation for, any additional differentiation. When, in Chapter Twelve, he comes nearer to the promised discussion, it is to assert that "I shall now proceed to the nature and genesis of the imagination"—still with no foreshadowing of a "secondary" imagination.[4] And in Chapter Thirteen itself, in an astonishing *volte face*, he writes himself a letter in which he says that

> I see clearly that you have done too much and yet not enough. You have been obliged to omit so many links, from the necessity of compression, that what remains, looks . . . like the fragments of the winding steps of an old ruined tower.[5]

While the reader who has lasted thus far is still bemused by the phrase about the "necessity of compression," Coleridge proceeds simply to dump upon him the threefold distinction, or as the book more elaborately puts it, to "content myself for the present with stating the main result of the Chapter, which I have reserved for that future publication"—that is, for the *magnum opus*.[6]

Not having the *magnum opus* to clarify matters, we must accordingly supply our own account of the "nature and genesis of the imagination," and such an account must necessarily be a tracing backwards more than a building up from first principles. I shall attempt here to supply the essentials of such an account by addressing myself to three questions. First of all, why is the threefold distinction simply deposited rather than deduced? Secondly, where in Coleridge's thought or reading does the secondary imagination originate? And thirdly, what is the context in which we should consider the secondary imagination?

We need not linger over the answer to the first of our questions, that is, why is the threefold distinction deposited rather than deduced? Briefly, the matter seems to stand this way: Coleridge had been following Schelling's line of reasoning, found himself unable to reconcile it with the threefold distinction—which neither comes from nor is paralleled by anything in Schelling—and so wrote himself a letter promising a later rethinking, while leaving as a down payment, as it were, the statements about primary imagination, secondary imagination, and fancy.

Coleridge had been involved, in Chapter Twelve, with an attempt to reconcile the subjective and the objective, which, transposed into his own terms of "I am" and "it is," was the consuming goal of his philosophical activity.[7] To this end he had translated substantial passages from Schelling's *System of Transcendental Idealism*, which seemed to promise such a reconciliation.[8] Coleridge had here accepted the thoroughly Schellingian notion that "the true system of natural philosophy places the sole reality of things in an ABSOLUTE . . . in the absolute identity of subject and object, which it calls nature, and which in its highest power is nothing else than self-conscious will or intelligence."[9]

In Chapter Thirteen, still following Schelling, who had been following Kant, Coleridge says that "the transcendental philosophy demands; first, that two forces should be conceived which counteract each other by their essential nature." [10] He goes on to speak of "this one power with its two inherent indestructible yet counteracting forces, and the results or generations to which their inter-penetration gives existence," [11] and moves ever closer to Schelling's own, pantheistic, theory of imagination. Coleridge's last statement, before breaking off and writing himself his explanatory letter, trembles on the very brink of pantheism: "Now this tertium aliquid can be no other than an inter-penetration of the counteracting powers, partaking of both." [12] Coleridge is here only a step from Schelling's openly pantheistic theses that "the system of Nature is at the same time the system of our Spirit," [13] and that "one might explain imagination as the power of transposing itself through complete self-activity into complete passivity." [14]

To Coleridge, whose entire intellectual life was bound up with the necessity of avoiding pantheism, such a reconciliation of subjective and objective came at too high a price. And so he abruptly refuses to press forward: "Thus far had the work been transcribed for the press," he interrupts, "when I received the following letter from a friend." [15]

There is perhaps an additional reason for Coleridge's merely depositing the threefold distinction. By doing so he makes his description, as Bate says, "cryptic"; and he probably was almost as content with this effect as he would have been with a clear demonstration. In any event, his letter's reference to the "many to whose *unprepared* minds your speculations on the esemplastic power would be utterly unintelligible" [16] seems almost to imply the Plotinian view that "holy things may not be uncovered to the stranger." [17] In general, by Coleridge, as by other Romantic thinkers, the fac-

ulty of imagination was treasured as something mysterious
and unfathomable. Wordsworth refers to it as an "awful
Power" that rises "from the mind's abyss." [18] Schelling calls it
a "wonderful faculty." [19] Baader says that it is "a wonder of
wonders," which is "no mere word, but a microcosmos of secret forces within us." [20] Coleridge, for his part, calls it a
"magical power," [21] and says that his investigation of its principle will follow the faculty to its "roots" only "as far as they
lift themselves above ground, and are visible to the naked eye
of our common consciousness." [22]

Such imprecision and emotional loading of the term in the
late eighteenth and early nineteenth centuries were results of
a protest against the mechanism and rationalism of Newton,
Locke, and what Coleridge calls the "impious and pernicious
tenets" of the "French fatalists or necessitarians." [23] As a
principle that stood against the passivity of mind, and against
the soul's domination by dead outer things, the imagination
possessed an importance that seemed actually to be enhanced
by a certain obscurity.[24] For obscurity allowed a sense of
vastness, mysteriousness, and incommensurability that precision and demonstration tended to reduce. Coleridge honors
such predilection for a *je ne sais quoi* in the concept of
imagination when he says that "Imagination, Fancy &c." are
"all poor & inadequate Terms" for "the sensuous Einbildungskraft." [25] We see the same sense of mysterious expansion, coupled with imprecision, in Herder's reference to
"*die Einbildungskraft,* or whatever we want to call this sea of
inner sensibility." [26] Indeed, Kant himself was content to be
vague on this issue. Jacobi rightly notes that Kant's "Einbildungskraft" is "a blind forward and backward connecting fac-

ulty" that rests upon "a spontaneity of our being, whose principle is entirely unknown to us." [27] As De Vleeschauwer says,

> Kant complicates the solution, so simple in its dualistic structure, by introducing imagination as an intermediary and mediating factor. It is the third element between the two original elements. It is capable of adopting this role because its nature is itself uncertain: Kant brings it into relation sometimes with sensibility, sometimes with understanding, and the schematism erects this confusion into a principle by making imagination participate both in sensibility and in understanding. Because of its confused nature the function delegated to it is not everywhere the same.[28]

Coleridge shows both his understanding of Kant's position and his ready acceptance of obscurities in the imagination by saying that "Fancy and Imagination are Oscillations, *this* connecting Reason and Understanding; *that* connecting Sense and Understanding." [29]

The word "connecting" in this last statement is significant both for Coleridge's breaking off of argument and for the function of imagination itself. For it seems clear that to Coleridge the imagination is less necessary as an element in an *a priori* theory of poetry than as a means of connecting poetic, philosophical, and theological interests. Most of all, it connects the inner world of "I am" with the outer world of "it is." [30]

The importance of systematic connection for Coleridge can scarcely be overemphasized. Indeed, as L. C. Knights has recently observed, "in the Coleridgean world everything is connected with everything else." [31] So in Chapter Nine of the

*Biographia Literaria* Coleridge asserts his need for an "abiding place for my reason," and it is evident that this could be found only in system: "I began to ask myself; is a system of philosophy, as different from mere history and historic classification, possible?" [32] To abandon the concept of system was, he then says, a "wilful resignation of intellect" against which "human nature itself fought." [33] And at the end of Chapter Twelve, just before a reference to "the imagination, or shaping and modifying power; the fancy, or the aggregative and associative power," [34] he speaks against those who dismiss "not only all system, but all logical connection." [35] "This, alas!," Coleridge continues, "is an irremediable disease, for it brings with it, not so much an indisposition to any particular system, but an utter loss of taste and faculty for all system and for all philosophy." [36]

Imagination is therefore primarily a connective developed because of Coleridge's commitment to systematic philosophizing. It would not appear to be rewarding, accordingly, to try to make very much critically of its presence in particular poems. But that is not to say that knowledge of the threefold distinction is wholly without value in the understanding of Coleridge's poetry. As a single illustration, which I shall try not to labor unduly, the widely held view that "Kubla Khan" is a poem about poetic or imaginative creation,[37] in which the major images are symbolic, would, in the light of the threefold distinction and Coleridge's systematic concerns, seem to be an un-Coleridgean reading, or at least only a partial reading.

"Kubla Khan" is, to be sure, an outstanding example of the secondary imagination at work. Furthermore, not only does the poem possess an unconscious but to us unmistakable undercurrent of sexual reference, but it would also certainly be Coleridgean to think of it as containing a consciously symbolic statement. Indeed, as Coleridge says in *The Statesman's Manual,* the imagination, "incorporating the reason in images of the sense," gives birth to "a system of symbols." [38]

As Bate has recently argued, however, in his sensitive volume in The Masters of World Literature series, theological preoccupations subsume all Coleridge's other concerns.[39] It is not merely idle chatter for Coleridge to say that "the primary imagination" is "a repetition in the finite mind of the eternal act of creation in the infinite I AM." The controlling symbolism of "Kubla Khan" is, I think, anagogic; it refers to the "eternal act"—which alone, in Coleridge's scheme, could be called an idea of "reason"—not to the repetitive act in the finite mind nor to the echoes of that act. A poem written by Coleridge that ends with the word "paradise," and begins with the creation of a garden, should be interpreted, I believe, as a poem about God and Eden. The loss of the garden affirms, as Coleridge said in 1815 that he had wanted Wordsworth's poetry to affirm, "a Fall in some sense, as a fact . . . the reality of which is attested by Experience & Conscience." [40] The Khan, wonderful, remote in space and time, heard about rather than seen, is what Sidney might call "a notable *prosopopeias*" that represents God himself.[41] Although the words in Purchas say that "*In Xamdu did Cublai Can* build *a stately* Palace," [42] Coleridge's Khan does not build, rather he creates by decree—that is, by a word, or divine fiat. And the garden, like Milton's Eden, is menaced from its beginning by conflicts arising from an ancestral past.[43]

Such a reading could be bulwarked by considerations

drawn from the extensive literature of commentary on the poem. Geoffrey Yarlott, for instance, suggests that "Alph, the sacred river," instead of being the Nile or the Alpheus, could "derive from 'Alpha,' the beginning—the sacred source of all things." [44] And the part of the poem that does seem to be about poetic creation, that is, where the speaker will revive within him the Abyssinian maid's "symphony and song" so as to rebuild the dome in air, and thereby show that he has "drunk the milk of paradise," is, as Elisabeth Schneider has pointed out, an echo of the *Ion*, which is the *locus classicus* for the connection of poetic act with divine things.[45]

In any case, and whether one agrees or disagrees with an interpretation of the poem that transfers the emphasis from imaginative creation to theology, it should be evident that the imagination, though it cannot be dismissed in the consideration of Coleridge's poetry, is a tool of only limited critical use. To a considerable extent it functions simply as another name for that which is poetic about a poem. Whatever that may happen to be, however, can be approached by general methods available to any critic. In the *Biographia Literaria*, a book that is largely about poetry, the definition of the secondary imagination emphasizes and honors poetic creation. But it operates more as a link between its author's poetic and his systematic theological and philosophical interests than as a program for how poetry should be written.

Perhaps this role can be more fully understood if we turn to the second of our stipulated questions, that is, where in Coleridge's thought or reading did the secondary imagination originate? With regard to the answer, a passage published by Ernest Hartley Coleridge in the *Anima Poetae* in 1895 is instructive, both in its own right and for what it indicates about the textual difficulties that have hindered Coleridgean interpretation. The passage runs as follows:

> In the preface of my metaphysical works, I should say—
> "Once for all, read Kant, Fichte, &c., and then you will trace, or, if you are on the hunt, track me." Why, then, not acknowledge your obligations step by step? Because I could not do so in a multitude of glaring resemblances without a lie, for they had been mine, formed and full-formed, before I had ever heard of these writers, because to have fixed on the particular instances in which I have really been indebted to these writers would have been hard, if possible, to me who read for truth and self-satisfaction, and not to make a book, and who always rejoiced and was jubilant when I found my own ideas well expressed by others—and, lastly, let me say, because . . . I seem to know that much of the *matter* remains my own, and that the *soul* is mine. I fear not him for a critic who can confound a fellow-thinker with a compiler.[46]

The statement, written in 1804, is clearly central to the whole question of Coleridge's intellectual indebtedness, and constitutes both a proud testament to his own mental vitality and also, more ambivalently, perhaps something of a license to engage in the borrowings or plagiarisms that he embarked upon during his period of dejection.

But the editor of *Anima Poetae* did not transcribe the passage correctly. When it was republished in 1961, in the second volume of Kathleen Coburn's monumental edition of the *Notebooks*, numerous changes in punctuation and spelling appeared. More importantly, an interloper appeared as well.

Where earlier "Kant, Fichte, &c." had been acknowledged by Coleridge as the masters of his thought, the opening sentence now read:

> In the Preface of my Metaphys. Works I should say—
> Once & all read Tetens, Kant, Fichte, &c—&
> there you will trace or if you are on the hunt, track me.[47]

We almost sympathize with Ernest Hartley Coleridge's discarding of the name. For who on earth was Tetens? And what conceivably did he have to do with Coleridge?

To answer the latter question first, Tetens was the thinker to whom we may trace or track Coleridge's theory of secondary imagination. For the rest, he was the most important German psychologist of the *Aufklärung*, exerted a major influence on the formation of Kant's *Critique of Pure Reason*,[48] was for a time Professor at the University of Kiel, and from there was given in 1789 a royal commission as a high official of state finance in Copenhagen. He was born, according to varying accounts, on September 16, 1736, or November 5, 1738, and he died in 1807 on August 15 (Danish reckoning) or August 19 (German reckoning).[49]

Although Tetens wrote a number of treatises, some of them in Latin, his fame and significance rest almost exclusively upon a two-volume work published in Leipzig in 1777 and entitled *Philosophische Versuche über die menschliche Natur und ihre Entwickelung*. Coleridge, the "library-cormorant," annotated both volumes, and his copies are at present in the British Museum. It seems likely that he studied Tetens over a considerable time, for the notebook entry in 1804 indicates enough enthusiasm to suggest a substantial period of prior reading, and a crossed-out statement on the flyleaf of the first volume, in which he laments his separation from the Words-worths, seems to have been written not only during his Malta sojourn but also after he learned, in the spring of 1805, of John Wordsworth's death. "O shall I ever see them again?" he asks, and then he exclaims, "O dear John! Would I had been thy substitute!" [50]

Indeed, such is the length of Tetens's volumes that reading them over a substantial period of time would be a normal procedure. Kant, who, according to De Vleeschauwer, de-layed his first *Critique* in order to complete a study of Te-tens,[51] says, in a gentle gibe, that Tetens, in his "long essay on freedom in the second volume," was hoping as he wrote that with the aid of uncertainly sketched ideas he would find his way out of "this labyrinth," but "after he had wearied himself and his reader," the matter remained the same as before.[52] And Coleridge, in a friendly note on the last page of the Pref-ace, seems obliquely to record as much dismay as anticipa-tion about the rest of the work. "Would to Heaven," he writes, "that all Folios & Quartos contained in their 7 or 800 pages as much meaning & good sense, as these 36 pages oc-tavo in large type." [53] As Tetens's first volume, exclusive of preliminary material, is 784 pages, and his second 834 pages, Coleridge's statement about "7 or 800" pages seems to apply very much to matters at hand.

But I suspect he read every word. Both volumes are anno-tated, although not copiously; the subject of freedom in the second volume, which elicited Kant's gibe to Markus Herz, receives a Coleridgean comment; most of all, however, I trust my own sense of how Coleridge read, built up from tracing or tracking him through numerous treatises. Quite in opposition to earlier views that had him dipping and skimming through works he barely understood, we must see him now as a man who was able to read when he was able to do nothing else.[54] He read the works of Kant, for instance, with an almost unholy attentiveness, and was able to do so straight through the most severe periods of his opium addiction.[55]

In any event, what he needed in Tetens he could find within the first quarter of the first volume. And what was there to be found was not only the formulation of the theory of secondary imagination, but also the entire threefold division of the imaginative faculty that he deposits at the end of the thirteenth chapter of the *Biographia Literaria.*

The significance of this aspect of Coleridge's use of Tetens has not, I believe, been fully realized as yet. E. L. Stahl, in an article on Coleridge and Goethe that appeared in 1952 in the *Festgabe* for Fritz Strich, broached the possibility of Tetens (along with Maass) as an influence on Coleridge's theory of imagination.[56] In 1955, René Wellek likewise mentioned the possibility.[57] And although Stahl did not see the full situation, and Wellek contented himself with part of a single sentence, an article by Walter Greiner, which appeared in *Die neueren Sprachen* in 1960, identified both the secondary imagination and the threefold distinction of Chapter Thirteen as stemming from Tetens.[58] Greiner, however, could not know the passage in the *Notebooks* that so conclusively points to Tetens as a Coleridgean source, nor was he, as a doctoral candidate, equipped to assess the meaning of his discovery. His article made no impression on established Coleridge scholarship.

Now Tetens, like Coleridge, and indeed almost everyone who has thought about the matter, initially dichotomizes the power of representation. He explains that we ascribe to the psyche not only a power to produce representations in themselves . . . but also a power of calling them forth again, a re-representing power, which is customarily termed fancy (*Phantasie*) or imagination (*Einbildungskraft*).[59]

As to these two latter terms, although Tetens says that "imagination" more truly indicates the re-representing power "in so far as it renews imagistic representations of sensation," [60] the words remain for him synonymous, and in his actual practice he seems to prefer the word "fancy." He is not satisfied, however, with the twofold division of "perceiving faculty" and "fancy." In a radical departure from previous psychologizing, he adds a third entity, which he calls *Dichtungsvermögen*— that is, the power of joining together, and also, ambivalently, the power of poetry. "The activities of representation," he now says,

can be conceived under three headings. *First* we produce original representations out of the sensations within us . . . this is *perception.* . . . *Secondly,* this power of sensation is reproduced even when those first sensations have ceased. . . . This effect is commonly ascribed to the . . . *fancy.* . . .

*Thirdly.* This reproduction of the ideas is still not all, however, that the human power of representation does with them. It does not merely reproduce them, it does not merely alter their previous co-existence . . . but it also creates new images and representations. . . . The psyche is able not only to arrange and order its representations, like the curator of a gallery of paintings, but is itself a painter, and invents and constructs new paintings.

These achievements belong to the *Dichtungsvermögen,* a creative power, whose sphere of activity seems to have a great scope. . . . It is the self-active fancy . . . and without doubt an essential ingredient of genius.[61]

Tetens's threefold division of the representing power or *Vorstellungskraft* into *Perceptionsvermögen, Dichtungsvermögen,* and *Phantasie*[62] is paralleled by Coleridge's threefold division of the imaginative powers into primary imagination, secondary imagination, and fancy. Moreover, there are striking similarities between Tetens's *Perceptionsvermögen* and Coleridge's primary imagination. To Coleridge, primary imagination is the "prime Agent of all human Perception"; to Tetens, the *Perceptionsvermögen* is the "*facultas percipiendi*" or faculty of perceiving.[63] Coleridge's faculty is a repetition of the "eternal act of creation"; Tetens's is called the "constituting power" (*Fassungskraft*).[64] It "produces the original representations out of the sensations in us, and maintains them during after-perceiving, and we preserve these after-perceptions as reproductions of the sensed objects in us."[65]

The similarities extend also to Coleridge's fancy and Tetens's fancy. For Coleridge, fancy "must receive all its materials ready made from the law of association"; for Tetens, fancy operates "nach der Regel der Association"—according to the rule of association.[66] For Coleridge, fancy is "the aggregative and associative power";[67] for Tetens, fancy reproduces sensations either according to "their previous coexistence in the senses" or according to the rule that "similar representations group themselves with one another." This, he says, is "the law of the association of ideas."[68]

Tetens's new third entity, the *Dichtungsvermögen,* intrudes into the activities of the law of association. Representations,

says Tetens, would occur strictly according to the "true association of ideas," that is, according to their similarity or their
coexistence, "if nothing comes in between." [69] But this "if," he
says, is "an if that permits exception." [70] "The self-active
*Dichtungsvermögen* comes between, and creates new representations out of those already there, makes new points of
union, new connections, and new series. The power of
thought discovers new relationships, new similarities, new co-
existences, and new dependences . . . and makes in this manner new channels of communication among ideas." [71]

The intruding *Dichtungsvermögen* is the source of an activity that Tetens calls *Dichtkraft,* and *Dichtkraft* seems to be
neither more nor less than Coleridge's secondary imagination.
Chapter Fourteen of Tetens's first essay is called "Concerning
the Law of the Association of Ideas," and the rubric continues
with the assurance that the "law of association" is "only a law
of the fancy in the reproduction of sensations; it is no law for
the combination of ideas in new series." [72] And then Chapter
Fifteen, which is called "Von der bildenden Dichtkraft"—that
is, on the plastic joining or poetic power—begins to discuss
how new series are formed. The ten sections of the discussion
are indicated just below the title of the chapter, and include
such headings as "laws of the creative *Dichtkraft,*" "influence
of the *Dichtkraft* on the order in which the reproductions of
the fancy follow," and "the *Dichtkraft's* effecting power extends through all classes of representations." [73]

In the discussion itself are to be found repeatedly the exact
words used by Coleridge. Coleridge says that the secondary
imagination "dissolves, diffuses, dissipates," that it struggles
"to unify"; [74] and elsewhere he says that imagination "blends,
and (as it were) *fuses.*" [75] Tetens says that *Dichtkraft* is char-

acterized by activities of "dissolving" (*Auflösen*) and "reuniting" (*Wiedervereinigen*), "diffusing" in the sense of intermingling (*Ineinandertreiben*) and "blending" (*Vermischen*).[76]

The similarities do not end here. In Chapter Thirteen of the *Biographia Literaria,* just before his threefold formulation, Coleridge refers to the imagination as "the esemplastic power"; [77] and at the beginning of Chapter Ten he opens with the famous statement: "*Esemplastic. The word is not in Johnson, nor have I met with it elsewhere.*" [78] Esemplastic, Coleridge then says, means "to shape into one," which is a "new sense" of the word "imagination." [79] The *Dichtkraft,* likewise, is not only a *bildende*—that is, shaping—power; it is also one whose "first law," Tetens says, is that "several simple representations" be "united into one" (*in Eine vereiniget*).[80]

By way of illustrating the difference between fancy and *Dichtkraft,* Tetens invokes the example of Linnaeus, on the one hand, and of Milton and Klopstock, on the other. For Tetens, Linnaeus has, as Coleridge said of Cowley, a fanciful mind; the imagination of Linnaeus, says Tetens, "conceives a countless multitude of clear representations of sensation from bodily objects, and a like multitude of heard and gathered shades and tones; receives them in their clarity and reproduces them." [81] The work of Milton, on the other hand, for Tetens as for Coleridge, is characterized by a different order of imagination—by *Dichtkraft,* which "with inner intensity reworks the imaginings, dissolves and blends, separates and draws together again, and creates new forms and appearances." [82]

Such passages could be adduced in great number, but perhaps these few serve to show that the plastic, shaping *Dicht-*

*kraft,* with its emphasis on dissolving, diffusing, blending, re-uniting, and forming into one, and its introduction as a third entity into a spectrum made up of a psychological theory of perception and re-representation, is almost certainly the source of the theory of secondary imagination.

We may approach the third and last of our stipulated questions from the perspective of this fact. What is the context in which we should consider the secondary imagination? Actually, the question might almost better be phrased: what is the context for the primary imagination? For the secondary imagination, although named as such only in Chapter Thirteen, seems really to be the imagination Coleridge customarily talks about elsewhere, and to be called secondary only because of the primary imagination. The latter is the true newcomer. Coleridge's earliest invocation of the distinction between imagination and fancy, for instance, speaks of "Fancy, or the aggregating Faculty of the mind" and of "*Imagination,* or the *modifying,* and *co-adunating* Faculty." [83] The imagination here described seems to be the secondary imagination, and the date of the formulation, September 10, 1802, puts it interestingly close to the notebook entry of 1804 with its retrospective praise of Tetens. Furthermore, the phrase "*co-adunating* Faculty"—the faculty that makes many into one—could serve as a literal translation of the German *Dichtungsvermögen,* with the verb *dichten,* meaning "to join together" or "to caulk," serving as an ambivalent root along with *dichten* meaning "to compose poetry." In any event, our last question might be restated this way: what is the context in which we should consider Coleridge's use of Tetens's threefold distinction?

The answer to this question involves Coleridge's old nemesis, association psychology. The *Biographia Literaria* contains an intellectual history of Coleridge's concern to extricate himself from association psychology and at the same time attempts to elaborate a theory of imagination. Tetens, significantly, not only investigated the faculties of representation, but did so in the context of current theories of association psychology. He was, as J. H. Randall says, "in the thick of the crucial questions about knowledge raised in the 1760's." [84] The *Philosophische Versuche,* in other words, was very much a professional piece of psychological analysis, as those terms might apply to the situation in the late eighteenth century.

This professionalism, or scientism, was extraordinarily important to Coleridge, in view both of his temperamental needs and of what he was trying to do in philosophy. The matter was, for Coleridge, not one of merely rejecting association psychology and affirming a theory of imagination against it. Blake, for instance, does that much. The attitudes of Locke and Newton were as repugnant to him as they were to Coleridge. As Blake says, "Mans perceptions are not bounded by organs of perception. he perceives more than sense (tho' ever so acute) can ever discover." [85] And he states that "To Me This World is all One continued Vision of Fancy or Imagination." [86] Imagination for Blake asserts the mind's freedom and is opposed to the hegemony of the external: "Natural Objects always did & now do Weaken deaden & obliterate Imagination in Me." [87] But Blake's opinions, though on these issues not very different from those of Coleridge, are formulated as insights, not as conclusions from argument or investigation. Instead of argument, Blake simply escalates, and indeed, exaggerates, his own statement:

> To cast off Bacon, Locke & Newton from Albions cover-
> ing
> To take off his filthy garments, & clothe him with
> Imagination [88]

As Northrop Frye notes, "Bacon, Newton and Locke do not look very convincing in the role of three-headed hellish Cerberus which Blake assigns them." [89] Blake, for his part, says with disarming candor that men and works such as "Locke on Human Understanding" inspire his "Contempt & Abhorrence"; "They mock Inspiration & Vision Inspiration & Vision was then & now is & I hope will always Remain my Element my Eternal Dwelling place. how then can I hear it Contemnd without returning Scorn for Scorn." [90]

Coleridge too looked on Locke with "Contempt & Abhorrence." [91] For him, however, it was important not merely to abuse Newton and Locke but to argue against them on their own cognitive terms. To use his own phraseology, it was necessary to remove "the sandy Sophisms of Locke, and the Mechanic Dogmatists" by "demonstrating that the Senses were living growths and developements of the Mind & Spirit in a much juster as well as higher sense, than the mind can be said to be formed by the Senses." [92] The important word here is "demonstrating." "I can assert," says De Quincey, "upon my long and intimate knowledge of Coleridge's mind, that logic the most severe was as inalienable from his modes of thinking as grammar from his language." [93] Blake, on the other hand, dismissing both demonstration and logic, felt that

> Hes a Blockhead who wants a proof of what he Can't
> Perceive
> And he's a Fool who tries to make such a Blockhead
> believe [94]

But Coleridge, committed to a systematic reconciliation of all elements of experience, could not proceed in such a peremptory way. As John Beer notes, in a passage that is increasingly recognized as going to the heart of Coleridge's interests,

> Side by side with his visionary world of speculation, there is in his mind a positivist world of rationalist investigation, which he no doubt hoped would eventually be harmonized with it.[95]

And Coleridge himself said that the sum total of his convictions would constitute a system such "that of all Systems that have ever been presented, this has the least of Mysticism, the very Object throughout from the first page to the last being to reconcile the dictates of common Sense with the conclusions of scientific Reasoning." [96] Indeed, as Richard Haven has recently emphasized, Coleridge

> shared the respect of his age for science and scientific theories, the confidence that human experience could be explained as physical nature could be explained, that there were laws of human nature as well as laws of motion. While he was drawn to various earlier visionaries, he was also well aware of what seemed to be their inadequacy, their inability, that is, to meet the challenge of "enlightened" analysis and criticism. What he required was a means of reconciling the experience of the oasis [i.e., of visionary insight] with acceptable conceptions of physical and psychological reality.[97]

So Coleridge could hardly fail to be attracted by the most scientific and soberly professional psychologist of the German enlightenment. Tetens's two formidable tomes begin with a statement that seems to promise God's plenty:

The following essays concern the workings of the human understanding, its laws of thought and its basic powers; furthermore, they concern the active power of will, the fundamental character of humanity, freedom, the nature of the soul, and its development.[98]

Tetens immediately makes this comprehensiveness still more attractive by declaring himself in favor of the most respectable scientific procedures. He states that he has "carefully sought to avoid the admixture of hypotheses among propositions of experience"; [99] and he says that

Concerning the method which I have utilized, I consider it necessary to explain myself at the beginning. It is the method of observation that Locke has pursued with regard to the understanding, and our psychologists have followed in the doctrine of psychic experience.[100]

Still another aspect of Tetens's procedure would doubtless have engaged Coleridge's attention. Tetens focuses not only on the tradition of Locke but specifically on Hartley and Priestley. Hartley's hypothesis, which Coleridge knew so well and from which he needed to free himself,[101] is brought forward almost at the outset. As Tetens says, "The Hartleyan hypothesis that movements of the brain . . . consist in certain vibrations of the brain fibres or even of the aether in the brain, has been set forth by Mr. Priestley in a new, somewhat altered, well executed, and most praiseworthy exposition. Since then people have accustomed themselves to regard ideas as above all vibrations in the brain." [102] Coleridge, who was "much pleased . . . with everything that overthrows & or illustrates the overthrow of that all-annihilating system of explaining every thing wholly by association," [103] would have been even more interested, however, in Tetens's further preliminary remarks about the "difficulties" of Hartley's view: for Tetens concludes that "it seems to me, nothing is less probable than that the whole sensible motion of the brain that constructs the material idea can consist purely and simply in vibration, as is hypothesized." [104]

If we inquire into the intellectual origin of this discontent on the part of Tetens with Hartley's psychology of association, we are led to a single source: Leibniz. Hartley's master, Locke, had supposed "the mind to be, as we say, white paper, void of all characters, without any ideas," and to be furnished by "EXPERIENCE." [105] "SENSATION" was the "great source of most of the ideas we have." [106] "External material things, as the objects of SENSATION, and the operations of our own minds within, as the objects of REFLECTION" were to Locke "the only originals from whence all our ideas take their beginnings." [107]

This view of the mind's nature dominated European psychology until the second part of the eighteenth century. In 1765, however, Leibniz's answer to Locke, the *Nouveaux essais sur l'entendement,* was found and first published by Raspe. The *Nouveaux essais* immediately began to exert the strongest kind of counterinfluence on European intellectuals; indeed, the book's historical effect can hardly be overestimated.[108] "In my opinion," said Tetens proudly in a work of 1775,

> our own Leibniz has seen far more deeply, acutely and correctly into the nature of the human understanding, its modes of thought, and in particular the transcendental knowledge of reason, than the more assiduously observing Locke. He has seen further than the otherwise clear-

sighted Hume, than Reid, Condillac, Beattie, Search, and Home.[109]

Such an endorsement implies an acceptance of the idea of inherent powers of mind, and thus for Coleridge's purposes a defense of the "I am" or irreducible sense of an autonomous self. For Leibniz had rejected the *tabula rasa* of the associationists as "a fiction," [110] and had urged that

> there are some ideas and principles which do not come to us from the senses, and which we find in ourselves without forming them, although the senses give us occasion to perceive them.[111]

Moreover, by his conception of *vis activa* (active force) or *vis insita* (inherent force) as the nature of the monad, Leibniz paved the way for a rejection of the mind's passivity.[112] As Cassirer notes, by way of inaugurating a discussion of Tetens:

> When the mind becomes a mirror of reality [as it did in Leibniz's monad doctrine] it is and remains a living mirror of the universe, and it is not simply a sum total of mere images but a whole composed of formative forces. The basic task of psychology and epistemology will henceforth be to elucidate these forces in their specific structure and to understand their reciprocal relations. . . . The psychological formulation and defense of the spontaneity of the ego now prepare the ground for a new conception of knowledge and of art.[113]

Of these late followers of Leibniz engaged in the psychological formulation and defense of the spontaneity of the ego, Tetens was, says Cassirer, "the most original and ingenious psychological analyst." [114]

Coleridge was as much aware of Leibniz as he was of

Tetens. Indeed, in Chapter Nine of the *Biographia Literaria,*
the position of Locke is adduced in the language of Leibniz:
"nihil in intellectu quod non prius in sensu"—nothing in the
mind which is not first in the senses. Coleridge also para-
phrases Leibniz's amendment of the position: "praeter ipsum
intellectum"—except the mind itself.[115] The amendment provides as good a programmatic statement as any of Coleridge's
arguments against the associationism of his youth. And it
takes on added significance in light of the fact that the two
massive volumes of Tetens represent a kind of enormously expanded gloss upon the position of Locke as criticized by
Leibniz's addendum.

It is in the empirical examination of two related edifices of
thought, science and poetry, that Tetens looks for his evidence for active powers of mind that stand outside the law of
association, and to which he gives the general name *Denkkraft.*[116] He finds particularly vulnerable the associationist account of the mental activities revealed in poetry:

> Psychologists commonly explain poetic creation as a
> mere analysis and synthesis of ideas that are produced in
> sensation and drawn forth again. But does this really
> quite account for fictions? If so, then poetic creation is
> nothing more than a mere transposition of phantasms,
> from which no new simple ideas can arise in our con-
> sciousness. According to this supposition, every discrete
> sensuous appearance must, if analyzed into the compo-
> nent parts that can be differentiated by reflection, consist
> of nothing but pieces, which taken individually are pure
> imaginings or renewed ideas of sense.[117]

But, says Tetens, such is not the case; and he proceeds to
examine a certain fiction used by poets, that of Pegasus. "The
representation of Pegasus," he says,

is an image of a winged horse. We have the image of a
horse from sensation, and also the image of wings. Both
are pure phantasms, sundered from other representations
and bound together with one another here in the image
of Pegasus. To that extent this is nothing but an effect of
the fancy. But this is only an analysis and a putting together again.[118]

Tetens continues:

It seems to me that there is more in the image than a
mere putting together. The wings of Pegasus might have
been a pure phantasm in the head of the first poet who
produced this image; likewise the representation of the
horse. But there is a place in the image, at the shoulders
of the horse, somewhat more obscure than the others,
where the wings are joined to the body; at that point the
images of the horse's shoulders and of the roots of the
wings flow into one another. There is accordingly a spontaneous appearance, which disappears if the image of the
horse and the image of the wings are again clearly separated from one another.[119]

By such form of empirical observation, which seems to prefig-
ure the "phi phenomenon" that lies at the basis of twentieth-century Gestalt psychology, Tetens concludes that

Dichtkraft can create no elements, no fundamental materials, can make only nothing out of nothing, and to that
extent is no creative power. It can only separate, dissolve, join together, blend; but precisely thereby it can
produce new images, which from the standpoint of our
faculty of differentiation are discrete representations.[120]

There is accordingly a "Selbstthätigkeit"—a spontaneous
activity—in "the receptivity of the psyche," and on this "the

ability to have secondary sensations depends." [121] The "receptivity of our psyche" passes over into a "percipirende, repro-
ducirende and dichtende Kraft"—a perceiving, reproducing
and co-adunating power.[122]

Tetens's argument for "Selbstthätigkeit" in mental process,
for "selbstbildende Dichtkraft," with such conceptions being
derived in the course of an examination of association psychology, must have seemed to Coleridge like a fountain in the
desert. As he wrote in 1801, perhaps shortly before encounter-
ing the *Philosophische Versuche:*

> Newton was a mere materialist—*Mind* in his system is
> always passive—a lazy Looker-on on an external World.
> If the mind be not *passive,* if it be indeed made in God's
> Image, & that too in the sublimest sense—the Image of
> the *Creator*—there is ground for suspicion, that any sys-
> tem built on the passiveness of the mind must be false, as
> a system.[123]

The phrase about the mind as "the Image of the *Creator*"
seems to be a foreshadowing of the primary imagination as a
"repetition in the finite mind" of the creative activity of "the
infinite I AM." But the tone of the passage does not suggest
that Coleridge at this moment had in hand the threefold elaboration of the mind's imaginative activity. The statement,
however, occurred in the same month as his declaration that
he had "overthrown the doctrine of Association, as taught by
Hartley, and with it all the irreligious metaphysics of modern
Infidels—especially, the doctrine of Necessity." [124] Apparently, then, some sort of intellectual conversion—which for
Coleridge must have seemed to be based on cognitive
demonstration—took place in March, 1801, against associa-

tion psychology and in favor of active powers of mind. Whether we suppose the reading of Tetens to have preceded and actually to have caused this change, or to have followed and confirmed it, it seems quite unarguable that those emphases of Tetens that we have described would be of central importance to Coleridge.[125]

They were still important when the *Biographia Literaria* came to be written, for there the problems are the same: to argue against association psychology and to affirm the spontaneous power of mind, although now in the specific form of imagination.[126] As Coleridge says in Chapter Eight of that work, association theory neither "involves the explanation, nor precludes the necessity of a mechanism and co-adequate force in the percepient, which at the more than magic touch of the impulse from without is to create anew for itself the correspondent object." [127] Such an active principle was not elaborated in association psychology before Tetens.[128] As Coleridge wryly says, "In Hartley's scheme, the soul is present only to be pinched or *stroked,* while the very squeals or purring are produced by an agency wholly independent and alien." [129] Tetens, in insisting that a third element, *Dichtkraft,* must be added to those accounted for by the law of association, provided exactly what Coleridge required.[130]

Therefore we must amend the theory, advanced by commentators such as D. G. James,[131] that sees Kant as the prototype for Coleridge's discrimination of the imaginative faculties. Whatever Kant's role, the correspondences between his descriptions of imagination and those of Coleridge are by no means so close as between those of Tetens and Coleridge.[132] There is, for instance, only a twofold, not a threefold division of imaginative activity in the first *Critique;* and

Kant's "productive imagination" does not emphasize dissolving, diffusing, and blending activities as do Coleridge's secondary imagination and Tetens's *Dichtkraft*. And in any case, Kant's own theories of imagination, as De Vleeschauwer demonstrates in his magisterial work on the transcendental deduction in Kant, were themselves derived from Tetens. "As to the theme of imagination," says De Vleeschauwer,

> it is evident, although Kant disguises it somewhat by its integration in the transcendental methodology, that it derives from the psychological work of the eighteenth century. The birth, in effect, of the imagination from the internal sense comes directly from the psychology contemporary to Kant, and discloses increasingly the influence of Lockian empiricism.[133]

But, as De Vleeschauwer points out, "the single memorable psychological event" [134] that occurred in Germany at this time was the publication of Tetens's *Philosophische Versuche*, and after exhaustive discussion he concludes as follows:

> We shall terminate this chapter by demonstrating that Kant studied the *Philosophische Versuche* of Tetens. Anticipating this conclusion, the legitimacy of which is guaranteed by the correspondence of Kant, we believe that it is not going beyond the bounds of prudence so necessary in this kind of discussion to say that in all probability the introduction of imagination as a factor in the critical philosophy was due to the reading of Tetens.[135]

Coleridge's secondary imagination, therefore, looks past Kant's productive imagination to the *Dichtkraft* of Tetens. Authorized by the empirical observation of poetry rather than by a critic's notion of what poetry should be, both secondary imagination and *Dichtkraft* are themselves articulations of the metaphysical *vis activa* of Leibniz.[136] Thus in a note of 1804 Coleridge speaks of the "*Ego/* its metaphysical Sublimity—& intimate Synthesis with the principle of Co-adunation—without *it* every where all things were a waste—nothing, &c—."[137] Although the "principle of Co-adunation" here invoked is clearly the secondary imagination or *Dichtkraft*, the phrase about the ego's "metaphysical Sublimity" can refer neither to poetry nor to psychology, but only to metaphysics—that is, not to Tetens, but to Leibniz.

Indeed, one of the epigraphs to Chapter Thirteen of the *Biographia Literaria*—a chapter, we may recall, bearing the subtitle "On the imagination, or esemplastic power"—is a Latin quotation from Leibniz's *Specimen dynamicum*.[138] It is, significantly, in this treatise that the conception of *vis activa* is most fully discussed. "Active force," says Leibniz there, is either "primitive or derivative"; the "primitive force" (which is what concerns us) is "nothing else than the first entelechy" or "the soul."[139] Coleridge's epigraph comes from a passage a few pages further on, and it stresses metaphysical rather than poetical principles: "in addition to considerations purely mathematical, and subject to the fancy, I have concluded that certain metaphysical principles must be admitted. . . . that a certain higher, and so to speak, formal principle must be added to that of material mass."[140]

The epigraph, however, is not drawn wholly from *Specimen dynamicum*. Its first sentence is from the *De ipsa natura*, the treatise in which Leibniz discusses active force in the alternative phrasing of *vis insita*, or inherent force. The sentence from this treatise refers to the Platonists as recognizing the necessity of formative powers as well as matter; [141] and elsewhere Leibniz speaks of Plato himself as supplying in his doctrine of *anamnesis* [142] a prototype of the doctrine of inherent mental force.[143]

So we may conclude that the lineage of the secondary imagination extends not only backward beyond Kant to Tetens, but also beyond Tetens to Leibniz, and finally beyond Leibniz to Plato. With antecedents of this kind, it is inevitable that Coleridge's threefold theory of imagination actually bears less on poetry than it does on those things that always mattered most to him—as they did to Leibniz and to Kant—that is, "the freedom of the will, the immortality of the soul, and the existence of God." [144]

## NOTES

1. *Biographia Literaria,* by S. T. Coleridge, edited with his Aesthetical Essays by J. Shawcross (London, 1907), I, 202.

2. "Coleridge on the Function of Art," *Perspectives of Criticism,* ed. Harry Levin (Cambridge, Mass., 1950), pp. 144, 145–46.

3. *Biographia,* I, 60, 62, 64.        4. *Ibid.,* p. 193.

5. *Ibid.,* p. 200.        6. *Ibid.,* pp. 201–2.

7. See my *Coleridge and the Pantheist Tradition* (Oxford, 1969), especially pp. 148–60.

8. See *ibid.,* pp. 24–26; and Shawcross's notes (*Biographia,* I, 268–71).

9. *Biographia,* I, 187.

10. *Ibid.,* p. 197. Cf. Schelling, e.g., "Die Philosophie geht aus von einer unendlichen Entzweiung entgegengesetzter Thätigkeiten . . ." (*Friedrich Wilhelm Joseph von Schellings sämmtliche Werke,* ed. K. F. A. Schelling [Stuttgart and Augsburg, 1856–61],

III, 626). This frequently expressed fundamental of Schelling's thought was largely derived from Kant's analysis of the metaphysical foundations of the dynamic (see *Kant's gesammelte Schriften,* ed. by the Prussian Academy of Sciences [Berlin and Leipzig, 1902–], IV, 511). Cf. Goethe's comment: "Since our excellent Kant says in plain words that there can be no material without attraction and repulsion (that is, without polarity), I am much reassured to be able, under this authority, to proceed with my view of the world according to my earliest convictions, in which I have never lost confidence" (*Werke,* Memorial Edition, ed. Ernst Beutler [Zurich, 1948–60], XIX, 732).

11. *Biographia,* I, 198.

12. *Ibid.* The tertium aliquid would metaphysically have to be God, so the solution would be pantheistic. I suspect, however, that Coleridge did not see this until the last moment because his mind was set on poetic imagination. Schelling had said that the "infinite opposition" could be resolved through "each individual representation of art." "What," he asks, "is that wonderful power" that can resolve an infinite opposition: "We have until now not been able to make this mechanism completely understandable, because it is only the power of art that can fully reveal it. That productive faculty is the same by which art also attains the impossible, that is, resolves an infinite opposition in a finite product. It is the faculty of poetry (*Dichtungsvermögen*) . . . it is the only thing by which we are able to think and unify the contradictory—that is, the imagination" (*Werke,* III, 626).

13. *Werke,* II, 39.  14. *Ibid.,* I, 332n.

15. *Biographia,* I, 198.  16. *Ibid.,* p. 201.

17. Plotinus, *Enneads,* VI.ix.11.

18. *The Prelude: A Parallel Text,* ed. J. C. Maxwell (Harmondsworth, Middlesex, 1971), p. 239 (Book VI, lines 592–94).

19. *Werke,* I, 332n; III, 626.

20. *Franz von Baader's sämmtliche Werke,* ed. Franz Hoffmann *et al.* (Leipzig, 1850–60), XI, 85.

21. *Biographia*, II, 12. We may see the same mysteriousness in Jean Paul's rubric of 1795: "Über die natürliche Magie der Einbildungskraft."

22. *Biographia*, I, 64.

23. *Ibid.*, p. 191. To make headway against the school of Locke, one needed to exploit all possibilities. In the words of one commentator, Locke was a "writer whose influence pervades the eighteenth century with an almost scriptural authority. . . . surely never has a secular writer obtained such universal recognition or been received with such unquestioning faith as Locke" (Alfred Cobban, *Edmund Burke and the Revolt Against the Eighteenth Century*, 2d ed. [London, 1960], p. 16). Moreover, "the French fatalists or necessitarians" opposed by Coleridge were still more insistent than was their master upon the chief point of Lockian thought: the theoretical diminution of the soul's autonomy. For instance Condillac, in the words of another commentator, "was a professional Lockian, more Lockian in his final system even than Locke himself" (Peter Gay, *The Enlightenment: An Interpretation*, II [New York, 1969], 178). In general, as Ernst Cassirer emphasizes, "the development of empirical philosophy from Locke to Berkeley and from Berkeley to Hume represents a series of attempts to minimize the difference between sensation and reflection, and finally to wipe it out altogether. French philosophical criticism of the eighteenth century hammered at this same point also in an attempt to eliminate the last vestige of independence which Locke had attributed to reflection" (*The Philosophy of the Enlightenment*, trans. Fritz A. C. Koelln and James P. Pettegrove [Boston, 1955], p. 100).

24. Cf. Coleridge in 1803: "Mix up Truth & Imagination so that the Imag. may spread its own indefiniteness over that which really happened" (*The Notebooks of Samuel Taylor Coleridge*, ed. Kathleen Coburn [New York, 1957–], I, 1541). Cf. Wordsworth: "Imagination . . . recoils from every thing but the plastic, the pliant, and the indefinite" (*Literary Criticism of William Wordsworth*, ed. P. M. Zall [Lincoln, Neb., 1966], p. 152). Geoffrey Hartman's description of Wordsworth's "Imagination" as *"consciousness of self raised to apocalyptic pitch"* well expresses the

emotional function of imagination for all Romantic thinkers (*Wordsworth's Poetry, 1787–1814* [New Haven and London, 1964], p. 17). This emblematic role was possible for imagination because of its unaccountability even to the associationists. Locke himself had conceded that in the "faculty of repeating and joining together its ideas, the mind has great power in varying and multiplying the objects of its thoughts"; that "the mind often exercises an *active* power in making . . . combinations"; that in "secondary perception . . . or reviewing again the ideas that are lodged in the memory, the mind is oftentimes more than barely passive; the appearance of those dormant pictures depending sometimes on the *will*" (*An Essay Concerning Human Understanding*, ed. A. C. Fraser [New York, 1959], I, 214, 382, 197). Such concessions were an Achilles heel, a crack which the historical progress toward Romanticism widened into an increasing recognition of the mysteriousness of active or imaginative function. Thus, for instance, La Mettrie, the most extreme of all those whom Coleridge called "the French fatalists or necessitarians," was fascinated by imagination. His notorious *L'Homme machine* of 1751 was the *ne plus ultra* of mechanism and fatalism: men, he said, "ne sont au fond que des Animaux, & des Machines perpendiculairement rampantes"; he argued that "l'Homme est une machine; & qu'il n'y a dans tout l'Univers qu'une seule substance diversement modifiée." But as he also says, "By the imagination . . . the cold skeleton of reason takes on living and ruddy flesh, by the imagination the senses flourish, the arts are adorned, the wood speaks, the echoes sigh, the rock weeps, marble breathes, and all inanimate objects gain life. . . . Foolishly decried by some, vainly praised by others, and misunderstood by all, . . . it not only describes, but also can measure nature." And he renders explicit homage to the mysteriousness of the faculty: "L'imagination, ou cette partie fantastique du cerveau, dont la nature nous est aussi inconnue, que sa manière d'agir" (*L'Homme machine*, ed. Aram Vartanian [Princeton, 1960], 191–92, 197, 165–66, 165).

25. Note on the flyleaf of J. G. E. Maass, *Versuch über die Einbildungskraft*, rev. ed. (Halle and Leipzig, 1797), now in the British Museum.

**26.** *Herders sämmtliche Werke,* ed. Bernhard Suphan (Berlin, 1877–1913), VIII, 190.

**27.** *Friedrich Heinrich Jacobi's Werke* (Leipzig, 1812–25), II, 306.

**28.** Herman-J. de Vleeschauwer, *The Development of Kantian Thought: The History of a Doctrine,* trans. A. R. C. Duncan (London, 1962), pp. 83–84.

**29.** *Coleridge on the Seventeenth Century,* ed. Roberta F. Brinkley (Durham, N.C., 1955), p. 694. For a critical application of the principle of imagination's oscillatory nature see the report of Coleridge's statement about a passage from *Romeo and Juliet:* ". . . there is an effort in the mind, when it would describe what it cannot satisfy itself with the description of, to reconcile opposites, and to leave a middle state of mind more strictly appropriate to the imagination than any other when it is hovering between two images: as soon as it is fixed on one it becomes understanding, and when it is waving between them, attaching itself to neither, it is imagination" (*Coleridge on Shakespeare: The Text of the Lectures of 1811–12,* ed. R. A. Foakes [London, 1971], p. 82).

**30.** See my *Coleridge and the Pantheist Tradition,* p. 157n 1: "Broadly speaking the function of the imagination for Coleridge was to connect the 'I am' with the 'it is,' while maintaining the primacy and independence of the 'I am.'"

**31.** *The New York Review of Books,* XVI (April 22, 1971), 55.

**32.** *Biographia,* I, 93.    **33.** *Ibid.*    **34.** *Ibid.,* p. 193.

**35.** *Ibid.,* p. 192.    **36.** *Ibid.,* pp. 192–93.

**37.** Thus George Watson: "What is 'Kubla Khan' about? This is, or ought to be, an established fact of criticism: 'Kubla Khan' is a poem about poetry" (*Coleridge the Poet* [London, 1966], p. 122). Cf. W. J. Bate: "The theme . . . is the hope and precarious achievement of the human imagination" (*Coleridge* [New York, 1968], p. 78); Marshall Suther: "More integral than any of these readings . . . is that which sees the poem as an introspective account of the elements of personality involved in the poetic experience, an anatomy, as it were, of the poetic experience. . . . Then we have the *poem* as symbol, partaking of the reality it would render intelligible, *being* what it is *about*" (*Visions of Xanadu* [New York and London, 1965], p. 287); Harold Bloom: ". . . *Kubla Khan,* a poem about poetry," ". . . not quite a 'poem about the act of poetic creation,' for it contains that theme as one element in a more varied unity" (*The Visionary Company* [Ithaca, N.Y., 1971], pp. 211, 218); Humphry House: "'Kubla Khan' is a poem about the act of poetic creation" (*Coleridge: The Clark Lectures 1951–52* [London, 1962], p. 115); Virginia L. Radley: "Coleridge attempts in 'Kubla Khan' to portray the world of Imagination pictorially in terms of sunlit caverns and floating pleasure-domes"; "'Kubla Khan' becomes clearly a recapitulation in poetry of Coleridge's concept of the secondary Imagination" (*Samuel Taylor Coleridge* [New York, 1966], pp. 78, 80).

38. *The Complete Works of Samuel Taylor Coleridge,* ed. W. G. T. Shedd (New York, 1853), I, 436. "An IDEA," notes Coleridge elsewhere, "in the *highest* sense of that word, cannot be conveyed but by a *symbol*" (*Biographia,* I, 100).

39. Theology was even more important to Coleridge than was poetry. As Bate says, "To begin with, no other poet . . . has devoted so little time and effort to his poetry. Second, and more important, none has considered it so incidental to his other interests, hopes, or anxieties. Failure to recognize these two facts alone . . . has led to misinterpretations . . . that are still accepted and passed on without examination. Most common among them is the stock premise that one of the major modern poets . . . hit his true stride in the 'Ancient Mariner,' 'Christabel,' and 'Kubla Khan,' and then, because of opium and general weakness of will, was forced to fritter away the next thirty-five years in chasing philosophical and theological will-of-the-wisps" (*Coleridge,* pp. 40–41). Cf. Coleridge in 1804: "When my Triplets you see / Think not of my Poesy / But of the holy Trinity" (*Notebooks,* II, 1904). The subordinate position of poetry in Coleridge's scheme of things is further implied by his "early study" of "the illustrious Florentine"—that is, Ficino (*Biographia,* I, 94); for as Eugenio Garin emphasizes, "in Ficino's view,

poetry loses its intrinsic value, for it becomes solely an incarnation
of the truth, a sensuous image of the One. But at the same time it
is clear that the whole of cosmic reality is seen as a poem by God"
(*Italian Humanism: Philosophy and Civic Life in the Renaissance*,
trans. Peter Munz [Oxford, 1965], p. 95). Coleridge's criticism too
was subordinate to his philosophical and theological concerns. As
J. R. de J. Jackson maintains: "There can be little doubt that philosophy was his central activity, and that the criticism . . . was a
digression from it. . . . his criticism was in fact . . . in the nature
of an inspired aside" (*Method and Imagination in Coleridge's Criticism* [Cambridge, Mass., 1969], p. 15).

40. *Collected Letters of Samuel Taylor Coleridge*, ed. Earl L.
Griggs (Oxford, 1956–71), IV, 575. Cf. *Table Talk*, May 1, 1830:
"A Fall of some sort or other—the creation, as it were, of the non-
absolute—is the fundamental postulate of the moral history of Man.
Without this hypothesis, Man is unintelligible."

41. I cannot agree with John Beer that "Kubla Khan is the Tartar
king of tradition: fierce and cruel, he bears the brand of Cain," or
that "Kubla Khan may seem a peaceful and prosperous ruler, but
his garden is not and cannot be the garden of Eden" (*Coleridge
the Visionary* [London, 1959], pp. 222, 228). Nor do I agree with
House that the Khan is "the Representative Man, or Mankind in
general" (*Coleridge*, p. 120). Nor again with Bate that "Kubla . . .
is man as he in general would be, . . . placed in an enviable position of power" (*Coleridge*, p. 79). I am more nearly in agreement
with G. Wilson Knight's view that Kubla is a symbol of "God: or
at least one of those 'huge and mighty forms,' or other intuitions of
mountainous power in Wordsworth"—although I disagree with
other points in Knight's interpretation (*The Starlit Dome* [London,
1941], p. 93).

42. As quoted in John Livingston Lowes, *The Road to Xanadu: A
Study in the Ways of the Imagination* (Boston and New York,
1927), p. 358.

43. Elisabeth Schneider emphasizes the extent to which Milton
"hovers over Coleridge's poem" (*Coleridge, Opium and* Kubla

Khan [Chicago, 1953], p. 264 *et passim*. Cf. House: "Of course we have in 'Kubla Khan' a fruit of Coleridge's Miltonising" (*Coleridge*, p. 119).

44. *Coleridge and the Abyssinian Maid* (London, 1967), p. 138n1.

45. *Coleridge, Opium* and *Kubla Khan*, pp. 245–46.

46. *Anima Poetae*, ed. Ernest Hartley Coleridge (London, 1895), p. 106.

47. *Notebooks*, II, 2375.

48. Kant's *Dissertatio* of 1770 influenced Tetens, and then Tetens's *Philosophische Versuche* of 1777 exerted influence back on Kant's *Kritik der reinen Vernunft* of 1781. See, e.g., Gustav Störring, *Die Erkenntnistheorie von Tetens: Eine historisch-kritische Studie* (Leipzig, 1901), p. 159. See further Arthur Seidel, *Tetens' Einfluss auf die kritische Philosophie Kants* (Würzburg, 1932); Max Brenke, *Johann Nicolas Tetens' Erkenntnistheorie vom Standpunkt des Kriticismus* (Rostock, 1901); Arthur Apitzsch, *Die psychologischen Voraussetzungen der Erkenntniskritik Kants dargestellt und auf ihre Abhängigkeit von der Psychologie C. Wolfs und Tetens' geprüft* (Halle a. S., 1897); Otto Ziegler, *Johann Nicolaus Tetens' Erkenntnistheorie in Beziehung auf Kant* (Leipzig, 1888). See also n. 135 below.

49. For details of Tetens's career see Wilhelm Uebele, *Johann Nicolaus Tetens nach seiner Gesamtentwicklung betrachtet, mit besonderer Berücksichtigung des Verhältnisses zu Kant* (Berlin, 1911), pp. 5–25.

50. The note has been printed in *Inquiring Spirit: A New Presentation of Coleridge from His Published and Unpublished Prose Writings*, ed. Kathleen Coburn (New York, 1951), p. 40.

51. *The Development of Kantian Thought*, p. 69.

52. Letter to Markus Herz, April, 1778, in *Kant's gesammelte Schriften*, X, 232. The criticism is tempered by Kant's preceding statement that "Tetens, in his vast and prolix work on human nature, has said much that is acute." Tetens, for his part,

frequently refers to Kant's achievements, calling him, for instance, "the profound philosopher who observes the understanding so keenly" (*Über die allgemeine speculativische Philosophie* [Bützow and Wismar, 1775], p. 56n).

53. Note at page xxxvi of Volume I of Johann Nicolas Tetens, *Philosophische Versuche über die menschliche Natur und ihre Entwickelung* (Leipzig, 1777), now in the British Museum. This work will hereafter be referred to as "Tetens."

54. Compare Dorothy Wordsworth's testimony, in a letter to Catherine Clarkson in 1810, during a time of virtual collapse on Coleridge's part: "As to Coleridge, . . . I hope you are sufficiently prepared for the worst. We have no hope of him. . . . If he were not under our Roof, he would be just as much the slave of stimulants as ever; and his whole time and thoughts, (except when he is reading and he reads a great deal), are employed in deceiving himself, and seeking to deceive others. He will tell me that he has been writing, that he *has* written half a Friend; when I *know* that he has not written a single line" (*The Letters of William and Dorothy Wordsworth. The Middle Years. Part I, 1806–1811*, ed. Ernest de Selincourt, revised by Mary Moorman [Oxford, 1969], pp. 398–99). Again, on June 2, 1810: "Coleridge is still at Keswick where, as at Grasmere, he has done nothing but read" (*ibid.*, p. 412).

55. Cf. *Notebooks*, I, 1517. See further George Whalley, "Coleridge Unlabyrinthed," *University of Toronto Quarterly*, XXXII (1963), 338.

56. "S. T. Coleridges Theorie der Dichtung im Hinblick auf Goethe," *Weltliteratur: Festgabe für Fritz Strich zum 70. Geburtstag*, ed. Walter Muschg and Emil Staiger (Bern, 1952), pp. 101–16. The references to Tetens are on p. 103.

57. *A History of Modern Criticism: 1750–1950* (New Haven, 1955–), II, 164.

58. Walter Greiner, "Deutsche Einflüsse auf die Dichtungstheorie von Samuel Taylor Coleridge," *Die neueren Sprachen*, n.f., IX (1960), 57–65.

59. Tetens, I, 24.      60. *Ibid.*      61. *Ibid.*, pp. 105–7.

62. "The power of representation is a main branch that shoots out into the different faculties . . . as into so many twigs, that of receiving representations, that of drawing them forth again, and that of transforming them—that is, into the *Perceptionsvermögen,* into the *Einbildungskraft,* and into the plastic *Dichtungsvermögen"* (Tetens, I, 26).

63. *Ibid.*, p. 24.      64. *Ibid.*, p. 105.

65. *Ibid.* Tetens's curious technical word, "after-perceiving" (*Nachempfinden*) is the original, I suspect, of Coleridge's statement about "distinct recollection, or as we may aptly express it, *after-consciousness"* (*Biographia,* I, 72). *Empfindung, Nachempfindung, Reproduktion,* and *Dichtkraft* are the functions of *Vorstellungskraft,* while *Apperception, Verstand,* and *Vernunft* are the functions of *Denkkraft*—a term corresponding closely to Descartes's *intellectio.*

66. Tetens, I, 140.      67. *Biographia,* I, 193.

68. Tetens, I, 106.      69. *Ibid.*, pp. 112–13.

70. *Ibid.*, p. 113.      71. *Ibid.*, p. 112.      72. *Ibid.*, p. 108.

73. *Ibid.*, p. 115.      74. *Biographia,* I, 202.

75. *Ibid.*, II, 12.      76. Tetens, I, 117.

77. *Biographia,* I, 201.      78. *Ibid.*, p. 107.      79. *Ibid.*

80. Tetens, I, 136. Coleridge also knew Jean Paul's view by which "Die Phantasie macht alle Teile zum Ganzen. . . . sie totalisiert alles"—imagination makes all parts a whole. . . . totalizes everything (*Jean Pauls sämtliche Werke,* Historical-critical Edition, ed. Eduard Berend [Weimar, 1927–], II, 38). This statement, however, was not even published until 1804, some two years after Coleridge had already defined *"Imagination"* as the *"modifying, and co-adunating* Faculty." Moreover, Jean Paul considered "Einbildungskraft" as a power inferior to "Phantasie"; and his contexts are not so close to Coleridge as those of Tetens.

81. Tetens, I, 159.

82. *Ibid.*, p. 160. Again, "*Dichtkraft* magnifies and reduces. . . . it heaps up the similar and of one sort, or diminishes it, and makes magnitudes, grades, degrees which are over or under the magnitudes of sensation. It creates Brobdingnagians and Lilliputians . . ." (I, 136). After citing three "laws" for *Dichtkraft*, Tetens says: "These are some of the laws and modes of action of *Dichtkraft*, which creates new simple representations. I have here intended to indicate only the first lines of this investigation. Are these all? I am not saying that" (I, 138). Such a statement constituted a virtual invitation for someone like Coleridge to make his own contribution.

83. *Collected Letters*, II, 865–66.

84. *The Career of Philosophy: Volume II: From the German Enlightenment to the Age of Darwin* (New York and London, 1965), p. 83.

85. *The Poetry and Prose of William Blake*, ed. David V. Erdman and Harold Bloom (New York, 1968), p. 2.

86. *Ibid.*, p. 677.

87. *Ibid.*, p. 655. See, e.g., Morton D. Paley, *Energy and the Imagination: A Study of the Development of Blake's Thought* (Oxford, 1970), pp. 200–60.

88. *Poetry and Prose of Blake*, p. 141.

89. Northrop Frye, *Fearful Symmetry: A Study of William Blake* (Princeton, 1969), p. 187.

90. *Poetry and Prose of Blake*, p. 650.

91. Henry Crabb Robinson, for instance, reports a typical conversation with Coleridge: "Of Locke he spoke as usual with great contempt. . . . He assented to my remark that atheism might be demonstrated out of Locke" (*Coleridge's Miscellaneous Criticism*, ed. T. M. Raysor [London, 1936], p. 390).

92. *Collected Letters*, IV, 574.

93. *The Collected Writings of Thomas De Quincey*, ed. David Masson (Edinburgh, 1889–90), II, 153.

94. *Poetry and Prose of Blake*, p. 499.

95. *Coleridge the Visionary*, p. 287.

96. *Collected Letters*, IV, 706.

97. *Patterns of Consciousness: An Essay on Coleridge* (Amherst, Mass., 1969), p. 81.

98. Tetens, I, iii.    99. *Ibid.*, p. xxix.    100. *Ibid.*, pp. iii–iv.

101. Coleridge speaks in the *Biographia Literaria* of "Hartley's hypothetical vibrations in his hypothetical oscillating ether of the nerves" (I, 74). As early as November, 1794, Coleridge writes of a "diligent, I *may* say, an intense study of Locke, Hartley and others who have written most wisely on the Nature of Man" (*Collected Letters*, I, 126). By December of that year he announces that "I am a compleat Necessitarian—and understand the subject as well almost as Hartley himself" (*Collected Letters*, I, 137).

102. Tetens, I, viii–ix. Forty years later Coleridge says that "it is fashionable to smile at Hartley's vibrations and vibratiuncles; and his work has been re-edited by Priestley, with the omission of the *material* hypothesis" (*Biographia*, I, 76).

103. *Notebooks*, II, 2093.    104. Tetens, I, ix.

105. *An Essay Concerning Human Understanding*, I, 121–22.

106. *Ibid.*, p. 123.    107. *Ibid.*, p. 124.

108. In fact, if one wishes to identify an event and a date as the origin of Romanticism, the publication of the *Nouveaux essais* in 1765 might be as good a candidate for this elusive honor as the outbreak of the French Revolution in 1789, the publication of *Lyrical Ballads* in 1798, or the appearance of Friedrich Schlegel's Fragment 116 in 1798. For not only did the *Nouveaux essais*, by its emphasis on "petites perceptions," open up a twilight world closed off by Descartes and undreamt of by Locke (*Die philosophischen Schriften von Gottfried Wilhelm Leibniz*, ed. C. J. Gerhardt [Berlin, 1875–90], V, 46–48), but the work called renewed attention to Leibniz's vision of "la matière organique par tout" (V, 65), and to his conception of "puissance active" or "la Force"—of

*"Forces agissantes primitives"* (V, 156). In his conception of "puissance active," both in matter and in the soul, Leibniz prepared the way both for the egotism and for the metaphorical, metaphysical, and physical dynamism that were hallmarks of Romanticism. In his conception of the organic he foreshadowed that emphasis on the organic view of nature that Whitehead has described as the essence of the Romantic reaction against eighteenth-century mechanism. And in his emphasis on "petites perceptions" he instituted the theory of the unconscious mind and of the importance of dreams—both of incalculable effect for Romanticism (see, e.g., Albert Béguin, *L'Ame romantique et le rêve* [Paris, 1939]). G. H. Schubert's *Symbolik des Traumes*, which was read by Coleridge and influenced Freud (see, e.g., Ernest Jones, *The Life and Work of Sigmund Freud* [New York, 1953–57], II, 312), arose out of ground fertilized by the *Nouveaux essais*. "The body," Leibniz said, "responds to all the soul's thought, rational or not, and dreams have also their marks in the brain as well as the thought of those who are awake" (*Philosophische Schriften*, V, 106).

109. *Uber die allgemeine speculativische Philosophie*, p. 91.

110. *Philosophische Schriften*, V, 99. This was not a new attitude on Leibniz's part. In 1686, some four years before the publication of Locke's *Essay Concerning Human Understanding*, he had declared himself against the *tabula rasa*: ". . . it is a bad habit we have of thinking as if our souls received certain *especes* as messengers and as if it had doors and windows. We have all these forms in our own minds, and even from all time, because the mind always expresses all its future thought and already thinks confusedly of everything of which it will ever think distinctly. Nothing can be taught us the idea of which is not already in our minds, as the matter out of which this thought is formed. This Plato has excellently recognized when he puts forward his doctrine of reminiscence. . . . Aristotle preferred to compare our souls to tablets that are still blank but upon which there is a place for writing and maintained that there is nothing in our understanding that does not come from the senses. This conforms more with popular notions, as Aristotle usually does, while Plato goes deeper" (*Philosophische Schriften*, IV, 451–52).

111. *Philosophische Schriften*, V, 67.

112. The "puissance active" of the *Nouveaux essais* (see above, n. 108) was the "vis insita" of *De ipsa natura*, which "produces immanent actions, or what is the same thing, acts immanently" (*Philosophische Schriften*, IV, 510). As Leibniz says in that treatise, his opinions "de vi insita" were "first published in the *Acta Eruditorum* of Leipzig in March, 1694, and further elaborated in my *Specimen dynamicum* in the same journal for April, 1695"—where the force was called "vis activa" (*Philosophische Schriften*, IV, 516). See below, n. 139.

113. Cassirer, *The Philosophy of the Enlightenment*, pp. 124–25. Cf. Leibniz, *Philosophische Schriften*, VI, 616; IV, 485.

114. Cassirer, *Philosophy of the Enlightenment*, p. 125. Cf. the statement of Lewis White Beck that Tetens provided "an important recognition of the activity involved in knowing, which from now on in the history of philosophy is to be seen as an activity, not as a passive contemplation of pictures in the mind. No one in the eighteenth century between Leibniz and Kant so clearly saw the active aspects of knowing" (*Early German Philosophy: Kant and His Predecessors* [Cambridge, Mass., 1969], p. 418).

115. *Biographia*, I, 93. Cf. Leibniz: "On m'opposera cet axiome receu parmy les Philosophes, *que rien n'est dans l'ame qui ne vienne des sens*. Mais il faut excepter l'ame meme et ses affections. *Nihil est in intellectu, quod non fuerit in sensu*, excipe: *nisi ipse intellectus*. Or l'ame renferme l'estre, la substance, l'un, le même, la cause, la perception, la raisonnement, et quantité d'autres notions, que le sens ne sauroient donner" (*Philosophische Schriften*, V, 100–1).

116. E.g. "Geometry, optics, astronomy—these works of the human mind, these irrefutable proofs of its greatness, are real and well-founded branches of knowledge. By what principles does human reason build such immense edifices?. . . . It is in such enterprises that *Denkkraft* must be revealed in its greatest energy" (Tetens, I, 428–29). For the place of *Denkkraft* in Tetens's scheme see above, no. 65.

117. Tetens, I, 116.

118. *Ibid.*, pp. 116–17. The winged horse is an image that appears elsewhere in philosophical discussion as to the nature of perception, e.g., in Spinoza, *Ethica* II. 49, Scholium, and in William James, *The Principles of Psychology* (New York, 1890), II, 289.

119. *Ibid.*, pp. 117–18.

120. *Ibid.*, p. 139. Cf. Burke in 1757: "Besides the ideas . . . which are presented by the sense; the mind of man possesses a sort of creative power of its own; either in representing at pleasure the images of things in the order and manner in which they were received by the senses, or in combining those images in a new manner, and according to a different order. This power is called Imagination; and to this belongs whatever is called wit, fancy, invention, and the like. But it must be observed, that this power of the imagination is incapable of producing any thing absolutely new; it can only vary the disposition of those ideas which it has received from the senses" (*A Philosophical Enquiry into the Origin of Our Ideas of the Sublime and Beautiful*, ed. James T. Boulton [London, 1967], pp. 16–17).

121. Tetens, I, 162.          122. *Ibid.*, p. 164.

123. *Collected Letters*, II, 709. To Thomas Poole, March 23, 1801.

124. *Ibid.*, p. 706. To Poole, March 16, 1801.

125. It is clear at any rate that by that time Coleridge was aware of Leibniz's opposition to the tradition of Locke; e.g., see his letter to Josiah Wedgwood in February, 1801: "Now Leibnitz not only opposed the Philosophy of Locke . . ." (*Collected Letters*, II, 702). I rather feel, however, that Kant, as is traditionally the view, should be ascribed a larger part in the conversion—mainly because Coleridge's passage about overthrowing the doctrine of association also talks of extricating the "notions of Time, and Space." The reference could, of course, be to Leibniz, but Kant seems more likely. It is important to remember, however, that Coleridge was reading Leibniz at the same time and as intensely as he was Kant; and to syncretize the two would have been a characteristic procedure on his part. As he writes, in February of 1801: "I turn at times half

reluctantly from Leibnitz or Kant even to read a smoking new newspaper/such a purus putus Metaphysicus am I become" (*Collected Letters*, II, 676). He had announced his intention to read Leibniz in June, 1800 (*ibid.*, I, 590), and was trying to see his works at the Durham library in July, 1801 (*ibid.*, II, 747).

126. We may see this in a letter written during the actual composition of the *Biographia*. Speaking in 1815 of his "Autobiographia literaria, or Sketches of my literary Life & opinions as far as Poetry and *poetical* Criticism is concerned," Coleridge says that one of "the foundation Stones of the Constructive or Dynamic Philosophy in opposition to the merely mechanic" will be "a disquisition on the powers of association, with the History of the Opinions on this subject from Aristotle to Hartley, and on the generic difference between the faculties of Fancy and Imagination" (*Collected Letters*, IV, 578–79; to R. H. Brabant, July 29, 1815). In the interests of our understanding of the continuity of Coleridge's intellectual endeavor, however, it must be stressed that the *Biographia*'s attempt to elucidate imaginative function elaborates, rather than rejects or replaces, a realization arrived at as early as 1796, by which "Fancy [i.e., imagination] is the power/That first unsensualises the dark mind . . ./ Emancipates it from the grosser thrall/ Of the present impulse" (*The Complete Poetical Works of Samuel Taylor Coleridge*, ed. Ernest Hartley Coleridge [Oxford, 1912], I, 134). Also by 1796 (a date, incidentally, clearly in advance of his knowledge either of Tetens or of Kant) Coleridge had seen that the "Doctrine of necessity" is "rendered not dangerous by the Imagination" (*Notebooks*, I, 156). See further my *Coleridge and the Pantheist Tradition*, pp. 157–58.

127. *Biographia*, I, 92.

128. Hartley's own view of imagination made no provision at all for *Dichtkraft* or for secondary imagination. "The Recurrence of Ideas," he says, "especially visible or audible ones, in a vivid manner, but without a regard to the Order observed in past Facts, is ascribed to the Power of Imagination or Fancy" (*Observations on Man, His Frame, His Duty, and His Expectations* [London, 1749], I, 383).

129. *Biographia*, I, 81. Hartley had said that *"Sensations"* were "those internal Feelings of the Mind, which arise from the Impressions made by external Objects upon the several Parts of our Bodies. . . . The Ideas which resemble Sensations, are called *Ideas:* All the rest may therefore be called *Intellectual Ideas.* It will appear in the Course of these Observations, that the *Ideas of Sensation* are the Elements of which all the rest are compounded" (*Observations on Man*, I, ii). Coleridge's objection to such a view was that it destroyed the meaning of human action and personality. "The assumption," he says, that ". . . all acts of thought . . . are parts and products of this blind mechanism, instead of being distinct powers, whose function is to controul, determine, and modify the phantasmal chaos of association," subordinates "final to efficient causes in the human being," and makes the "soul" a mere "ens logicum," something "worthless and ludicrous" (*Biographia*, I, 81).

130. We can see very clearly the superimposition of "I am"-controlled secondary imagination on associationist fancy in Coleridge's statement that "images, however beautiful, though faithfully copied from nature . . . do not of themselves characterize the poet. They become proofs of original genius only as far as they are modified by a predominant passion . . . or when they have the effect of reducing multitude to unity . . . or lastly, when a human and intellectual life is transferred to them from the poet's own spirit" (*Biographia*, II, 16). Compare Tetens's statements about Linnaeus and Milton adduced on p. 212 above. *Dichtkraft* intrudes into the law of association (see p. 211 above), and this, for Coleridge, was what the activity of thought itself did. Crabb Robinson reports his conversation: "Thought . . . is a laborious breaking through the law of association" (*Miscellaneous Criticism*, p. 389). Again, in December, 1803: ". . . the *streamy* Nature of Association, which Thinking = Reason, curbs & rudders" (*Notebooks*, I, 1770). Indeed, if we substitute Tetens's *Denkkraft*, or rational power of thought, for *Dichtkraft*, Coleridge's statements would agree identically with the opinion of Tetens. For the intrusion of *Dichtkraft* itself, cf. the question posed by Tetens: "For

how many moments does the fancy operate in a vital man merely as fancy, according to the rule of association, without having the busy *Dichtkraft* mix itself in, and join together the series of images in a new way?" (Tetens, I, 140).

131. *Scepticism and Poetry: An Essay on the Poetic Imagination* (London, 1937), pp. 18–24. E.g., p. 23: "Such we may believe was the essence of Kant's doctrine in the *Critique of Pure Reason,* and we may reasonably regard it as the source of Coleridge's reflections on the imagination." Cf. James Volant Baker, *The Sacred River: Coleridge's Theory of the Imagination* (Baton Rouge, 1957), e.g., p. 29: "Kant administered the *coup-de-grace* to Hartley."

132. Shawcross, however, goes too far when he says that "it is evident . . . that Coleridge's conception of the imagination was not fundamentally affected by his study of Kant" (Introduction to *Biographia Literaria,* I, xliii). For example, a statement in Chapter Seven of the *Biographia* sounds thoroughly Kantian: "There are evidently two powers at work, which relatively to each other are active and passive; and this is not possible without an intermediate faculty, which is at once both active and passive. (In philosophical language, we must denominate this intermediate faculty in all its degrees and determinations, the IMAGINATION)" (*Biographia,* I, 86). See further my *Coleridge and the Pantheist Tradition,* pp. 33–34, 306–10. Coleridge, impelled by his commitment to system and his urge to reconcile, customarily syncretized his sources. His major ideas exhibit a blending of his own thought with these syncretisms rather than an exclusive allegiance to a single source. For instance, though his insistence that the imagination "dissolves, diffuses, dissipates" (*Biographia,* I, 202) utilizes terms unique to Tetens (see above, n. 76), his statement that the imagination is a "synthetic" power (*Biographia,* II, 12) takes up a term emphasized not by Tetens but by Kant, e.g.: "Synthesis in general . . . is the mere result of the power of imagination, a blind but indispensable function of the soul, without which we should have no knowledge whatsoever . . ."; ". . . the pure synthesis of imagination"; "the reproductive synthesis of the imagination is to be counted among the transcendental acts of the mind"; "we must assume a pure transcendental

synthesis of imagination as conditioning the very possibility of all experience" (*Kant's gesammelte Schriften*, IV, 64, 88, 79, 78).

133. H. J. de Vleeschauwer, *La Déduction transcendentale dans l'oeuvre de Kant* (Antwerp, Paris, The Hague, 1934–37), I, 290.

134. *Ibid.*, p. 299.

135. *Ibid.*, p. 315. As Hamann wrote to Herder in May, 1779: "Kant is at work on his Ethics of Pure Reason and always has Tetens lying before him" (*Johann Georg Hamann Briefwechsel*, ed. Arthur Henkel, IV [Wiesbaden, 1959], 81).

136. For Leibniz, "each monad is a living mirror, or a mirror endowed with an internal action (*action interne*) . . . it represents the universe according to its point of view"; it is "the nature of the monad to represent" (*Philosophische Schriften*, VI, 599, 617). Thus the representational activity or *vis representativa* is a form of the *vis activa* or primary substance. Cf. Beck, *Early German Philosophy*, p. 282: "Leibniz . . . had emphasized the spontaneous creativity of consciousness in its representations, even in its perception of the world; the representative power (*vis representativa*), with the emphasis upon the power, has its most natural and characteristic function in the creation of images not given ready-made to the senses." Furthermore, this power of representation is an image of God's, and thus prefigures Coleridge's description of the secondary imagination as an echo of the primary, which is itself a "repetition in the finite mind of the eternal act of creation in the infinite I AM." As Leibniz says, "The spirit not only has a perception of the works of God but is even capable of producing something which resembles them, though in miniature"; "In its own realm and in the small world in which it is allowed to act, the soul imitates what God performs in the great world" (*Philosophische Schriften*, VI, 604, 605). This, of course, is a Platonic thought of venerable antiquity, and Coleridge could know it from sources other than Leibniz. See, e.g., Sir Philip Sidney: "but rather give right honor to the heavenly maker of that maker, who having made man to his owne likenes, set him beyond and over all the workes of that second nature, which in nothing he sheweth so much as in Poetry;

when with the force of a divine breath, he bringeth things foorth surpassing her doings" (*The Prose Works of Sir Philip Sidney*, ed. Albert Feuillerat, III [Cambridge, 1963], 8–9). For Coleridge's knowledge of the phrase *vis representativa* see *Biographia*, I, 90.

137. *Notebooks*, II, 2057. Note the similarity of this statement to the passages at nn. 140 and 141 below.

138. *Biographia*, I, 195.

139. *Leibnizens mathematische Schriften*, ed. C. I. Gerhardt, VI (Halle, 1860), 236: "Duplex autem est *Vis Activa* . . . nempe ut *primitiva*, quae in omni substantia corporea per se inest . . . aut *derivativa*. . . . Et primitiva quidem (quae nihil aliud est quam ἐντελέχεια ἡ πρώτη) *animae* vel *formae substantiali* respondet. . . ." Cf. *Philosophische Schriften*, IV, 512. It seems possible and even perhaps probable that Coleridge's "primary" imagination owes its name to Leibniz's "primitive" active force, and equally so that "secondary" imagination reflects in its own name Locke's concession of a "secondary perception" that depends on "will" (see above, n. 24).

140. *Biographia*, I, 195; *Leibnizens mathematische Schriften*, VI, 241–42. Coleridge, significantly, changes Leibniz's Latin word "imaginationi" to "phantasiae."

141. *Philosophische Schriften*, IV, 509: "Surely if corporeal things contained nothing but matter, they could most truly be said to consist of a flux and to have nothing substantial, as the Platonists long ago recognized."

142. *Phaedo* 72E-75E; *Meno* 81C-D.

143. E.g., *Philosophische Schriften*, IV, 451–52; V, 42.

144. *Kant's gesammelte Schriften*, III, 518. Cf. Coleridge: "God created man in his own image. . . . gave us REASON . . . gave us CONSCIENCE—that law of conscience, which . . . unconditionally *commands* us attribute *reality*, and actual *existence*, to those ideas and to those only, without which the conscience itself would be baseless and contradictory, to the ideas of Soul, of Free-will, of Im-

mortality, and of God!" (*The Friend,* ed. Barbara E. Rooke [London, 1969], I, 112.) It is, furthermore, significant that the first epigraph to Chapter Thirteen of the *Biographia* is Milton's "O Adam, One Almighty is, from whom/ All things proceed, and up to him return . . ." (I, 195). Again, see Coleridge's statement that "the free-will" is "our only absolute *self*" (*Biographia,* I, 80), or the concluding words of the *Biographia* about preserving "the Soul steady and collected in its pure *Act* of inward adoration to the great I AM and to the filial WORD that re-affirmeth it from Eternity to Eternity . . ." (II, 218). Cf., e.g., Leibniz, *Philosophische Schriften,* V, 65.

HAROLD BLOOM

COLERIDGE: THE ANXIETY OF INFLUENCE

*Coleridge* observed that "psychologically, Consciousness is the problem," and he added somberly: "almost all is yet to be achieved." How much he achieved, Kathleen Coburn and others are showing us. My concern here is the sadder one of speculating yet again why he did not achieve more as a poet. Walter Jackson Bate has meditated, persuasively and recently, upon Coleridge's human and literary anxieties, particularly in regard to the burden of the past and its inhibiting poetic splendors. I swerve away from Mr. Bate to center the critical meditation upon what might be called the poetics of anxiety, the process of misprision by which any latecomer strong poet attempts to clear an imaginative space for himself. Coleridge could have been a strong poet, as strong as Blake or Wordsworth. He could have been another mighty antagonist for the Great Spectre Milton to engage and, yes, to overcome, but not without contests as titanic as *The Four Zoas* and *The Excursion,* and parental victories as equivocal as *Jerusalem* and *The Prelude*. But we have no such poems by Coleridge. When my path winds home at the end of this essay, I will speculate as to what these poems should have been. As critical fathers for my quest I invoke first, Oscar Wilde, with his glorious principle that the highest criticism sees the object as in itself it really is not, and second, Wilde's critical father, Walter Pater, whose essay of 1866 on "Coleridge's Writings" seems to me still the best short treatment of Coleridge, and this after a century of commentary. Pater, who knew his debt to Coleridge, knew also the anxiety Coleridge caused him, and Pater therefore came to a further and subtler knowing. In the Organic Analogue, against which the entire soul of the great Epicurean critic rebelled, Pater recognized the product of Coleridge's profound anxieties as a creator. I begin therefore with Pater on Coleridge, and then will move immediately deep into the Coleridgean interior, to look upon Coleridge's fierce refusal to take on the ferocity of the strong poet.

This ferocity, as both Coleridge and Pater well knew, expresses itself as a near-solipsism, an Egotistical Sublime, or Miltonic godlike stance. From 1795 on, Coleridge knew, loved, envied, was both cheered and darkened by the largest instance of that Sublime since Milton himself. He studied constantly, almost involuntarily, the glories of the truly modern strong poet, Wordsworth. Whether he gave Wordsworth rather more than he received, we cannot be certain; we know only that he wanted more from Wordsworth than he received, but then it was his endearing though exasperating weakness that he always needed more love than he could get, no matter how much he got: "To be beloved is all I need,/ And whom I love, I love indeed."

Pater understood what he called Coleridge's "peculiar charm," but he resisted it in the sacred name of what he called the "relative" spirit against Coleridge's archaizing "absolute" spirit. In gracious but equivocal tribute to Coleridge he observed:

> The literary life of Coleridge was a disinterested struggle against the application of the relative spirit to moral and religious questions. Everywhere he is restlessly scheming to apprehend the absolute; to affirm it effectively; to get it acknowledged. Coleridge failed in that attempt, happily even for him, for it was a struggle against the increasing life of the mind itself. . . . How did his choice of a controversial interest, his determination to affirm the absolute, weaken or modify his poetic gift?

To affirm the absolute, Pater says, or as we might say, to reject all dualisms except those sanctioned by orthodox Christian thought; this is not *materia poetica* for the start of the nineteenth century, and if we think of a poem like the "Hymn before Sunrise in the Vale of Chamouni," then we are likely to agree with Pater. We will agree also when he contrasts Wordsworth favorably with Coleridge, and even with Goethe, commending Wordsworth for "that flawless temperament . . . which keeps his conviction of a latent intelligence in nature within the limits of sentiment or instinct, and confines it to those delicate and subdued shades of expression which perfect art allows." Pater goes on to say that Coleridge's version of Wordsworth's instinct is a philosophical idea, which means that Coleridge's poetry had to be "more dramatic, more self-conscious" than Wordsworth's. But this in turn, Pater insists, means that for aesthetic success ideas must be held loosely, in the relative spirit. One idea that Coleridge did not hold

loosely was the Organic Analogue, and it becomes clearer as
we proceed in Pater's essay that the aesthetic critic is building toward a passionate assault upon the Organic principle.
He quotes Coleridge's description of Shakespeare as "a nature
humanized, a genial understanding, directing self-consciously
a power and an implicit wisdom deeper even than our consciousness." "There," Pater comments, with bitter eloquence,
" 'the absolute' has been affirmed in the sphere of art; and
thought begins to congeal." With great dignity Pater adds
that Coleridge has "obscured the true interest of art." By lik-
ening the work of art to a living organism, Coleridge does
justice to the impression the work may give us, but he "does
not express the process by which that work was produced."

M. H. Abrams, in his *The Mirror and the Lamp,* defends
Coleridge against Pater by insisting that Coleridge knew his
central problem: "was to use analogy with organic growth to
account for the spontaneous, the inspired, and the self-evolv-
ing in the psychology of invention, yet not to commit himself
as far to the elected figure as to minimize the supervention of
the antithetic qualities of foresight and choice." Though
Abrams called Pater "short-sighted," I am afraid the critical
palms remain with the relative spirit, for Pater's point was
not that Coleridge had no awareness of the dangers of using
the Organic Analogue, but rather that awareness, here as
elsewhere, was no salvation for Coleridge. The issue is
whether Coleridge, not Shakespeare, was able to direct
"self-consciously a power and an implicit wisdom deeper
than consciousness." Pater's complaint is valid because Coleridge, in describing Shakespeare, Dante, Milton, keeps repeating his absolute formula that poems grow from within

themselves, that their "wholeness is not in vision or conception, but in an inner feeling of totality and absolute being." As Pater says, "that exaggerated inwardness is barren" because it "withdraws us too far from what we can see, hear, and feel," because it cheats the senses and the emotions of their triumph. I urge Pater's wisdom here not only against Coleridge, though I share Pater's love for Coleridge, but against the formalist criticism that continued in Coleridge's absolute spirit.

What is the imaginative source of Coleridge's disabling hunger for the Absolute? On August 9, 1831, about three years before he died, he wrote in his Notebook: "From my earliest recollection I have had a consciousness of Power without Strength—a perception, an experience, of more than ordinary power with an inward sense of Weakness. . . . More than ever do I feel this now, when all my fancies still in their integrity are, as it were, drawn *inward* and by their suppression and compression rendered a mock substitute for Strength." Here again is Pater's barren and exaggerated inwardness, but in a darker context than the Organic principle provided.

This context is Milton's "universe of death," where Coleridge apprehended death-in-life as being "the wretchedness of *division*." If we stand in that universe, then "we think of ourselves as separated beings, and place nature in antithesis to the mind, as object to subject, thing to thought, death to life." To be so separated is to become, Coleridge says, "a soul-less fixed star, receiving no rays nor influences into my Being, *a Solitude which I so tremble at, that I cannot attribute it even to the Divine Nature.*" This, we can say, is Coleridge's

Counter-Sublime, his answer to the anxiety of influence in strong poets. The fear of solipsism is greater in him than the fear of not individuating his own imagination.

As with every other major Romantic, the prime precursor poet for Coleridge was Milton. There is a *proviso* to be entered here; for all these poets—Blake, Wordsworth, Shelley, Coleridge (only Keats is an exception)—there is a greater Sublime poetry behind Milton, but as its author is a people and not a single poet, and as it is far removed in time, its greatness does not inhibit a new imagination, not unless it is taken as the work of the Prime Precursor Himself, to whom all creation belongs. Only Coleridge acquired a doubly Sublime anxiety of influence, among these poets. Beyond the beauty that has terror in it of Milton was beauty more terrible. In a letter to Thelwall, December 17, 1796, Coleridge wrote: "Is not Milton a *sublimer* poet than Homer or Virgil? Are not his Personages more sublimely cloathed? And do you not know, that there is not perhaps *one* page in Milton's Paradise Lost, in which he has not borrowed his imagery from the *Scriptures?*—I allow, and rejoice that *Christ* appealed only to the understanding & the affections; but I affirm that, after reading Isaiah, or St. Paul's Epistle to the Hebrews, Homer & Virgil are disgustingly *tame* to me, & Milton himself barely tolerable." Yet these statements are rare in Coleridge. Frequently, Milton seems to blend with the ultimate Influence, which I think is a normal enough procedure. In 1796, Coleridge also says, in his review of Burke's *Letter to a Noble Lord:* "It is lucky for poetry, that Milton did not live in our days." Here Coleridge moves toward the center of his concern, and we should remember his formula: "Shakespeare was all men, potentially, except Milton." This leads to a more ambiguous formula, reported to us of a lecture that Coleridge gave on November 28, 1811: "Shakespeare became all things well into which he infused himself, while all forms, all things became Milton—the poet ever present to our minds and more than gratifying us for the loss of the distinct individuality of what he represents." Though Coleridge truly professes himself more than gratified, he admits loss. Milton's greatness is purchased at the cost of something dear to Coleridge, a principle of difference he knows may be flooded out by his monistic yearnings. For Milton, to Coleridge, is a mythic monad in himself. Commenting upon the apostrophe to light at the commencement of the third book of *Paradise Lost,* Coleridge notes: "In all modern poetry in Christendom there is an under consciousness of a sinful nature, a fleeting away of external things, the mind or subject greater than the object, the reflective character predominant. In the Paradise Lost the sublimest parts are the revelations of Milton's own mind, producing itself and evolving its own greatness; and this is truly so, that when that which is merely entertaining for its objective beauty is introduced, it at first seems a discord." This might be summarized as: where Milton is not, nature is barren, and its significance is that Milton is permitted just such a solitude as Coleridge trembles to imagine for the Divine Being.

Humphry House observed that "Coleridge was quite unbelievably modest about his own poems; and the modesty was of a curious kind, sometimes rather humble and over-elaborate." As House adds, Coleridge "dreaded publication" of his poetry, and until 1828, when he was fifty-six, there was nothing like an adequate gathering of his verse. Wordsworth's attitude was no help, of course, and the Hutchinson girls and

Dorothy no doubt followed Wordsworth in his judgments. There was Wordsworth, and before him there had been Milton. Coleridge presumably knew what "Tintern Abbey" owed to "Frost at Midnight," but this knowledge nowhere found expression. Must we resort to psychological speculation in order to see what inhibited Coleridge, or are there more reliable aids available?

In the *Biographia Literaria* Coleridge is not very kind to his pre-Wordsworthian poetry, and particularly to the "Religious Musings." Yet this is where we must seek what went wrong with Coleridge's ambitions, here, and if there were space, in "The Destiny of Nations" fragments (not its arbitrarily yoked-together form of 1817), and in the "Ode to the Departing Year" and "Monody on the Death of Chatterton" in its earlier versions. After Wordsworth had descended upon Coleridge, supposedly as a "know-thyself" admonition from heaven, but really rather more like a new form of the Miltonic blight, then Coleridge's poetic ambitions sustained another kind of inhibition. The Miltonic shadow needs to be studied first in early Coleridge, before a view can be obtained of his maturer struggles with influence.

With characteristic self-destructiveness, Coleridge gave "Religious Musings" the definitive subtitle: "A Desultory Poem, Written on the Christmas Eve of 1794." The root-meaning of "desultory" is "vaulting," and though Coleridge consciously meant that his poem skipped about and wavered, his imagination meant "vaulting," for "Religious Musings" is a wildly ambitious poem. "This is the time," it begins, in direct recall of Milton's "Nativity" Hymn, yet it follows not the Hymn but the most sublime moments of *Paradise Lost*, particularly the invocation to Book III. As with the 1802 "Hymn

before Sunrise," its great fault as a poem is that it never stops
whooping; in its final version I count well over one hundred
exclamation-points in just over four hundred lines. Whether
one finds this habit in Coleridge distressing or endearing
hardly matters; he just never could stop doing it. He whoops
because he vaults; he is a high-jumper of the Sublime, and
psychologically he could not avoid this. I quote the poem's
final passage, with relish and with puzzlement, for I am uncertain as to how good after all it may not be, though it does
seem palpably awful. Yet its awfulness is at least Sublime; it
is not the drab, flat awfulness of Wordsworth at *his* common
worst in *The Excursion* or even (heresy to admit this!) in so
many passages of *The Prelude* that we hastily skip by, with
our zeal and relief in getting at the great moments. Having
just shouted out his odd version of Berkeley, that "Life is a
vision shadowy of truth," Coleridge sees "the veiling clouds
retire" and God appears in a blaze upon His Throne. Raised
to a pitch of delirium by this vision, Coleridge soars aloft to
join it:

> Contemplant Spirits! ye that hover o'er
> With untired gaze the immeasurable fount
> Ebullient with creative Deity!
> And ye of plastic power, that interfused
> Roll through the grosser and material mass
> In organizing surge! Holies of God!
> (And what if Monads of the infinite mind?)
> I haply journeying my immortal course
> Shall sometime join your mystic choir! Till then
> I discipline my young and novice thought
> In ministeries of heart-stirring song,
> And aye on Meditation's heaven-ward wing

> Soaring aloft I breathe the empyreal air
> Of Love, omnific, omnipresent Love,
> Whose day-spring rises glorious in my soul
> As the great Sun, when he his influence
> Sheds on the frost-bound waters—The glad stream
> Flows to the ray and warbles as it flows.

Scholars agree that this not terribly pellucid passage some-how combines an early Unitarianism with a later orthodox overlay, as well as quantities of Berkeley, Hartley, Newton, Neo-Platonism, and possibly more esoteric matter. A mere reader will be reminded primarily of Milton, and will be in the right, for Milton counts here and the rest do not. The Spirits Coleridge invokes are Miltonic Angels, though their functions seem to be more complicated. Coleridge confidently assures himself and us that his course is immortal, that he may end up as a Miltonic angel, and so perhaps also a Monad of the infinite mind. In the meantime, he will study Milton's "heart-stirring song." Otherwise, all he needs is Love, which is literally the air he breathes, the sunrise radiating out of his soul in a stream of song, and the natural Sun toward which he flows, a Sun that is not distinct from God. If we re-flect on how palpably sincere this is, how wholehearted, and consider what was to be Coleridge's actual poetic course, then we will be moved. Moved to what? Well, perhaps to re-member a remark of Coleridge's: "There are many men, espe-cially at the outset of life, who, in their too eager desire for the end, overlook the difficulties in the way; there is another class, who see nothing else. The first class *may* sometimes fail; the latter rarely succeed." Whatever the truth of this for other men, no man becomes a strong poet unless he starts out with a certain obliviousness of the difficulties in the way. But soon enough he will meet those difficulties, and one of them will be that his precursor and inspirer threatens to subsume him, as Coleridge is subsumed by Milton in "Religious Musings" and his other pre-Wordsworthian poems. And here, I shall digress massively, before returning to Coleridge's poetry, for I enter now upon the enchanted and baleful ground of poetic influence, through which I am learning to find my way by a singular light, which will bear a little explanation.

I do not believe that poetic influence is simply something that happens, that it is just the process by which ideas and images are transmitted from earlier to later poets. On that view, whether or not influence causes anxiety in the later poet is a matter of temperament and circumstance. Poetic influence thus reduces to source-study, of the kind performed upon Coleridge by Lowes and later scholars. Coleridge was properly scornful of such study, and I think most critics learn how barren an enterprise it turns out to be. I myself have no use for it as such, and what I mean by the study of poetic influence turns source-study inside out. The first principle of the proper study of poetic influence, as I conceive it, is that no strong poem has sources and no strong poem merely alludes to another poem. The meaning of a strong poem *is* another strong poem, a precursor's poem which is being misinterpreted, revised, corrected, evaded, twisted askew, made to suffer an inclination or bias which is the property of the later and not the earlier poet. Poetic influence, in this sense, is actually poetic misprision, a poet's taking or doing amiss of a parent-poem that keeps *finding* him, to use a Coleridgean turn-of-phrase. Yet even this misprision is only the first step that a new poet takes when he advances from the early phase where his precursor floods him, to a more Promethean phase where he quests for his own fire, which nevertheless must be stolen from his precursor.

I count some half-dozen steps in the life-cycle of the strong poet, as he attempts to convert his inheritance into what will aid him without inhibiting him by the anxiety of a failure in priority, a failure to have begotten himself. These steps are revisionary ratios, and for the convenience of shorthand, I find myself giving them arbitrary names, which are proving useful to me, and perhaps can be of use to others. I list them herewith, with descriptions but not examples, as this can only be a brief sketch, and I must get back to Coleridge's poetry, but I hope, with this list helpfully in hand, to find my examples in Coleridge:

1. *Clinamen,* which is poetic misprision proper; I take the word from Lucretius, where it means a "swerve" of the atoms so as to make change possible in the universe. The later poet swerves away from the precursor, by so reading the parent-poem as to execute a *clinamen* in relation to it. This appears as the corrective movement of his own poem, which implies that the precursor poem went accurately up to a certain point, but then should have swerved, precisely in the direction that the new poem moves.

2. *Tessera,* which is completion and antithesis; I take the word not from mosaic-making, where it is still used, but from the ancient Mystery-cults, where it meant a token of recognition, the fragment, say, of a small pot which with the other fragments would reconstitute the vessel. The later poet antithetically "completes" the precursor, by so reading the parent-poem as to retain its terms but to mean them in an opposite sense, as though the precursor had failed to go far enough.

3. *Kenosis,* which is a breaking-device similar to the

defense mechanisms our psyches employ against repetition-compulsions; *kenosis,* then, is a movement toward discontinuity with the precursor. I take the word from St. Paul, where it means the humbling or emptying-out of Jesus by himself, when he accepts reduction from Divine to human status. The later poet, apparently emptying himself of his own afflatus, his imaginative godhood, seems to humble himself as though he ceased to be a poet, but this ebbing is so performed in relation to a precursor's poem-of-ebbing that the precursor is emptied out also, and so the later poem of deflation is not as absolute as it seems.

4. *Daemonization,* or a movement toward a personalized Counter-Sublime, in reaction to the precursor's Sublime; I take the term from general Neo-Platonic usage, where an intermediary being, neither Divine nor human, enters into the adept to aid him. The later poet opens himself to what he believes to be a power in the parent-poem that does not belong to the parent proper, but to a range of being just beyond that precursor. He does this, in his poem, by so stationing its relation to the parent-poem as to generalize away the uniqueness of the earlier work.

5. *Askesis,* or a movement of self-purgation which intends the attainment of a state of solitude; I take the term, general as it is, particularly from the practice of pre-Socratic shamans like Empedocles. The later poet does not, as in *kenosis,* undergo a revisionary movement of emptying, but of curtailing; he yields up part of his own and imaginative endowment, so as to separate himself from others, including the precursor, and he does this in his poem by so stationing it in regard to the parent-poem as to make that poem undergo an *askesis* also; the precursor's endowment is also truncated.

6. *Apophrades,* or the return of the dead; I take the word from the Athenian dismal or unlucky days upon which the dead returned to reinhabit the houses in which they had lived. The later poet, in his own final phase, already burdened by an imaginative solitude that is almost a solipsism, holds his own poem so open again to the precursor's work that at first we might believe the wheel has come full circle, and that we are back in the later poet's flooded apprenticeship, before his strength began to assert itself in the revisionary ratios of *clinamen* and the others. But the poem is now *held* open to the precursor, where once it *was* open, and the uncanny effect is that the new poem's achievement makes it seem to us, not as though the precursor were writing it, but as though the later poet himself had written the precursor's characteristic work.

These then are six revisionary ratios, and I think they can be observed, usually in cyclic appearance, in the life's work of every post-Enlightenment strong poet, which in English means, for practical purposes, every post-Miltonic strong poet. Coleridge, to return now where I began, had the potential of the strong poet, but declined the full process of developing into one, unlike Blake, Wordsworth, and the major poets after them down to Yeats and Stevens in our time. Yet his work, even in its fragmentary state, demonstrates this revisionary cycle in spite of himself. My ulterior purpose in this discussion is to use Coleridge as an instance because he is apparently so poor an example of the cycle I have sketched. But that makes him a sterner test for my theory of influence than any other poet I could have chosen.

I return to Coleridge's first mature poetry, and to its *clina-*

*men* away from Milton, the Cowperizing turn that gave Coleridge the Conversation Poems, particularly "Frost at Midnight." Hazlitt quotes Coleridge as having said to him in the spring of 1798 that Cowper was the best modern poet, meaning the best since Milton, which was also Blake's judgment. Humphry House demonstrated the relation between "Frost at Midnight" and *The Task*, which is the happy one, causing no anxieties, where a stronger poet appropriates from a weaker one. Coleridge used Cowper as he used Bowles, Akenside, and Collins, finding in all of them hints that could help him escape the Miltonic influx that had drowned out "Religious Musings." "Frost at Midnight," like *The Task*, swerves away from Milton by softening him, by domesticating his style in a context that excludes all Sublime terrors. When Coleridge rises to his blessing of his infant son at the poem's conclusion he is in some sense poetically "misinterpreting" the beautiful declaration of Adam to Eve: "With thee conversing I forget all time," gentling the darker overtones of the infatuated Adam's declaration of love. Or, more simply, like Cowper he is not so much humanizing Milton—that will take the strenuous, head-on struggles of Blake, Wordsworth, Shelley, Keats —as he is making Milton more childlike, or perhaps better, reading Milton as though Milton loved in a more childlike way.

The revisionary step beyond this, an antithetical completion or *tessera,* is ventured by Coleridge only in a few pantheistic passages that sneaked past his orthodox censor, like the later additions to "The Eolian Harp," or the veiled vision at the end of the second verse paragraph of "This Lime-Tree Bower My Prison." With his horror of division, his endless quest for unity, Coleridge could not sustain any revisionary impulse which involved his reversing Milton, or daring to complete that sacred father.

But the next revisionary ratio, the *kenosis* or self-emptying, seems to me almost obsessive in Coleridge's poetry, for what is the total situation of the Ancient Mariner but a repetition-compulsion, which his poet breaks for himself only by the writing of the poem, and then breaks only momentarily. Coleridge had contemplated an Epic on the Origin of Evil, but we may ask: where would Coleridge, if pressed, have located the origin of evil in himself? His Mariner is neither depraved in will nor even disobedient, but is merely ignorant, and the spiritual machinery his crime sets into motion is so ambiguously presented as to be finally beyond analysis. I would ask the question: what was Coleridge trying (not necessarily consciously) to do for himself by writing the poem? and by this question I do not mean Kenneth Burke's notion of trying to do something for oneself as a person. Rather, what was Coleridge the poet trying to do for himself as poet? To which I would answer: trying to free himself from the inhibitions of Miltonic influence, by humbling his poetic self, and so humbling the Miltonic in the process. The Mariner does not empty himself out; he starts empty and acquires a Primary Imagination through his suffering. But, for Coleridge, the poem is a *kenosis*, and what is being humbled is the Miltonic Sublime's account of the Origin of Evil. There is a reduction from disobedience to ignorance, from the self-aggrandizing consciousness of Eve to the painful awakening of a minimal consciousness in the Mariner.

The next revisionary step in clearing an imaginative space for a maturing strong poet is the Counter-Sublime, the attaining of which I have termed *daemonization,* and this I take to be the relation of "Kubla Khan" and "Christabel" to *Paradise Lost.* Far more than "The Rime of the Ancient Mariner," these poems demonstrate a trafficking by Coleridge with powers that are daemonic, even though the "Rime" explicitly invokes Neo-Platonic daemons in its marginal glosses. Opium was the avenging daemon or *alastor* of Coleridge's life, his Dark or Fallen Angel, his experiential acquaintance with Milton's Satan. Opium was for him what wandering and moral taletelling became for the Mariner—the personal shape of repetition-compulsion. The lust for paradise in "Kubla Khan," Geraldine's lust for Christabel; these are manifestations of Coleridge's revisionary daemonization of Milton, these are Coleridge's Counter-Sublime. Poetic Genius, the genial spirit itself, Coleridge must see as daemonic when it is his own, rather than when it is Milton's.

It is at this point in the revisionary cycle that Coleridge begins to back away decisively from the ferocity necessary for the strong poet. He does not sustain his daemonization, closes his eyes in holy dread, stands outside the circumference of the daemonic agent, and is startled by his own sexual daring out of finishing "Christabel." He moved on to the revisionary ratio I have called *askesis,* or the purgation into solitude, the curtailing of some imaginative powers in the name of others. In doing so, he prophesied the pattern for Keats in *The Fall of Hyperion,* since in his *askesis* he struggles against the influence of a composite poetic father, Milton-Wordsworth. The great poems of this *askesis* are "Dejection: An Ode" and "To William Wordsworth," where criticism has demonstrated to us how acute the revision of Wordsworth's stance is, and how much of himself Coleridge purges away to make this revision justified. I would add only that both poems misread Milton as sensitively and desperately as they do Wordsworth; the meaning of "Dejection" is in its relation to "Lycidas" as much as in its relation to the "Intimations" Ode, even as the poem "To William Wordsworth" assimilates *The Prelude* to *Paradise Lost*. Trapped in his own involuntary dualisms, longing for a monistic wholeness such as he believes he is found by in Milton and Wordsworth, Coleridge in his *askesis* declines to see how much of his composite parent-poet he has purged away also.

After that, sadly enough, we have only a very few occasional poems of any quality by Coleridge, and they are mostly not the poems of a strong poet, that is, of a man vaulting into the Sublime. Having refused the full exercise of a strong poet's misprisions, Coleridge ceased to have poetic ambitions. But there is a significant exception, the late manuscript fragment "Limbo" and the evidently still-later fragment "Ne Plus Ultra." Here, and I think here only, Coleridge experiences the particular reward of the strong poet in his last phase, what I have called the *apophrades* or return of the dead, not a Counter-Sublime but a negative Sublime, like the *Last Poems* of Yeats or *The Rock* of Stevens. Indeed, negative sublimity is the mode of these Coleridgean fragments, and indicates to us what Coleridge might have become had he permitted himself enough of the perverse zeal that the great poet must exhibit in malforming his great precursor. "Limbo" and "Ne Plus Ultra" show that Coleridge could have become, at last, the poet of the Miltonic abyss, the bard of Demogorgon. Even as they stand, these fragments make us read Book II of *Paradise Lost* a little differently; they enable Coleridge to claim a corner of Milton's Chaos as his own.

Pater thought that Coleridge had succumbed to the Organic Analogue, because he hungered too intensely for eternity, as Lamb had said of his old school-friend. Pater also quoted De Quincey's summary of Coleridge: "he wanted better bread than can be made with wheat." I would add that Coleridge hungered also for an eternity of generosity between poets, as between people, a generosity that is not allowed in a world where each poet must struggle to individuate his own breath, and this at the expense of his forebears as much as his contemporaries. Perhaps also, to modify De Quincey, Coleridge wanted better poems than can be made without misprision.

I suggest then that the Organic Analogue, with all its pragmatic neglect of the processes by which poems have to be produced, appealed so overwhelmingly to Coleridge because it seemed to preclude the anxiety of influence, and to obviate the poet's necessity not just to unfold like a natural growth but to develop at the expense of others. Whatever the values of the Organic Analogue for literary criticism—and I believe, with Pater, that it does more harm than good—it provided Coleridge with a rationale for a dangerous evasion of inner steps he had to take for his own poetic development. As Blake might have said, Coleridge's imagination insisted upon slaying itself on the stems of generation, or to invoke another Blakean image, Coleridge lay down to sleep upon the Organic Analogue as though it were a Beulah-couch of soft, moony repose.

What was our loss in this? What poems might a stronger Coleridge have composed? The Notebooks list *The Origin of Evil, an Epic Poem, Hymns to the Sun, the Moon, and the Elements—six hymns,* and more fascinating even than these,

a scheme for an epic on "the destruction of Jerusalem" by the
Romans. Still more compelling is a March, 1802, entry in the
Notebooks: "Milton, a Monody in the metres of Samson's
Choruses—only with more rhymes / —poetical influences—
political-moral-Dr. Johnson/" Consider the date of this entry,
only a month before the first draft of "Dejection," and some
sense of what *Milton, a Monody* might have been begins to
be generated. In March, 1802, William Blake, in the midst of
his sojourn at Hayley's Felpham, was deep in the composition
of *Milton: A Poem in 2 Books, to Justify the Ways of God to
Men.* In the brief, enigmatic notes for *Milton, a Monody*
Coleridge sets down "—poetical influences—political-moral-
Dr. Johnson," the last being, we can assume, a refutation of
Johnson's vision of Milton in *The Lives of the Poets,* a refutation that Cowper and Blake would have endorsed. "Poetical
influences" Coleridge says, and we may recall that this is one
of the themes of Blake's *Milton,* where the Shadow of the
Poet Milton is one with the Covering Cherub, the great
blocking-agent who inhibits fresh human creativity by em-
bodying in himself all the sinister beauty of tradition. Blake's
*Milton* is a kind of monody in places, not as a mourning for
Milton, but as Milton's own, solitary utterance, as he goes
down from a premature Eternity (where he is unhappy) to
struggle again in fallen time and space. I take it though that
*Milton, a Monody* would be modeled upon Coleridge's early
"Monody on the Death of Chatterton," and so would have
been Coleridge's lamentation for his Great Original. Whether,
as Blake was doing at precisely the same time, Coleridge
would have dared to identify Milton as the Covering Cherub,
as the angel or daemon blocking Coleridge himself out from

the poet's paradise, I cannot surmise. I wish deeply that Coleridge had written the poem.

It is ungrateful, I suppose, as the best of Coleridge's recent scholars keep telling us, to feel that Coleridge did not give us the poems he had it in him to write. Yet we have, all apology aside, only a double handful of marvelous poems by him. I close therefore by attempting a description of the kind of poem I believe Coleridge's genius owed us, and which we badly need, and always will need. I would maintain that the finest achievement of the High Romantic poets of England was their humanization of the Miltonic Sublime. But when we attend deeply to the works where this humanization is most strenuously accomplished—Blake's *Milton* and *Jerusalem, The Prelude, Prometheus Unbound,* the two *Hyperions,* even in a way *Don Juan*—we sense at last a quality lacking, in which Milton abounds, for all his severity. This quality, though not in itself a tenderness, made Milton's Eve possible, and we miss such a figure in all her Romantic descendants. More than the other five great Romantic poets, Coleridge was able, by temperament and by subtly shaded intellect, to have given us a High Romantic Eve, a total humanization of the tenderest and most appealing element in the Miltonic Sublime. Many anxieties blocked Coleridge from that rare accomplishment, and of these the anxiety of influence was not the least.

MEETING HONORING RUDOLF KIRK

AND ROBERT SPILLER

On Wednesday, September 8, 1971, the chairman, Samuel Hynes, called the Institute to order for its afternoon session and made the following preliminary remarks:

*This* is the thirtieth meeting of the English Institute, and the Supervising Committee has thought it an appropriate occasion on which to pause and pay tribute to some of the men who created the Institute, and have helped it through three decades.

Actually, though this is the thirtieth meeting, the Institute is older than that—it began in 1938. If you fancy gynecological metaphors you might say that it was conceived on a subway platform in Manhattan, and brought to birth on the Upper West Side (which should make the Institute a true citizen of New York). The father of the Institute is here today, and I think he should stand and acknowledge his thirty-two-year-old offspring. Professor Rudolf Kirk.

The first meeting was in session at Columbia in September, 1939, when the German invasion of Poland started the Second World War; after the fourth meeting, 1942, the Institute, like butter and tires and other good things, disappeared for a time. It reappeared when the war ended, and has been going ever since, though, like butter and tires, it has gotten steadily more expensive. If I read the records correctly, the space for the first meeting was provided by Columbia without charge, and the first volume of Institute essays seems to have been published without a subsidy.

The annual volumes of essays are one of the Institute's great distinctions, and a severe test of the serious substance of our meetings, for what sounded persuasive from the lectern doesn't always convince in print. The man behind the essays was Robert Spiller; I would like him to rise and take credit for a very good idea.

I wish, just now, that the Institute were a monarchy, and that we could create life peerages for these distinguished creators of our organization. Since we can't create Lord Kirk, or Baron Spiller of Chestnut Hill, we have done the best we could, and have made them both Life Members of the Institute, the first in the history of the group.

Looking back over the early history of the Institute, one must conclude that there was more money then, and also a good deal more time. The first meeting lasted two weeks; there were twenty-four papers on four subjects, and ten evening lectures. As one old-timer recalls, everyone had plenty of time to take in the World's Fair out in Flushing. The dates —which have from the first meeting been in early September —were originally chosen because "the trans-Atlantic expeditions to European libraries, which in former years would have been a serious obstacle to meetings at this season, were removed from consideration this year (1939) by the embargo imposed by the war." And that's the way traditions get started. At the second meeting, the papers had shrunk to

twenty (there was no World's Fair that year), and gradually
the shrinkage was continued, until at last we have reached a
level that we can all tolerate. It is useful to remind ourselves that these changes have taken place; for it seems likely
that new academic calendars will require further changes. But
a capacity for change is a sign of organic health, and this organism seems very healthy indeed.

Not everything has changed, though. On the first meeting's
program two items are of special note now: a paper by James
Clifford on "Editorial Revisions of Letters," and a lecture by
James Osborn, "Finding Literary Documents." Both Jim Clifford and Jim Osborn have been long-time supporters of the
Institute, and both are now Trustees. The survival of Rudolf
Kirk's good idea owes much to them. It also owes much, of
course, to the loyalty and presence of its regular, continuing
members. According to our records, there is only *one* member
who has been registered for every session. His name leads all
the rest on the first list of participants, for alphabetical reasons, but it now must lead all the rest for loyalty. Professor G.
S. Alleman, of Rutgers University at Newark.

No doubt it is because such men have continued to guide
and support the Institute that it has not only survived but has
maintained its first principles. The first volume of Essays contains this statement, which I think remains true:

> The English Institute . . . is not, as its name might sug-
> gest, an association or an organization; it is simply an as-
> semblage of persons interested in the serious study of Eng-
> lish and American language and literature. The primary
> purpose of the institute is not to provide a forum for
> presenting the results already achieved by individual in-
> vestigators, but to consider essential problems which

must be faced by those undertaking various phases of literary and linguistic research.

This assumes that literary criticism is not a system but an activity, and that our annual meetings are progress reports on that activity, or perhaps the activity itself in action. So it is appropriate that we should celebrate our first thirty years by proceeding with the activity of criticism.

# THE ENGLISH INSTITUTE, 1971

ARCHIVIST

David V. Erdman,
  *State University of New York, Stony Brook, and
  New York Public Library*

CHAIRMAN, 1971 NOMINATING COMMITTEE

Norman Rabkin, *University of California, Berkeley*

## THE PROGRAM

I. Pastoral Modes in Modern Literature
*Directed by Isabel MacCaffrey, Tufts University*

Tues.  9:30 A.M.  The Idyllic Moment: On Pastoral and
Romanticism
*Herbert Lindenberger, Stanford
University*

Tues.  11:00 A.M.  Playful and Prophetic Modes of
Romantic Pastoral
*Lore Metzger, Emory University*

Wed.  9:30 A.M.  Pastoralism as Culture and Counter-
Culture in English Fiction, 1800–1916:
From a View to a Death
*Julian Moynahan, Rutgers University*

Wed.  11:00 A.M.  Notes on Revolutionary Pastoralism
in America
*Leo Marx, Amherst College*

II. The Poetry of Samuel Taylor Coleridge
*Directed by Harold Bloom, Yale University*

Tues.  1:45 P.M.  The Manipulation of Space in
Coleridge's Poetry
*Michael Cooke, Boston University*

| | | |
|---|---|---|
| Tues. | 3:15 P.M. | Origin and Significance of Coleridge's Theory of Secondary Imagination<br>*Thomas McFarland, Graduate Center of the City University of New York* |
| Wed. | 1:45 P.M. | "Positive Negation": Threshold, Sequence, and Personification in the Later Poetry of Coleridge<br>*Angus Fletcher, State University of New York at Buffalo* |
| Wed. | 3:15 P.M. | Coleridge: The Anxiety of Influence<br>*Harold Bloom, Yale University* |

III. Recent Linguistics and Literary Study
*Directed by W. K. Wimsatt, Yale University*

| | | |
|---|---|---|
| Thurs. | 9:30 A.M. | Theory-based Grammars and Traditional Grammar<br>*Ralph B. Long, University of Puerto Rico* |
| Thurs. | 11:00 A.M. | After Babel: Whorf and Chomsky and the Study of Literature<br>*George Steiner, Churchill College, Cambridge University* |
| Fri. | 9:30 A.M. | Sign, Sense, and Roland Barthes<br>*Hugh M. Davidson, The Ohio State University* |
| Fri. | 11:00 A.M. | Roman Jakobson: The Grammar of Poetry and the Poetry of Grammar<br>*Victor Erlich, Yale University* |

IV. The Literature of Fantasy: Children's Literature
*Directed by G. Armour Craig, Amherst College*

| | | |
|---|---|---|
| Thurs. | 1:45 P.M. | The Invention of Childhood<br>*Peter Brooks, Yale University* |
| Thurs. | 3:15 P.M. | Death in Children's Literature<br>*Francelia Butler, University of Connecticut* |

| | | |
|---|---|---|
| Fri. | 1:45 P.M. | Child Reading and Man Reading: Oz, Babar, and Pooh |
| | | *Roger Sale, University of Washington* |
| Fri. | 3:15 P.M. | Women in Fairy Tale and Fiction |
| | | *Alison Lurie, Cornell University* |

Maurianne S. Adams, Smith College; Burt Alimansky, University of California at Berkeley; Gellert S. Alleman, Rutgers University at Newark; Marcia Allentuck, City College, CUNY; Valborg Anderson, Brooklyn College, CUNY; Thomas L. Ashton, University of Massachusetts at Amherst

George W. Bahlke, Kirkland College; James E. Barcus, Houghton College; J. Robert Barth, s.j., Harvard University; Bertrice Bartlett, Stephens College; Phyllis Bartlett, Queens College, CUNY; Adrianne Baytop, Douglass College, Rutgers University; John E. Becker, Fairleigh Dickinson University; Maurice Beebe, Temple University; D. L. Bergdahl, Ohio University; Warner Berthoff, Harvard University; J. Birje-Patil, Yale University; Harold Bloom, Yale University; Max Bluestone, University of Massachusetts at Boston; Julia B. Boken, State University of New York at Oneonta; W. F. Bolton, Douglass College, Rutgers University; Hoyt E. Bowen, Huntingdon College; John D. Boyd, s.j., Fordham University; Frank Brady, Graduate Center, CUNY; Richard E. Brantley, University of Florida; Barbara Breasted, Wellesley College; Nancy Brilliant, Newark State College; Leslie Brisman, Yale University; Paula Brody, State University of New York at Albany; Peter

Brooks, Yale University; Reuben A. Brower, Harvard University; Judith Brown, New York City; Jean R. Buchert, University of North Carolina at Greensboro; James Bunn, State University of New York at Buffalo; Francelia Butler, University of Connecticut

Joseph Cady, Rutgers University; Ronald Campbell, Harcourt, Brace, Jovanovich; James Van Dyck Card, Old Dominion University; Dorothy Carter, Bank Street College of Education; Thomas H. Chalfant, Alabama State University; James L. Clifford, Columbia University; Richard Cody, Amherst College; Sister Anne Gertrude Coleman, College of St. Elizabeth; Arthur N. Collins, State University of New York at Albany; David B. Comer III, Georgia Institute of Technology; Albert S. Cook, State University of New York at Buffalo; Michael Cooke, Boston University; Rosemary Cowler, Lake Forest College; James M. Cox, Dartmouth College; G. Armour Craig, Amherst College; Irving Cummings, University of Connecticut

Curtis Dahl, Wheaton College; Irene Dash, Columbia University; Hugh M. Davidson, Ohio State University; Winifred M. Davis, Columbia University; Robert Adams Day, Queens College, CUNY; Paul De Man, Yale University; Leonard W. Deen, Queens College, CUNY; Daniel A. Dervin, Mary Washington College, University of Virginia; Muriel Dollar, Caldwell College; E. Talbot Donaldson, Yale University; Sister Rose Bernard Donna, c.s.j., College of St. Rose; James Downey, Carleton University; Marya M. Dubose, Augusta College; Georgia Dunbar, Manhattan Community College

Thomas R. Edwards, Rutgers University; Scott Elledge, Cornell University; M. S. Elliott, York University; W. R. Elton, Graduate Center, CUNY; Martha Winburn England, Queens College, CUNY; David V. Erdman, State University of New York and New York Public Library; Victor Erlich, Yale University; Sister Marie Eugenie, Immaculata College

Angus Fletcher, State University of New York at Buffalo; Leslie D. Foster, Northern Michigan University; Robert Foulke, Skidmore College; Charles E. Frank, Illinois College; Barbara Friedberg, Columbia University; Albert B. Friedman, Claremont Graduate

School; William Frost, University of California at Santa Barbara; Northrop Frye, Massey College, University of Toronto

Frederick Garber, State University of New York at Binghamton; Harry R. Garvin, Bucknell University; Michael T. Gasman, Catholic University of America; Marilyn Gaull, Temple University; Blanche H. Gelfant, State University of New York; Janet K. Gezari, Connecticut College; Harry Girling, York University at Toronto; Malcolm Goldstein, Queens College, CUNY; Alfred C. Goodson, Jr., State University of New York at Buffalo; David J. Gordon, Hunter College; Sister Mary Eugene Gotimer, College of Mount St. Vincent; Matthew Grace, Bernard M. Baruch College, CUNY; M. E. Grenander, State University of New York at Albany; Ernest G. Griffin, York University at Ontario; John C. Guilds, University of South Carolina; Allen Guttmann, Amherst College

Robert Hacke, Newark State College; Margaret R. Hale, University of Connecticut; Robert G. Hallwachs, Drexel University; Robert Halsband, University of California at Riverside; Richard Harrier, Washington Square College; Joan E. Hartman, Staten Island Community College; Richard Haven, University of Massachusetts at Amherst; Susan L. Hawk, University of Iowa; Carol A. Hawkes, Finch College; Allen T. Hazen, Columbia University; William W. Heath, Amherst College; James L. Hill, Michigan State University; William Bernard Hill, s.j., University of Scranton; Sister Marion Hoctor, Nazareth College of Rochester; Daniel Hoffman, University of Pennsylvania; Frank S. Hook, Lehigh University; Vivian C. Hopkins, State University of New York at Albany; J. Paul Hunter, Emory University; Kathryn Hunter, Morehouse College; Samuel Hynes, Northwestern University

Helen Irvin, Transylvania University

Mary Lynn Johnson, Georgia State University; Kenneth R. Johnston, Indiana University

Robert P. Kalmey, Shippensburg State College; Hugh T. Keenan, Georgia State University; Robert Kellogg, University of Virginia; Ellen D. Kiehl, State University of New York at Albany; Clara Kirk, University of Illinois at Chicago Circle; Rudolph Kirk, Rutgers University; Frank Krutzke, Colorado College

J. Craig La Driere, Harvard University; Roy Lamson, Massachusetts Institute of Technology; Robert Langbaum, University of Virginia; Jack Levenson, University of Virginia; Claudia Lewis, Bank Street College of Education; Thomas S. W. Lewis, Skidmore College; Herbert Lindenberger, Stanford University; Dwight H. Lindley, Hamilton College; Lawrence Lipking, Princeton University; Lois Anne Logemann, Tufts University; Ralph B. Long, University of Puerto Rico; George de F. Lord, Yale University; Joseph P. Lovering, Canisius College; Sister Alice Lubin, College of Saint Elizabeth; Eben W. Ludlow, Harcourt, Brace, Jovanovich; Alison Lurie, Cornell University

Isabel MacCaffrey, Harvard University; Frank D. McConnell, Northwestern University; Thomas McFarland, Graduate Center, CUNY; Patricia McFate, University of Illinois at Chicago Circle; Thomas A. McGowan, Charlottesville, Virginia; Warren J. MacIsaac, Catholic University of America; Mother Mary Dolores Mackay, Mount St. Ursula; Terence J. McKenzie, U.S. Coast Guard Academy; Irving Malin, CUNY; Alice S. Mandanis, Catholic University of America; Daniel Marder, University of Tulsa; Donald G. Marshall, University of California at Los Angeles; Leo Marx, Amherst College; John Kelly Mathison, University of Wyoming; Donald C. Mell, Jr., University of Delaware; Lore Metzger, Emory University; John H. Middendorf, Columbia University; J. Hillis Miller, Johns Hopkins University; Takuo Miyake, Kyoto University, Japan; Geoffrey Moore, University of Hull, England; Julian Moynahan, Rutgers University; Robert D. Moynihan, State University of New York at Oneonta; Thomas V. Mulvey, St. Francis College

Lowry Nelson, Jr., Yale University; George L. Nesbitt, Hamilton College; William T. Noon, s.j., Le Moyne College; John Norton, University of California at Riverside

Myron Ochshorn, University of South Florida; Richard Ohmann, Wesleyan University; M. Thomas Aquinas O'Reilly, o.s.u., College of New Rochelle; Carol Orr, Princeton University Press; James M. Osborn, Yale University; Charles A. Owen, Jr., University of Connecticut; Patricia Owen, CUNY

Ward Pafford, West Georgia College; Reeve Parker, Cornell University; Robert W. Parker, University of Rochester; Felix L. Paul, West Virginia State College; Harry Pauley, Shippensburg State College; Roy Harvey Pearce, University of California at San Diego; Norman Holmes Pearson, Yale University; Daniel Peck, University of Iowa; Robert Peck, Union College; Marjorie G. Perloff, University of Maryland at Collége Park; Donald Petersen, State University of New York at Oneonta; Henry H. Peyton III, Memphis State University; Barry Phillips, Wellesley College; Robert O. Preyer, Brandeis University; Martin Price, Yale University; William H. Pritchard, Amherst College

Paula J. Quint, Children's Book Council, Inc.

Norman Rabkin, University of California at Berkeley; James Raimes, Oxford University Press; Isabel E. Rathborne, Hunter College; Allen Walker Read, Columbia University; Donald H. Reiman, The Carl H. Pforzheimer Library; P. Gila Reinstein, Northeastern University; Thomas P. Roche, Princeton University; Sally Ronsheim, C. W. Post College; Rebecca D. Ruggles, Brooklyn College, CUNY

Roger Sale, University of Washington; Phillips Salman, Cleveland State University; Irene Samuel, CUNY; James L. Sanderson, Rutgers University; Bernard N. Schilling, University of Rochester; Helene Maria Schnabel, New York City; H. T. Schultz, Dartmouth College; John Seelye, University of Connecticut; Susan Field Senneff, Columbia University; Richard J. Sexton, Fordham University; A. Paul Shallers, Temple University; Harold I. Shapiro, Hofstra University; F. Parvin Sharpless, Germantown Friends School; Norman Silverstein, Queens College, CUNY; Lowell L. Simmons, Florida A. and M. University; Sister Mary Francis Slattery, George Washington University; Carol H. Smith, Douglass College, Rutgers University; Paul Smith, Trinity College; Nelle Smither, Douglass College, Rutgers University; Ian Sowton, York University at Toronto; Mark Spilka, Brown University; Robert Spiller, University of Pennsylvania; Thomas F. Staley, University of Tulsa; Nathan C. Starr, New School for Social Research; George Steiner, Churchill College, Cambridge University; Milton R. Stern, University of

Connecticut; A. Wilbur Stevens, Prescott College; Holly Stevens, Yale University; David L. Stevenson, Hunter College, CUNY; John W. Stevenson, Converse College; Fred E. Stockholder, University of British Columbia; Katherine Stockholder, University of British Columbia; Donald R. Stoddard, Skidmore College; Maureen Sullivan, University of Pennsylvania; Donald R. Swanson, Wright State University; Rosemary Hope Sweetapple, University of Adelaide and Yale University

E. W. Tayler, Columbia University; Ruth Z. Temple, Brooklyn College, CUNY

John Unterecker, Columbia University

Virginia Walker Valentine, University of South Florida; Rosemary T. Van Arsdel, University of Puget Sound; John Van Sickle, Brown University; Helen Vendler, Boston University; Sister M. Vincentia, O.P., Albertus Magnus College

Marshall Waingrow, Claremont Graduate School; Eugene M. Waith, Yale University; Emily M. Wallace, Philadelphia, Pennsylvania; Sister Betsy Walsh, R.S.C.J., Manhattanville College; Sister Mary Anthony Weining, Rosemont College; Ronald A. Wells, U.S. Coast Guard Academy; Alexander Welsh, University of Pittsburgh; Ronald C. Wendling, Hamilton College; Christian S. Wenger, Elizabethtown College; Robert L. White, York University at Toronto; Joseph J. Wiesenfarth, University of Wisconsin at Madison; Marilyn L. Williamson, Oakland University; Dorothy M. Willis, New Haven, Connecticut; James I. Wimsatt, University of North Carolina at Greensboro; Mary Ann Wimsatt, Greensboro College; William K. Wimsatt, Yale University; Philip Withim, Bucknell University

James Dean Young, Georgia Institute of Technology

Vivian Zinkin, Glassboro State College.